Praise for *Driving Like Crazy*:

“With the car industry under attack, both socially and economically, it is pleasing to read O’Rourke’s trenchant analysis of all the good things the automobile has brought to American society, even as his tongue is firmly planted in cheek. . . . A great book for summer reading; thumbing through it elicits a laugh at almost any point.” —*Library Journal*

“Worth a read . . . When [O’Rourke’s] using his wit to probe a bit deeper into his world, his writing is frequently superb.”
—*The Philadelphia Inquirer*

“Libertarian satirist P. J. O’Rourke has built a best-selling career by celebrating his own politically incorrect intemperance. So it’s only fitting that he’s devoted some of his best writing to that gaudy metaphor for excess, the gas-guzzling muscle car. . . . The collapse of the auto industry makes the book poignantly timely.” —*SmartMoney*

“Readers looking for insights and laughs will not be disappointed by *Driving Like Crazy* . . . [it] is a ride worth taking, even for readers who don’t know an oil pan fro[illegible] a frying pan.”
—*T*[illegible]*ngton Times*

“*Driving Like Crazy* isn’t just a [illegible] greatest hits. P.J. has written new le[illegible] fresh meat even for those wh[illegible] all before. . . . This book is a must-read. [illegible] *tomobile Magazine*

DRIVING LIKE CRAZY

ALSO BY P. J. O'ROURKE

Modern Manners
The Bachelor Home Companion
Republican Party Reptile
Holidays in Hell
The American Spectator's Enemies List
Parliament of Whores
Give War a Chance
All the Trouble in the World
Age and Guile Beat Youth, Innocence, and a Bad Haircut
Eat the Rich
The CEO of the Sofa
Peace Kills
On The Wealth of Nations

P. J.
O'ROURKE

DRIVING LIKE CRAZY

Thirty Years of Vehicular Hell-bending, Celebrating America the Way It's Supposed to Be—With an Oil Well in Every Backyard, a Cadillac Escalade in Every Carport, and the Chairman of the Federal Reserve Mowing Our Lawn

Grove Press
New York

Published simultaneously in Canada
Printed in the United States of America

ISBN-13: 978-0-8021-4479-9

Grove Press
an imprint of Grove/Atlantic, Inc.
841 Broadway
New York, NY 10003

Distributed by Publishers Group West

www.groveatlantic.com

10 11 12 13 10 9 8 7 6 5 4 3 2 1

To David E. Davis Jr.

Boss, mentor, road trip comrade, hunting companion, and—first, last, and always—friend

We drive our cars because they make us free. With cars we need not wait in airline terminals, or travel only where the railway tracks go. Governments detest our cars: they give us too much freedom. How do you control people who can climb into a car at any hour of the day or night and drive to who knows where?

— D.E.D. Jr.

Contents

Acknowledgments

Car journalism is not a solitary artistic endeavor. Obviously. You need a car to write about cars. And if that car is going to be more than four inches long and do something beside roll across the playroom floor for the amusement of my five-year-old son, Buster, then it has to be made by people other than me. Nor is there much that's artistic about car journalism. Cars are a broad subject with all sorts of sociological, political, and even aesthetic ramifications. But a car is still a car. And there are only so many ways to say "some lunk did something in a clunker." Thus there is a certain strain upon the language in car journalism. Take the accelerator just for instance. This must be pressed hundreds of times in even a cursory test of a car. As a result, to press the accelerator becomes:

Put the pedal to the metal
Push the go-fast pump
Lead foot it
Slip it the big shoe
Give it the boot
Give it some Welly
Stand on it
Crank it up
Ramp it up
Gin it up
Wind the speedometer . . . the tach . . . the gears
Wind it up like a Hong Kong wristwatch
Drop the bottle and grab the throttle
Floor it

And so forth. For this I apologize to the reader. And to the extent that such euphuistic rodomontade does not drive you crazy in the following pages, credit must be given to car journalism's editors. Credit must also be given to fellow car journalists, car jockeys, and car nuts who can be counted upon for genuinely clever turns of phrase, which I can be counted on to swipe.

For some reason automobiles attract good people, the kind of people with whom you'd gladly go on road trips. And that's the secret right there. You need a car to go on a road trip, and the kind of people you wouldn't take on a road trip aren't in the car.

Over the past thirty-odd years I've had the pleasure of going on road trips with all sorts of good people. Many are named in the text and more are named below. But I have neither the space nor the memory left to list them all. My apologies to anyone whom I've forgotten. I promise to pick you up if the Obama administration reduces you to hitchhiking on your road trips.

At *Car and Driver* and *Automobile* there variously are and were David E. Davis Jr., Jeannie Davis, Jim Williams, Brock Yates, Bruce McCall, Humphrey Sutton, William Jeans, Don Sherman, Patrick Bedard, Don Coulter, Michael Jordan, Mike Knepper, John Phillips, Kathy Hoy, Jean Lindamood/Jennings, Csaba Csere, Rich Ceppos, Aaron Kiley, Larry Griffin, Philip Llewellin, Harriet Stemberger, Trant Jarman, Greg Jarem, Mark Gilles, and Bill Neale. They can drive like crazy, every one of them.

At *Esquire* there were Terry McDonell and David Hirshey, the last two *Esquire* editors worthy of having the publication attach itself to their names.

And at *Forbes FYI* there was the inimitable Christopher Buckley who founded *FYI* because his father's publication, *National Review,* did not devote adequate space to good food, good drink, good cars, and high living. Thus the question was raised, "What the hell are conservatives conserving?" At *FYI* Christopher had, fittingly for a conservative, two right hands: Patrick Cooke and Thomas Jackson. Let me shake (not stir) them both.

This book is a mixture of old things and new, not to say a mishmash. Mostly it's a collection of car journalism from 1977 to the present, a sort of social history with all the social science crap left out. I've reworked many of the pieces because the writing—how to put this gently to myself? —sucked. I may not have become a better writer over the years but I've become a less bumptious and annoying one, I think. Also many of the original articles dealt at length with then-current minutiae that now has to be explained or, better, deleted. A couple manuscripts (especially "The Rolling Organ Donors Motorcycle Club") were so bad that my old tear sheets served as little more than aide-mémoirs for the present chapters.

Anyway, to give the publishing history that is required by copyright law or publishers' custom or some damn thing, the aforementioned motorcycle saga, the journal of a trip across America in a 1956 Buick, the story of Rent-A-Wreck, the tale of an off-road drive from Canada to Mexico, my record of discovering Jeep worship in the Philippines, the log of my trudge to Denver in a station wagon full of children, and the first two parts of the Baja memoirs were originally published in *Car and Driver*.

The third and most disaster-filled saga of the Baja ran in *Esquire* about the time that Terry McDonell and David Hirshey were getting out of there. The whole article is about what a godforsaken, star-crossed hell the Baja is, and some idiot from the *Esquire* promotion department called to ask me if I could write a sidebar about wonderful places to stay and fun things to do there.

The piece on NASCAR appeared in *Rolling Stone*, also under the editorship of Terry McDonell.

Automobile published the essays about buying a family car and about traveling across India in a Disco II.

Forbes FYI printed the description of the California Mille where the Fangio Chevy was codriven by Fred Schroeder, who was the world's bravest investment banker until collateralized debt obligations and credit swaps came around and showed that other bankers were more foolhardy than he. The California Mille is the brainchild of the estimable Martin Swig, whose car nut credentials can be summed up in the following anecdote: I was looking for the proper model designation of the Tatra T87, the Czech car from which Ferdinand Porsche stole the Volkswagen design. The Tatra looks like an over-scale VW Bug but has a big metal fin on the back, earning it the nickname "Land Squid." I called Martin, described the Land Squid, and he said, "I own one."

FYI also underwrote my Kyrgyzstan horseback ride where I discovered the six-wheel-drive Soviet Zil truck.

My obnoxious defense of SUV obnoxiousness was written for the London *Sunday Times,* and given the number of times the MG I owned in college broke down, the Brits had it coming.

And my proposal for a linear National Park went off into the ether of some Webzine called Winding Road that never paid me. The Internet in a nutshell.

I confess to a bit of self-plagiarism in this volume. The chapter about my trip across India was, in part, previously anthologized in *The CEO of the Sofa*. I've re-reprinted it because I wrote two versions, one for *Rolling Stone* emphasizing culture, politics, and economics in India and one for *Automobile* emphasizing the Land Rover Discovery II, out the window of which I was seeing the culture, politics, and economics of India. In *CEO* I mainly used the *Rolling Stone* article. Here I've combined both and written more about the driving. The driving was gruesome. "If it bleeds, it leads," is always a wise rule in journalism. Another reason for giving India a second chance between book covers was that *The CEO of the Sofa*—an assortment of light and frivolous sketches from the happy-go-lucky Clinton era—had a publication date of 9/10/01.

I also palmed an item from *Republican Party Reptile*. It's an instructional tract called "How to Drive Fast on Drugs While Getting Your Wing-Wang Squeezed and Not Spill Your Drink." I couldn't collect my automotive writing and not include this.

Plus I've wanted an opportunity to respond to my youthful ravings ever since I turned fifty and my drug of choice became blood pressure medicine.

Speaking of age, my friends seem to be getting older. I don't know what's the matter with them. A number of the good people mentioned in this book have passed on the double yellow line of lifespan's highway. Most notably the car world feels the loss of Jim Williams, Humphrey Sutton, Trant Jarman, and Bill Neale. Fortunately they were all careful to live so as to never miss a drink, a romance, or a fast drive. Every pleasure that you forego on Earth is a pleasure you won't get in heaven.

One of my deceased friends had a brain tumor. He was lucky enough—or perhaps worthy enough—that his tumor seemed to destroy the parts of the brain that generate sadness, anger, irritation, and regret. He went off into unconsciousness with a smile on his face. He was blessed with a loving wife and she took care of him at home even after he became comatose. She used to speak to him as if he could hear, though he showed no sign of response. One day, as she was leaving the house, she reflexively asked her husband, "Is there anything I can get for you?"

He spoke for the first time in months. "Yes," he said, "a ten-thousand-dollar blow job."

I thank him for his inspiration. And there is one more thanks I need to give. For nineteen years she's been with me through thick and thin. She's vivacious and exciting. She's a little unpredictable but she has a solid core of common sense. She's glamorous but not flashy, powerful but not pushy about it. I can rely on her absolutely. And she's more beautiful than ever, my 1990 Porsche Carrera 2. (And my wife is also fabulous.)

Introduction

The End of the American Car

The feminists grabbed our women,
The liberals banned our guns,
The health cops snuffed our cigarettes,
The bailout has our funds,
The laws of Breathalyzing
Put an end to our roadside bars,
Circle the Fords and Chevys, boys,
THEY'RE COMING TO TAKE OUR CARS

It's time to say . . . how shall we put it? . . . sayonara to the American car. The American automobile industry—GM, Ford, even Chrysler—will live on in some form, a Marley's ghost dragging its corporate chains at taxpayer expense. The fools in the corner offices of Detroit (and the fool officials of Detroit's unions) will retire to their vacation homes in Palm

Beach (and St. Pete). They no more deserve our sympathy than the malevolent trolls under the Capitol dome. But pity the poor American car when Congress and the White House get through with it—a lightweight vehicle with a small carbon footprint, using alternative energy and renewable resources to operate in a sustainable way. When I was a kid we called it a Schwinn.

Oh well, it's been a great run these past 110-odd years since the Duryea brothers built the first American car in Springfield, Massachusetts. If the Duryea Motor Wagon Company had been a success, Springfield, Massachusetts, might be today's Motor City, full of abandoned houses, unemployment, drug dealing, violent crime, and racial tensions, which Springfield, Massachusetts, is full of anyway. But we owe the American car a lot more than just the entertaining spectacle of Detroit's felon mayor Kwame Kilpatrick. In fact many people my age owe their very existence to the car, or to the car's backseat, where—if our birth date and our parents' wedding anniversary are a bit too close for comfort—we were probably conceived.

There was no premarital sex in America before the invention of the internal combustion engine. You couldn't sneak a girl into the rec room of your house because your mom and dad were unable to commute so they were home all day working on the farm. And your farmhouse didn't have a rec room because recreation had not been discovered due to all the farmwork. You could take a girl out in a buggy, but it was hard to get her in the mood to let you bust into her corset because the two of you were seated facing a horse rectum. It spoils the atmosphere.

Cars let us out of the barn and, while they were at it, destroyed the American nuclear family. As anyone who has had an American nuclear family can tell you, this was a relief to all concerned. Cars also caused America to be paved. There are much worse things you can do to a country than pave it, as the Sudanese are proving in Darfur. (And do we car nuts ever hear a word of thanks for this largesse from the scatter-skulled, face-skinned, limbs-in-casts skateboarders?)

Cars fulfilled the ideal of America's founding fathers. Of all the truths we hold self-evident, of all the unalienable rights with which we're endowed, what's most important to the American dream? It's right there, front and center, in the Declaration of Independence: freedom to *leave*! Founding fathers, can I have the keys?

The car provided Americans with an enviable standard of living. You could not get a steady job with high wages and health and retirement benefits working on the General Livestock Corporation assembly line putting udders on cows.

The American car was a source of intellectual stimulation. Think of the innovation, the invention, the sheer genius that transformed the 1908 Model T Ford into the 1968 Shelby Cobra GT500 in the course of a single human lifetime full of speeding tickets. Compare this to progress in the previously fashionable mode of human transportation. Equine design and production have remained much the same for three thousand years. And when it came to creativity nobody thought to put a stirrup on a saddle until about 500 AD. If the engineering development of the automobile had proceeded at that pace we'd be powering ourselves down the road by running with our feet stuck through a hole in the floor like Fred Flintstone. (Although it may come to that in the 2010 Obamamobile.)

And upon the fine arts the American car has had a welcome effect. The minute the house lights dim for a symphony, opera, or play, we can run out, start the car, and *effect* a welcome escape.

The saga of the American car is no abstract matter to me, no subject of fanciful theories. Nancy Pelosi and Harry Reid may think they were transported home from the maternity ward on pink, fluffy clouds supported by cherubs but I know that the car got me to where I am.

My grandfather Jacob Joseph ("J.J.") O'Rourke was born in 1877 on a patch of a farm outside Lime City, Ohio. He was one of ten kids. They grew up in a one-room unpainted shack. I have a photograph of them, lined up by age, staring at the photographer, amazed to see someone in shoes. My great-grandfather Barney was a woodcutter and a drunk and an illiterate. I have a copy of the marriage certificate with his X. Barney's only accomplishment—aside from the ten prizes he won on the corn-shuck stuffing of the poor man's roulette wheel—was to train a pair of draft horses to haul him home dead drunk, flat on his back, in his unsprung "Democrat wagon." He died a pauper in a charity hospital run by the Little Sisters of the Poor.

Grandpa Jake left home armed with a fifth-grade education, heading for the bright lights of Toledo. It's a short drive, as I remember from Grandpa taking me to see Lime City. But it's a damn long walk. Grandpa went to work as a mechanic for a buggy maker. When horseless buggies came along he fixed them too. For the rest of his life he called cars "buggies." It didn't take him long to realize that cleaner hands were to be had and more money was to be made selling the things instead of repairing them. (And my uncle Arch's birth date and my grandparents' wedding anniversary were a bit too close for comfort.)

The upshot—by the time I arrived in the 1940s—was O'Rourke Buick. Grandpa and Uncle Arch owned the dealership. My father was the sales manager. Dad's younger brother, Joe, ran the used car lot. Baby brother Jack was a salesman. Cousin Ide was in charge of the parts department. Various aunts and girl cousins worked in the office. The boy cousins and I got our first jobs cleaning and waxing cars. (Shorty, the old black man in charge, told me, "Always leave some lint in the corners of the windows, that way they know you washed 'em.")

Arch's son-in-law, my cousin Hep, would go on to run the Ohio Car Dealers Association and I would go on to do what I'm doing here. Which has something to do with cars, but there are times I wished I'd stayed in Toledo and starred in late-night local TV commercials: "Arrrgh, mateys, sail on down to Pirate Pat's Treasure Island Buick, where prices walk the plank! And don't miss our Pieces of V-8 used car lot! Free chocolate doubloons for the kiddies!"

Grandpa died in 1960, full of years and honors (albeit honors from Rotary, Kiwanis, and Lions clubs, Elk and Moose lodges, and the Shriners, as befits a good car dealer). My family owes everything to the American car. What with the inability to read and write and no food and all, O'Rourke family history does not begin until the beginnings of the American car. Now some O'Rourkes have even gone to college.

I take the demise of the American car personally. I'm looking around furiously for someone or something to blame. Ralph Nader for instance. What fun it would be to jump on him with both feet and send the pink Marxist goo squirting out of his cracked egghead. And let's definitely do that even though Ralph is seventy-five and insane. But it took more than one man and his ignorant and ill-written book *Unsafe at Any Speed* to wreck the most important industry in the nation. (My high school girlfriend Connie had a Corvair. Connie was the worst driver in the world—and one of the fastest. If Connie couldn't get that rear-engine, swing-axle setup to spin out and flip, nobody could.)

Pundits say there's plenty of blame to be shared for the extinction of the American car. But I'm not so sure about that either. True, car executives are knuckleheads. But *all* executives are knuckleheads. Look at Bill Gates. If you were worth eleventy bazillion wouldn't you give up on your *That Seventies Show* optometrist look and go to a barber college and get a decent $5 haircut? Labor union leadership is maddening. But it's one thing to be mad at union leaders and another thing to expect them to stand on a chair at the UAW hall and shout, "We demand less money from the bosses!"

Car company workers are making $600 an hour plus overtime—or so it's claimed. In the first place, these people get laid off every time a camel farts at an OPEC meeting. Maybe their pay is too high, but it's not like they're getting that pay. And their jobs are harder than being president. All Barak Obama has to do is look cool. If a couple hundred armed Secret Service agents had my back and were also ready to run down to the corner store and get me a pack of smokes, I'd look cool too. (And when you're president you can't get laid off. We know, because we tried with Clinton.)

American car designers and engineers are supposedly at fault because American cars fell behind foreign cars in sophistication of design and engineering. American cars fell especially behind during the 1960s era of chrome and tailfin excess that car-hating Volvo-butts still like to natter on about. Too much jogging has addled their brains. There's little chrome and barely a fin to be seen on American cars after 1960, excepting the modest lark tails on Cadillac rear fenders and the shark attack of the 1961 Chryslers. In fact, early '60s American cars exhibit some of the cleanest, crispest, most restrained lines in automotive design history—the 1962 Lincoln Continental; the Avanti; the last of the Studebaker Hawks; the 1964 Buick Electra, Oldsmobile 98, and Pontiac Grand Prix hardtops; the 1965 Buick Riviera; those maligned Corvairs, including the Corvair Greenbriar precursor to the minivan; Mustangs; the 1965 Pontiac GTO and similar early muscle cars; and the 1964 Rambler American sedan in its own oddball way. Then, when it comes to down-and-dirty, gnarly, totally unrestrained lines, there's the Corvette Stingray.

As for engineering you'll note that Carroll Shelby did not create the Shelby Cobra by taking a 1961 AC Ace and sticking an AC Ace engine in it. America made the best engines in the world—compact, powerful, gas-station-mechanic-proof V-8s that were overbored, understressed, and delivered terrifying horsepower at comforting rpms. American engines were cheap to make, simple to fix, and easy to hot-rod. Europe was producing more complicated and—to be fair—more efficient engines. But Europe had to. European cars were taxed by engine size as though performance were a disease of the liver. European gasoline cost more per liter than Château Lafite 1961. And European racing formulas stipulated a volume of displacement that wouldn't get an American eighth grader drunk if it were filled with bourbon.

European chassis and running gear were more complicated as well—birdcages, monocoques, unibodies, four-wheel independent suspensions, five-speed synchromeshes, rack-and-pinion steering, and disc brakes that squealed like a girl. Wonderful stuff—light, nimble, and damned near useless in

America. Useless, that is, when it wasn't broken. American roads, American weather, and Americans took that fancy European engineering and smashed it to bits as if it were a dainty Dresden china teacup.

Among people who have no idea what they're talking about there is an idea that nifty, thrifty, and brilliant automobiles were being manufactured first in Europe and then in Japan. Meanwhile America was turning out clunking, profligate, and stupid lead sleds. That's crap. And so were—and are—most of the cars made in Europe and Japan.

By the end of the 1950s American cars were so reliable that their reliability went without saying even in car ads. Thousands of them bear testimony to this today, still running on the roads of Cuba though fueled with nationalized Venezuelan gasoline and maintained with spit and haywire. This was a big change from just a few years before (as readers of a following chapter on a trip across the United States in a 1956 Buick will note).

American cars were sophisticated when sophistication was called for. Foreigners have yet to figure out how to make decent power steering or a worthwhile automatic transmission. But American carmakers have always favored solidity, plain mechanicals, and sturdy overbuilding. (And, P.S., that 1964 Electra hardtop could be had new for four grand.)

There's nothing special about a leaf-spring-mounted solid rear axle. However, it's the thing to have if you decide to use your Fairlane 500 to pull a wheat combine. Americans have been known to do that. Disc brakes are better than drum brakes, but drum brakes are less expensive to make and assemble. Drum brakes fade but they do work the first time you use them. As the great American car journalist Brock Yates has pointed out, car journalists tend to forget that the point of brakes in an emergency stop is to stop you *once.* If you have to make emergency stop after emergency stop, you have a problem worse than your brakes.

American carmakers made—and, after dozing at the wheel in the '70s and '80s, still make—cars well suited to their country and their customers (and particularly well suited to the size of both).

Foreign carmakers, on the other hand, were making my 1960 MGA with foot wells constructed of wooden boards that rotted, leaving me running with my feet stuck through a hole in the floor like Fred Flintstone. At an SCCA time trial, one of the MG's ridiculous, untuneable SU side-draft carburetors sprayed gasoline all over my red-hot exhaust headers causing a very rapid clearing of the pit area. Also, as I was pulling out of the driveway one day, the MG's radio caught fire. "Home by Dark" was the motto of the Lucas Electrical Company, which also made the parts on a friend of mine's Riley roadster. The Riley's battery exploded when we tried to give the car a jump-start because some idiot Englishman had specified positive grounding.

Noted car photographer Humphrey Sutton drove a Mini (an original 1960s Austin one) over a protruding New York City manhole cover and tore the oil pan and crankcase out of the car. Another time, in Scotland, Humphrey got a Fiat 600 so firmly jammed in reverse gear that it had to be driven (Humphrey swore this was true) backward from Glasgow to Edinburgh.

Car and Driver editor David E. Davis and Brock Yates drove a 1964 Rover 2000TC from Chicago to New York and were so impressed they called it "the best sedan we have ever tested," resulting in loud reader complaints and a major falloff in subscription renewals. "We made that claim," said

David E., "before we discovered the screw under the Rover's hood that, if given a quarter-turn counterclockwise, caused everything to fall off the car."

In college, after my MG imploded, I had a 1960 Mercedes 190 sedan that blew a head gasket because it had had its head gasket replaced. The mechanic hadn't tightened the head bolts correctly. I mean, he'd tightened them with the correct amount of torque but he hadn't tightened them in the correct *order*. By way of contrast, the next car I had was a 1959 Plymouth Belvedere with Chrysler Corporation's ancient L-head 6. There was a leak in the radiator hose. I didn't notice because the bong was blocking my view of the temperature gauge. Anyway, I ran every ounce of coolant out of the cooling system and the engine seized. I duct-taped the radiator hose and filled the radiator with a bystander's garden house. The Plymouth started on the first try and ran for years.

I could go on. And I will if you get me started on the rice-burner junk prior to Datsun's 510 and 240Z. Early generations of Japanese cars were styled by the Hello Kitty factory and had model designations such as "Sapsucker," "Blowfly," and "Hello Kitty." Early generations of Japanese motorcycles weren't much better. My 250cc Suzuki X6 Hustler (there's a name) fried a spark plug every hour. The only way the plug could be changed was by using a 15/16ths box-end wrench with a dip. This awkward bugger of a tool had to be carried bungee-corded to the rear fender of the X6 along with a box of spare Champions. As for other highlights of Japanese engineering, remember the Honda Dream with square shock absorbers?

No, the American car industry was not destroyed by its cars. The American car industry was destroyed by the Fun-Suckers. You know the Fun-Suckers. You may be married to one. The Fun-Suckers go around saying how unsafe this fun thing is and how unhealthy that fun thing is and how unfair, unjust, uncaring, insensitive, divisive, contagious, and fattening every other thing that's fun is.

The Fun-Suckers are a bit too careful, a bit too concerned, a bit too scrupulous. That's bullshit. They're evil and they hate us. The motive behind spoiling things for others and then throwing a wet blanket over the rained-on parade is a matter of neither caution nor morals. The Fun-Suckers suck the fun out of life in order to gain control. They've found a way to achieve power without merit. Nothing requires less information, education, or accomplishment than saying that everything's wrong. It's wrong to risk lives, wrong to use up earth's resources, wrong to pollute air, wrong to support an economic system that heightens income inequalities, wrong to own a big, expensive car, drive it fast, and vote Republican.

The Fun-Suckers have been around forever. But they didn't used to have the influence they have now. The ruling class of yore was too fond of its dangerous fun. The nobility was having a ball (and PETA be damned) chasing game animals through the serfs' standing corn and chasing serfs as well if any buxom serf lasses were spied. Dukes and princes spent their days warring with infidels and each other and their nights feasting themselves into oblivion. The Fun-Suckers had to rely on religious zealotry to make others miserable and themselves important. Fun-Suckers were reduced to burning a few books and witches, pestering Copernicus and Galileo, and making everyone eat carp pie on Fridays. (Although, to judge by the cumbersome impracticality of medieval armor, knights and squires may have had to deal with a Ralphius Naderum.)

Even the threat of damnation failed the Fun-Suckers when the Enlightenment dawned, and elite thinkers like Voltaire gave up the idea of hell for the idea of a hell of a good time. And yet Fun-Sucking was not to be thwarted. The invention of democracy gave the Fun-Suckers a party platform. What better way to gain power without merit than by being the kind of pea-brained, unaccomplished Fun-Sucker who runs for political office? And what makes a better stump speech than saying that everything's wrong? Elect the Fun-Sucker.

Cars were a perfect opportunity for Fun-Sucking. Ruining cars could produce an even bigger sensation (and government) than the Fun-Suckers' previous golden oldie, Prohibition. After all, at any given moment there are a few people on the wagon and hence not affected by Prohibition. But Americans *never* get out of their cars.

Cars were everyplace. We couldn't do without them. The car business was too big, complicated, and socially prominent to go on the lam. Cars were a way for the Fun-Suckers to clamp their lamprey jaws onto everybody's seat upholstery.

The Fun-Suckers started small, with seat belts to make sure we'd be trapped inside flaming car wrecks and padded dashboards so we wouldn't injure our knuckles while pounding the dash in frustration as we burned to death. Then the Middle East's predatory goat molesters gave Fun-Suckers the excuse they were looking for, with the 1973 oil embargo.

The Fun-Suckers were able to turn the automobile into a public enemy, an outlaw they could persecute without compunction. Cars were shackled with five-mph bumpers that spoiled the styling of everything from 3.OCS BMWs to landau-style vinyl-roofed opera-windowed Gauche DeVilles. The idea was to make us fun-lovers look ridiculous, to turn us into objects of popular ridicule and scorn. The Fun-Suckers are doing the same thing to our kids by making them wear bike helmets, knee and elbow pads, shin guards, safety goggles, and steel-toed boots to use the teeter-totter at the playground, after which they have to wipe themselves all over with Purell hand disinfectant.

Our children tamely submit to this because they were torn from our fun-filled arms as babies and strapped, belted, buckled, and bound into lonely, isolated rear-facing infant carriers where they grew up without normal social contact or human interaction, causing them to become the passive teen video-gaming thumb-twiddlers and pasty Facebookers who are tweeting, texting, iPhoning, and Wii-wiggling like Internet-wits while they sprawl in front of the high-def TV in our homes. These pallid adolescents are easy prey to the brandishers of Nerf hope and the loose change makers who are sucking fun in the Obama administration.

The fifty-five-mile-per-hour speed limit had a similar intent. The dreary and tedious rate of travel was meant to produce "highway hypnosis" in the American electorate so that the Carter White House's pointy-headed grand wizards of the Fun Sux Klan could employ posthypnotic suggestion to make people do their bidding. Americans would be rendered so zombielike and devoid of free will that, heedless of all pangs of conscience or instincts for self-preservation, they'd reelect Jimmy Carter. Fortunately, Jimmy's brother Billy had too many beers, told all, and the plot was foiled.

CAFE standards were imposed to make American cars use less gas and thereby keep the oil crisis going longer. If American cars used less gas the world wouldn't run out of oil. And as long as the world didn't run out of oil the sheep-humped sheikhs of the Mideast's giant kitty-litter tray—the

Fun-Suckers' most important allies—would remain rich, powerful, and happily mutton-buggered.

Pollution controls were installed on automobiles to increase the amount of pollution. You'll recall that, at first, air pollution from cars was nothing but a wisp of smog in the sky, easily remedied with a tune-up and positive crankcase ventilation. Then the atmosphere filled with lead that damaged our brains, followed by carbon monoxide that poisoned our bodies. Now hydrocarbons cook the planet and melt the ice caps and cause us all to die of heat prostration and drowning. That's no fun. Truly the Fun-Suckers are wicked, wicked people.

Next came the DUI hysteria with legal blood-alcohol levels lowered to the point where you can't drive a car all Sunday if you received communion at 8 A.M. Mass. This was the Fun-Suckers' most obvious attempt to create a police state since it takes one full-time police officer for each adult male in America to enforce current DUI laws.

Drinking and driving is not a problem and never has been. Bravery and driving is the problem. And beer makes young men brave. The answer isn't more cops. The answer is more drugs. Give those young men some peyote and mescaline and LSD with their beer and watch their bravery vanish. Mile markers jump out from the berm, hopping on their single legs and forming into packs. Their rectangular, numbered heads flash with green reflective menace. The centerline rises from the pavement. The giant yellow-striped serpent coils to strike. Meanwhile, a highway overpass gapes—the jaws of hell. Abandon all joyriding ye who enter here. Those young men will be crawling down I-40 at fifteen miles an hour the way I was forty years ago.

And then there is the air bag. It kills short people when it deploys. It kills short people, but what it does to short people who are smoking big cigars is too horrible to contemplate. I'm about the height of New York's Mayor Bloomberg. I do love my double-corona Havanas with a ring guage equal to my number of years on the planet. I don't think I have to spell out who is #1 on the Fun-Suckers' hit list.

1

How to Drive Fast on Drugs While Getting Your Wing-Wang Squeezed and Not Spill Your Drink

When it comes to taking chances, some people like to play poker or shoot dice; other people prefer to parachute jump, go rhino hunting, or climb ice floes, while still others engage in crime or marriage. But I like to get drunk and drive like a fool. Name me, if you can, a better feeling than the one you get when you're half a bottle of Chivas in the bag with a gram of coke up your nose and a teenage lovely pulling off her tube top in the next seat over while you're going a hundred miles an hour down a suburban side street. You'd have to watch the entire Iranian air force crash-land in a liquid petroleum gas storage facility to match this kind of thrill. If you ever have much more fun than that, you'll die of pure sensory overload, I'm here to tell you.

But wait. Let's pause and analyze *why* this particular matrix of activities is perceived as so highly enjoyable. I mean, aside from the teenage lovely pulling off her tube top in the next seat over. Ignoring that for a moment, let's look at the psychological factors conducive to placing positive emotional values on the sensory end product of experientially produced excitation of the central nervous system and smacking into a lamppost. Is that any way to have fun? How would your mother feel if she knew you were doing this? She'd cry. She really would. And that's how you know it's fun. Anything that makes your mother cry is fun. Sigmund Freud wrote all about this. It's a well-known fact.

Of course, it's a shame to waste young lives behaving this way—speeding around all tanked up with your feet hooked in the steering wheel while your date crawls around on the floor mat opening zippers with her teeth and pounding on the accelerator with an empty liquor bottle. But it wouldn't be taking a chance if you weren't risking *something*. And even if it is a shame to waste young lives behaving this way, it is definitely cooler than risking *old* lives behaving this way. I mean, so what if some fifty-eight-year-old butt head gets a load on and starts playing Death Race 2000 in the rush-hour traffic jam? What kind of chance is he taking? He's just waiting around to see what kind of cancer he gets anyway. But if young, talented you, with all of life's possibilities at your fingertips, you and the future Cheryl Tiegs there, so fresh, so beautiful—if the two of *you* stake your handsome heads on a single roll of the dice in life's game of stop-the-semi—now *that's* taking chances! Which is why old people rarely risk their lives. It's not because they're chicken, they just have too much dignity to play for small stakes.

Now a lot of people say to me, "Hey, P.J., you like to drive fast. Why not join a responsible organization, such as the Sports Car Club of America, and enjoy participation in sports car racing? That way you could drive as fast as you wish while still engaging in a well-regulated spectator sport that is becoming more popular each year." No thanks. In the first place, if you ask me, those guys are a bunch of tweedy old barf mats who like to talk about things like what necktie they wore to Alberto Ascari's funeral. And in the second place, they won't let me drive drunk. They expect me to go out there and smash into things and roll over on the roof and catch fire and burn to death when I'm sober. They must think I'm crazy. That stuff scares me. I have to get completely shit-faced to even think about driving fast. How can you have a lot of exciting thrills when you're so terrified that you wet yourself all the time? That's not fun. It's just not *fun* to have exciting thrills when you're scared. Take the heroes of the *Iliad*, for instance. They really had some exciting thrills, and were they scared? No. They were drunk. Every chance they could get. And so am I, and I'm not going out there and having a horrible car wreck until somebody brings me a cocktail.

Also, it's important to be drunk because being drunk keeps your body all loose, and that way, if you have an accident or anything, you'll sort of roll with the punches and not get banged up so bad. For example, there was this guy I heard about who was really drunk and was driving through the Adirondacks. He got sideswiped by a bus and went head-on into another car, which knocked him off a bridge, and he plummeted 150 feet into a ravine. I mean, it killed him and everything, but if he hadn't been so drunk and loose, his body probably would have been banged up a lot worse—and you can imagine how much more upset his wife would have been when she went down to the morgue to identify him.

Even more important than being drunk, however, is having the right car. You have to get a car that handles really well. This is extremely important, and there's a lot of debate on this subject—about what kind of car handles best. Some say a front-engined car; some say a rear-engined car. I say a *rented* car. Nothing handles better than a rented car. You can go faster, turn corners sharper, and put the transmission into reverse while going forward at a higher rate of speed in a rented car than in any other kind. You can also park without looking, and you can use the trunk as an ice chest. Another thing about a rented car is that it's an all-terrain vehicle. Mud, snow, water, woods—you can take a rented car anywhere. True, you can't always get it back, but that's not your problem, is it?

Yet there's more to a good-handling car than just making sure it doesn't belong to you. It has to be big. It's really hard for a girl to get her clothes off inside a small car, and this is one of the most important features of car handling. Also, what kind of drugs does it have in it? Most people like to drive on speed or cocaine with plenty of whiskey mixed in. This gives you the confidence you want and need for plowing through red lights and passing trucks on the right. But don't neglect downs and 'ludes and codeine cough syrup either. It's hard to beat the heavy depressants for high-speed spinouts, backing into trees, and a general feeling of not giving two fucks about man and his universe.

Overall, though, it's the bigness of the car that counts the most. Because when something bad happens in a big car—accidentally speeding through the middle of a gang of unruly young people who have been taunting you in a drive-in restaurant, for instance—it happens very far away, way out at the end of your fenders. It's like a civil war in Africa; you know, it doesn't really concern you too much. On the other hand, when something happens in a little bitty car it happens right in your face. You get all involved in it and have to give everything a lot of thought. Driving around in a little bitty car is like being one of those sensitive girls who writes poetry. Life is just too much to bear. You end up staying at home in your bedroom and thinking up sonnets that don't get published till you die, which will be real soon if you keep driving around in little bitty cars like that.

Let's inspect some of the basic maneuvers of drunken driving while you've got crazy girls who are on drugs with you. Look for these signs when picking up crazy girls: pierced ears with five or six earrings in them, unusual shoes, white lipstick, extreme thinness, hair that's less than an inch long, or clothing made of chrome and leather. Stay away from girls who cry a lot or who look like they get pregnant easily or have careers. They may want to do weird stuff in cars, but only in the backseat, and it's really hard to steer from back there. Besides, they'll want to get engaged right away afterward. But the other kinds of girls—there's no telling what they'll do. I used to know this girl who weighed about ninety pounds and dressed in skirts that didn't even cover her underwear, when she wore any. I had this beat-up old Mercedes and we were off someplace about fifty miles from nowhere on Christmas Eve in a horrible sleet storm. The road was a mess, all curves and big ditches, and I was blotto, and the car kept slipping off the pavement and sliding sideways.

And just when I'd hit a big patch of glare ice and was frantically spinning the wheel trying to stay out of the oncoming traffic, she said, "I shaved my crotch today, wanna feel?"

That's really true. And then about half an hour later the head gasket blew up and we had to spend I don't know how long in this dirt-ball motel, although the girl walked all the way to the liquor store through about a mile of slush and got all kinds of wine and did weird stuff with the bottlenecks later. So it was sort of okay, except that the garage where I left the Mercedes burned down and I used the insurance money to buy a motorcycle.

Now, girls who like motorcycles will do *anything*. I mean, really, *anything you can think of*. But it's just not the same. For one thing, it's hard to drink while you're riding a motorcycle —there's no place to set your glass. And cocaine's out of the question. And personally, I find that pot makes me too sensitive. You smoke some pot and the first thing you know you're pulling over to the side of the road and taking a break to dig the gentle beauty of the sky's vast panorama, the slow, luxurious interplay of sun and clouds, the lulling trill of breezes midst leafy tree branches—and what kind of fun is that? Besides, it's tough to "get it on" with a chick (I mean in the biblical sense) and still make all the fast curves unless you let her take the handlebars with her pants off and come on doggy style or something, which is harder than it sounds; also, pantless girls on motorcycles attract the highway patrol, so usually you don't end up doing anything until you're both off the bike, and by then you may be in the hospital. Like I was after this old lady pulled out in front of me in an Oldsmobile, and the girl I was with still wanted to do anything you can think of, but there was a doctor there and he was squirting antiseptic all over me and combing little bits of gravel out of my face with a wire brush, and I just couldn't get into it. So take it from me and don't get a motorcycle. Get a big car.

Usually, most fast-driving maneuvers that don't require crazy girls call for use of the steering wheel, so be sure your car is equipped with power steering. Without power steering, turning the wheel is a lot like work, and if you wanted work you'd get a job. All steering should be done with the index finger. Then, when you're done doing all the steering you want to do, just pull your finger out of there and the wheel will come right back to wherever it wants to. It's that simple. Be sure to do an extra lot of steering when going into a driveway or turning sharp corners. And here's another important tip: always roll the window down before throwing bottles out, and don't try to throw them through the windshield unless the car is parked and you're outside it.

Okay, now say you've been on a six-day drunk and you've just made a bet that you can back up all the way to Cleveland, plus you've got a buddy who's getting a blow job on the trunk lid. Well, let's face it, if that's the way you're going to act, sooner or later you'll have an accident. This much is true. But that doesn't mean you should sit back and just let accidents happen to you. No, you have to go out and cause them yourself. That way you're in control of the situation.

You know, it's a shame, but a lot of people have the wrong idea about accidents. For one thing, they don't hurt nearly as much as you'd think. That's because you're in shock and can't feel pain or, if you aren't in shock, you're dead, and that doesn't hurt at all so far as we know. Another thing is that they make great stories. I've got this friend—a prominent man in the automotive industry—who flipped his MG

TF back in the fifties and slid on his head for a couple hundred yards, then had to spend a year with no eyelids and a steel pin through his cheekbones while his face was being rebuilt. Sure, it wasn't much fun at the time, but you should hear him tell about it now. What a fabulous tale, especially during dinner. Besides, it's not all smashing glass and spurting blood, you understand. Why, a good sideswipe can be an almost religious experience. The sheet metal doesn't break or crunch or anything—it flexes and gives way as the two vehicles come together with a rushing liquid pulse as if two giant sharks of steel were mating in the perpetual night of the sea primordial. I mean, if you're on enough drugs. Also, sometimes you see a lot of really pretty lights in your head.

One sure way to cause an accident is with your basic "moonshiner's" or "bootlegger's" turn. Whiz down the road at about sixty or seventy, throw the gearshift into neutral, cut the wheel to the left, and hit the emergency brake with one good wallop while holding out the brake release with your left hand. This'll send you spinning around in a perfect 180-degree turn right into a culvert or a fast-moving tractor-trailer rig. (The bootlegger's turn can be done on dry pavement, but it works best on top of loose gravel or schoolchildren.) Or, when you've moved around backward, you can then spin the wheel to the right and keep on going until you've come around a full 360 degrees and are headed back the same way you were going; still, it probably would have been easier to have just kept going that way in the first place and not have done anything at all, unless you were with somebody you wanted to impress—your probation officer, for instance.

An old friend of mine named Joe Schenkman happens to have just written me a letter about another thing you can do to wreck a car. Joe's on a little vacation up in Vermont (and will be until he finds out what the statute of limitations on attempted vehicular homicide is). He wrote to tell me about a fellow he met up there, saying:

> . . . This guy has rolled (deliberately) over thirty cars (and not just by his own account—the townfolks back him up on this story), inheriting only a broken nose (three times) and a slightly black-and-blue shoulder for all this. What you do, see, is you go into a moonshiner's turn, but you get on the brakes and stay on them. Depending on how fast you're going, you roll proportionately. Four or five rolls is decent. Going into the spin, you have one hand on the seat and the other firmly on the roof so you're sprung in tight. As you feel the roof give on the first roll, you slip your seat hand under the dash (of the passenger side, as you're thrown hard over in that direction to begin with) and pull yourself under it. And here you simply sit it out, springing yourself tight with your whole body, waiting for the thunder to die. Naturally, it helps to be drunk, and if you have a split second's doubt or hesitation through any of this you die.

This Schenkman himself is no slouch of a driver, I may say. Unfortunately, his strong suit is driving in New York City, a place that has a great number of unusual special conditions, which we just don't have the time or the space to get into right here (except to note that the good part is how it's real easy to scare old ladies in new Cadillacs and the bad part is that Negroes actually *do* carry knives, not to mention Puerto Ricans, and everybody else you hit turns out to be a lawyer or married to somebody in the mob). However, Joe is originally from the South, and it was down there that he discovered huffing glue and sniffing industrial solvents and such. These give you a really spectacular hallucinatory type of a high where you think, for instance, that you're driving through an overpass guardrail and landing on a freight-train flatcar and being hauled to Shreveport and loaded into a container ship headed for Liberia with a crew of homosexual Lebanese, only to come to find that it's true. Joe is a commercial artist who enjoys jazz music and horse racing. His favorite color is blue.

There's been a lot of discussion about what kind of music to listen to while staring doom square in the eye and not blinking unless you get some grit under your contacts. Watch out for the fellow who tunes his FM to the classical station. He thinks a little Rimsky-Korsakov makes things more dramatic—like in a foreign movie. That's pussy style. This kind of guy's idea of a fast drive is a seventy-five-mile-an-hour cruise up to the summer cottage after one brandy and soda. The true skid-mark artist prefers something cheery and upbeat—"Night on Disco Mountain" or "Boogie Oogie Oogie" or whatever it is that the teenage lovely wants to shake her buns to. Remember her? So what do you care what's on the fucking tape deck? The high, hot whine of the engine, the throaty pitch of the exhaust, the wind in your beer can, the gentle slurping noises from her little bud-red lips—that's all the music your ears need, although side two of the first Velvet Underground album is nice if you absolutely insist. And no short jaunts either. For the maniacal high-speed driver endurance is everything. Especially if you've used that ever popular pickup line, "Wanna go to Mexico?" Especially if you've used it somewhere like Boston. Besides, teenage girls can go a long, long time without sleep, and believe me so can the police and their parents. So just keep your foot on it. There's no reason not to. There's no reason not to keep going forever, really. I had this friend who drove a whole shitload of people up from Oaxaca to Cincinnati one time, nonstop.

I mean, he stopped for gas but he wouldn't even let anybody get out. He made them all piss out the windows, and he says that it was worth the entire drive just to see a girl try to piss out the window of a moving car.

Get a fat girlfriend so you'll have plenty of amphetamines and you'll never have to stop at all. The only problem you'll run into is that after you've been driving for two or three days you start to see things in the road, great big scaly things twenty-feet high with nine legs. But there are very few great big scaly things with nine legs in America anymore, so you can just drive right through them because they probably aren't really there, and if they are really there you'll be doing the country a favor by running them over.

Yes, but where does it all end? Where does a crazy life like this lead? To death, you say. Look at all the people who've died in car wrecks: Albert Camus, Jayne Mansfield, Jackson Pollock, Tom Paine. Well, Tom Paine didn't actually die in a car wreck, but he probably would have if he'd lived a little later. He was that kind of guy. Anyway, death is always the first thing that leaps into everybody's mind—sudden violent death at an early age. If only it were that simple. God, we could all go out in a blaze of flaming aluminum alloys formulated specially for the Porsche factory race effort like James Dean did! No ulcers, no hemorrhoids, no bulging waistlines, soft dicks, or false teeth . . . *Bash! Kaboom! Watch this space for paperback reprint rights auction and movie option sale!* But that's not the way it goes. No. What actually happens is you fall for that teenage lovely in the next seat, fall for her like a ton of Trojans, and before you know it you're married and have teenage lovelies of your own—getting felt up in a Pontiac Trans Am this very minute, no doubt—plus a six-figure mortgage, a liver the size of the Bronx, and a Country Squire that's never seen the sweet side of sixty.

It's hard to face the truth but I suppose you yourself realize that if you'd had just a little more courage, just a little more strength of character, you could have been dead by now. No such luck.

2

How to Drive Fast When the Drugs Are Mostly Lipitor, the Wing-Wang Needs More Squeezing Than It Used to Before It Gets the Idea, and Spilling Your Drink Is No Problem If You Keep the Sippy Cups from When Your Kids Were Toddlers and Leave the Baby Seat in the Back Seat so that When You Get Pulled Over You Look Like a Perfectly Innocent Grandparent

Chapter 1 was published in the *National Lampoon* in 1978 or '79 when I was half my age. To not despise yourself when you were a twerp of thirty-one requires a more philosophical mind than this old fart possesses. The more so when that twerp was right. And he—that is, I—*was* right, especially about getting married, having a family, the mortgage, the liver, and the Country Squire (or, as it turned out, the SUV). Of course I didn't marry the teenage lovely in the tube top. (Gosh, tube tops . . . As Alzheimer's creeps upon me, please God, let that be the last memory I lose.) True love and common sense intervened to make sure that I gained a beautiful spouse who can read and write and stuff and who does not want to drive from Boston to Mexico without stopping at several Ritz-Carltons. The other reason I didn't wed the teenage lovely in the tube top was that she didn't exist. I mean, she existed. I saw her every day on the summer streets of New York. But she didn't see me. I was dweeby, Brooks Brothers–clad, and invisible to her ilk. And so I have remained these thirty years. All for the best, I suppose.

Yet families do slow you down. I'll be power sliding through some mountain pass with a bottomless ravine yawning inches from my tire treads and suddenly images of my children—Muffin, Poppet, and Buster—will flash before my eyes. Even so, I don't press the accelerator, yank the wheel, and plunge to eternal rest. This must be some paternal instinct or maybe a drug that the life insurance companies slip us.

Speaking of drugs, let me get back to mocking my shavetail self. Yes, it was the 1970s. Yes, I indulged in "youthful experimentation," which is to say I smoked, snorted, or otherwise consumed every illegal drug I could get my hands on. Alas, my reach exceeded my grasp. I had trouble getting my hands on *any* drugs. Mayor Koch had better drug connections than I did. And I, for Pete's sake, knew John Belushi personally. I loved the drugs, but I had no head for the drug business. Again, this was all for the best, I suppose.

The fact that I was incapable of mastering brokerage trading at even such a basic level as entering one side of Washington Square Park with a five-dollar bill and leaving the other side with a matchbox full of oregano is what kept me from venturing—as so many of my drug-addled pals did—onto Wall Street. Thus I am spared the shame of responsibility for the current global financial meltdown (and the extra-shameful billions in skimmed profits that, with a guilt so strong it might *almost* cause me to make restitution, I would have salted away in the Cayman Islands). So I'm not writing this via satellite uplink from my two-hundred-foot yacht in international waters, beyond the reach of the FBI and Treasury agents, darn it.

The smirky knowingness about drugs, like the teenage lovely in the tube top, were products of wishful thinking or whatever the equivalent of thinking is that you do at that age between your knees and navel. My exegesis on the handling properties of rental cars, however, was the product of careful research. Because rental cars were the only cars I had. Here I was exhorting readers to drive like Steve McQueen in *Bullitt*, plus with a snootful, a blindfold, and an erection, and *I didn't own an automobile*.

I hadn't had a functioning four-wheeled motor vehicle since the beat-up Mercedes that carried the miniskirted ninety-pound early adapter of porn star deforestation. I crashed my motorcycles. (The motorcycle is a device created by the team of God and Darwin to rid the world of useless young males.) I was just conniving to get my last motorcycle wreck repaired when the eleven thousand votive candles lit by my mother at Sacred Heart caused it to be stolen by archangels.

By then I'd moved to New York so that many of the adventures I've recounted—when true at all—took place in Yellow cabs. Such a pigeon dick of a city brat had I become that I actually let my driver's license lapse. I was forced to go to night school and take driver's education every Tuesday and Thursday for six weeks. There were fifteen or eighteen of us in the class: a group of Chinese who spoke Chinese and nothing but Chinese, half a dozen elderly Russian Jewish ladies too shy to make a peep, and a bunch of black guys in the back of the class talking loudly among themselves and giving one another complicated handshakes. The class was taught by an old and embittered veteran of the New York City public school system who had the looks and the attitude of, come to think of it, me these days. His form of instruction was Socratic, and relentlessly so.

"What is the purpose of the steering wheel?" he asked.

The elderly Jewish ladies looked at their shoes. The Chinese stared into space. The black guys continued slanging each other.

"What is the purpose of the steering wheel?" the teacher asked again and got the same response.

"What is the purpose of the steering wheel?" he asked once more without changing his tone or expression.

Finally, to put an end to this—no offense to the Chinese—Chinese water torture, I raised my hand. The teacher called on me. "The purpose of the steering wheel," I said, "is to guide the direction of the car."

"What is the purpose of the brake pedal?" the teacher asked. Jewish ladies looked at shoes. Chinese stared. Black guys jived.

"What is the purpose of the brake pedal?" the teacher asked.

I raised my hand. The teacher called on me. "The purpose of the brake pedal," I said, "is to slow or stop the car."

"What is the purpose of the gearshift lever?" the teacher asked.

And so it went for a month and a half. The teacher asked a painfully simple question. Nobody said anything. The teacher repeated the painfully simple question. Nobody said anything. And eventually I gave the painfully simple answer. Sometimes I'd answer each question right away to see if this would speed the end of our ninety-minute class. It didn't. Sometimes I'd let the teacher ask and ask. I believe the record was ten times. There was never any acknowledgment that I was the only person answering the questions. We all passed the course.

I went to the New York State Department of Motor Vehicles to take the written portion of my driver's license exam. This was available in so many languages that there was quite a shuffling of paper to find one in English. I was sent to a room full of school-style table-armed chairs. An immense woman occupied a desk at the front.

The immense woman gave us forty-five minutes to complete our multiple choice test, which asked questions such as, "What is the purpose of the steering wheel?" I completed the test in ten minutes and presented it to the immense woman. She laid a stencil atop the blacked-in multiple choice circles, looked at me, and asked, "D'ju cheat?"

"I most certainly did not cheat," I said.

"Ain't nobody ever got them all right before," the immense woman said.

And this tells us everything we need to know about New York City driving, including my own (and Joe Schenkman's—who, last time I checked, was the respectable proprietor of a commercial printing and publishing firm).

I borrowed a coworker's Volvo to take the driving part of the exam. It had an automatic transmission, and all I can say to excuse myself is that I'd never owned a car that wasn't a stick. The driving test examiner and I got to the point where I had to parallel park. This involved backing up a slight incline. I maneuvered the car to the turn-in position, put the shift lever into what I thought was reverse, cocked the wheels, and gave the gas pedal an extra pat to compensate for the rearward rise in pavement. The Volvo jumped toward the car parked in front of my designated parking space (a police cruiser as I recall but that may be the exaggeration of memory). I slammed on the Volvo's brakes, which were too excellent. The driving test examiner (who, let it be noted, was not wearing his seat belt) lurched forward. His clipboard hit the dash and his head hit the clipboard, leaving a large, red Egyptian ankh-shaped mark in the middle of his forehead. I didn't pass.

Later, a rattle bucket of an old Beetle was commandeered and I got a valid driver's license. I got a car too, a really bad idea of a car, sort of a teenage lovely in a tube top car. It was gorgeous, a 1965 Alfa Romeo GTC, the convertible version of the champion sedan racing GTA coupe. The GTC model was never imported to the United States. All the gauges were in Italian: *olio, benzina, ziti*. A fabulous car, except for a few small problems such as the sheet metal having rusted away completely leaving only the red paint in place. If you exhaled hard you could blow a hole in the fender. The Morelli electrical system was having its own small, private Three Mile Island incident, which caused total power shutdown, and if you touched any of the wiring it would kill you. Also, nothing inside the engine moved.

I was standing at the bar in Brew's on Thirty-fourth Street where all the car guys in New York—and me—hung out. Jim Williams, then the sport editor of *Car and Driver*, said, "I heard you just bought an old Alfa." I said I had. "Great," said Jim, "because I happen to have an old Alfa repair kit—a truckload of money to follow you everywhere you go."

The truck was soon emptied. The Alfa was sold shortly before I wrote "How to Drive Fast." And shortly after I wrote "How to Drive Fast" I bought—prepare to gasp with envy—a 1975 six-cylinder Chevy fleet-side pickup with three on the column and one hundred thousand on the odometer. It was fully capable of fifty-five miles per hour once I replaced the studded snow tires and had the front wheels aligned and the tie rods straightened. This was my main ride until I purchased a 1981 Subaru wagon, which was followed by a VW Rabbit convertible, the latter at least being a hetero-girlie car.

Now, mind you, I'm not saying that the tenderfoot who wrote Chapter I was without a certain wisdom. I'm just trying to put his naif ideas and half-formed theories into better order and give him the benefit of perspective and experience that seniority provides.

For example, no one drinks and drives anymore, me in particular. I'm holding a hand over one eye because of cataracts and I'm weaving all over the road due to the palsy of age. Merely admitting to DUI in print is a Class A felony in all blue states. But I take the fledgling me's point, and I've seen a lot more of the world than he had. I've never yet gone to a war zone, a divorce court, an election campaign, a childbirth delivery room, a corporate board meeting, or a parent-teacher conference sober if I could help it.

Indulge me, kind reader, and let me address a few words to my neophyte self.

Your psychological analysis of fun was way off. Freudianism has been thoroughly discredited. Fun has nothing to do with the oedipal complexities of making your mother cry. Not that mothers aren't involved. Fun is what makes your wife go back to *her* mother.

It isn't true that old people don't risk their lives because such a gamble antes up nothing of value. It's hard to imagine a less valuable life than the plugge-nickel one you were leading when you wrote that nonsense. The reason we geriatrics rarely put our lives on the line is that we can afford to have you youngsters do it for us. And a tip of the hat to the United States Marine Corps.

Your cancer joke was not very amusing, as you, my pimply forerunner, will find out in twenty-nine years. (The painkillers, however, turn out to be better than anything you were able to score.)

That is not a "tweedy barf mat," you callow slob. That is a "Harris tweedy barf mat," hand tailored in London (albeit when the pound was at a friendly exchange rate). It cost more than you made in six months. And one wore a black silk tie to Alberto Ascari's funeral. What else *would* one wear?

Let me note that your insight concerning "big cars" was something you stole without credit (or much of a tip) from a wise (and naturally) old gentleman who shined shoes at the Baltimore train station. You had gone to Baltimore, you'll recall, to make the foolish purchase of the Alfa GTC. It was not—as it never would be—running, so you took the train back to New York. You were getting your shoes shined when you and the dignitary doing the work began to talk about cars.

"I just bought a car," you said.

"You did?" he asked. "What kind of car?"

"An Alfa Romeo convertible."

"Alfa Romeo," he said. "That would be one of those small cars."

"Yes," you said.

"No," he said. "You should always drive a big car. Now, me, I got a Buick Electra deuce-and-a-quarter. That's the kind of car you ought to buy. Always drive a big car."

"Why's that?" you asked. "Small cars are more maneuverable, and they get better gas mileage."

"No, no, no," he said. "Always drive a big car."

"But why?"

"Because," he said, "when you drive a big car and you get yourself in trouble—get yourself in an accident or something—the trouble happens *way out there,* where you don't hardly care about it. Whereas when you drive a small car, trouble happens *right in yo' face*!"

On the other hand, I must give you credit for the Rimsky-Korsakov observation. Didn't like him then. Don't like him now. That said, I remember you at CBGB, pogoing in shirtsleeves and skinny tie, pretending to like a band called the Stupids. And side two of the first Velvet Underground album? You *were* kidding? Maybe *Scheherezade* deserves another listen.

There's just one other little detail: I can blow your doors off. You didn't know for squat how to drive fast. I was there in 1976 when you went to race-car driving school on assignment for *Esquire* (in the last of its respectable Arnold Gingrich days). It was the same thing that happened with the immense woman at the New York State DMV. You got the highest score of any student on the written exam. And then, on the track, you might as well have been in that Volvo automatic. You were the slowest, the dead last slowest. What did your fellow students have to say about your exam score then, huh? (An exam that was provided by the SCCA, in case anyone was wondering where the animus toward that organization came from.)

I have a million miles and more under my Todd loafers since then. I can blow your doors off, kid. And I've got the off-door-blowing machinery that you didn't. It's nothing fancy. I have old cars. Why not? I'm an old guy. I have old shotguns too. And they kill birds, something else you couldn't do back then. My rubbed and loved 1990 911 was made back when Porsche still aspired to quickness, lightness, simplicity, and handling that would make your silly Hall and Oates–era haircut stand on end. I bought it almost new from a dentist who'd scared his fillings loose and decided a Lexus coupe was more his speed. The 911 will do the job, although I drive my near-classic gently these days, rarely taking it over 140.

Or, if that's too much for your jumpy juvenile nerves, I can whip your butt in my wife's car—a 1989 3-Series BMW convertible that's as taunt and firm as my wife (who's nearer your age than mine, incidentally). The BMW handles curves like Parisian lingerie.

Come to that, I'll take you on in my barn-door, dog-caged, gun-racked, hunting and fishing '99 Chevy Suburban beater towing a travel trailer. There's a forty-mile stretch of the Salmon River Road through the middle of New Brunswick from Gaspereau Forks straight east to Harcourt. From where I live to where the Gaspereau and Salmon rivers meet is an eight- or nine-hour drive. If I want to spend the next day hunting the good bird covers on the far side of Harcourt, I have to get down the Salmon River Road before the sun sets. Because, after the sun sets, no one drives the Salmon River Road and lives.

It's October. We're at a latitude north of Montreal. The sun *is* setting. The forty miles is all but uninhabited. The forest comes down to the edge of the roadside ditches. There is no shoulder. The ditches are deep enough to swallow a fully loaded logging truck, let alone a Suburban. The logging trucks are all the traffic we'll see. And they are roaring straight at us in pay-hole gear, taking their half of the road out of the middle, and trying to get to Gaspereau Forks before they're stone blind from the setting sun. The road is crowned like the dome of St. Peter's, and it was last repaved when New Brunswick was a main source of strip-mined coal for embattled Britain during World War II. Seeing a logging truck and a Suburban with a fish-tailing trailer get past each other here at top speed is like seeing an NFL dream game between Tom Brady's Pats and Mean Joe Greene's Steelers, and after the ball is snapped the New England offense misses the Pittsburgh defense, and the Pittsburgh defense misses the New England offense, and no one gets hit by anyone, and at the end of the play all the linemen are left untouched, wandering around under the opposing team's goalposts.

But that's the least of it. The Salmon River Road is a regular Marlin Perkins *Zoo Parade*. As dusk gathers, critters are everywhere—moose, deer, bears, and raccoons, plus geese, ducks, and ruffed grouse all flying at windshield altitude. Mainly it's the moose and deer that kill you. The deer if you swerve to avoid hitting them and go into the ditch, the moose if you don't. The bears are usually too smart to slam into you, but raccoons can do a surprising amount of damage (the nearest reliable radiator shop is in Toronto) and a game bird can turn your windshield into peace in the Middle East.

The moose is another example of God and Darwin ganging up on us. Obviously the moose existed before the automobile. But the moose's only discernible biological purpose—other than providing passable steaks and oversize lodge decorations—is to kill automobile drivers. Talk about seeing big things in the road. True, moose aren't scaly and they have only four feet. But I don't recommend running them over. The moose stands on legs the exact average height of a car hood. These legs are fragile appendages, just temporary props holding fifteen hundred pounds of car-spanning body weight at eye level. Be your car ever so big, and the advice of the gentleman who used to shine shoes in the Baltimore train station notwithstanding, whatever happens when you collide with a moose happens "right in yo' face."

So, youngin', let's have a little cocktail-hour race from Gaspereau Forks to Harcourt. Pick any car you want, although I'd advise against Lamborghinis or anything else low-slung. You might find out that a raccoon *can* kill you. Choose your weapon, and try to catch this old duffer with his dimming eyesight and reflexes a half century past their prime. I'm going to put the hammer down on the big, fat nine-mile-a-gallon Chevy V-8. Then tons of shuddering Suburban are going to eat that ugly pavement at 90, 100, 110 mph, no matter the shot shocks, the wiggling bait-worm steering, the travel trailer doing the ten-dollar whore walk out back, and the off-brand recapped meat on the wheels.

I long for my camp, my whiskey, and my chance to let the farting bird dogs out to take a dump. I rage, rage against the dying of the light, to quote a poet you may dimly remember from college but whom I have read for pleasure and with adult understanding. Can you keep up? Or will you be creeping along at thirty-five with your brights on, pressing your nose against the windshield, searching frantically for lethal wildlife, and trying to remember the difference between Bob Dylan and Dylan Thomas? I am racing against that darkness Dylan Thomas so feared. And, hell, he'd never even seen a moose.

And let me say in closing that the ode to dying young, with which you closed your essay, was crap, my little pal. Dying young is fine, for young people. And from what I can see of young people—tongue studded, tramp stamped, and wearing their Playskool shorts and SpongeBob T-shirts to the office—more power to the notion. But dying old is the Grand

Prix. To be young is to be driving in the figure-eight races and demo derbies of life. There's better fun to be had as you head toward the finish line at Monte Carlo.

Die young? If I'd died young I never would have lived to see the glory of lard-assed President Clinton getting impeached by Congress for following the very advice you gave years ago in the *National Lampoon,* right down to the detail of the fat girlfriend. Although it is interesting to note—given the amount you knew about women, narcotics, and cars at the time you were dispensing your advice—that President Clinton did it all without drugs, alcohol, or even so much as turning an ignition key.

3

Sgt. Dynaflo's Last Patrol

The fervor of automotive brand loyalty in the 1950s must puzzle today's young car enthusiasts no matter how much they love their Honda tuners. It was an era when the wraparound windshield was considered a major technological breakthrough by the American car industry. So what was the Chevy versus Plymouth versus Fix-Or-Repair-Daily argument about? And partisan issues were intracorporational as well. There were Impala families and Bonneville families, and there may well have been Eldorado Brougham families, but the kids in my neighborhood would have beaten up the kids from those families. Boys of ten or eleven got in heated arguments about the relative merits of cars that were, even then, largely interchangeable and would soon become completely so. I am trying to imagine how I could explain, to someone born in 1999, the fine shade of difference between owning an Oldsmobile and owning a Buick. And what's an Oldsmobile anyway?

I was a Buick brat, born that way, no choice in the matter since my dad sold them for a living. My pulse still races when I see portholes on a fender, though I prefer them on the fender of a Maserati Gran Turismo S rather than on the fender of a Special, Super, Century, or Roadmaster. But I'm getting ahead of myself, passing on a curve, narratively speaking.

In the summer of 1977, I was pleased to hear that Tom Sargent, publisher of *Car and Driver*'s brother magazine *Cycle*, wanted someone to drive his 1956 Buick Special four-door sedan from Florida to Los Angeles.

I'd never written for *Car and Driver*, but on the strength of some drinks I'd had with its new editor, David E. Davis Jr., and the inebriated Oldsmobile/Buick quarrel that had ensued, I volunteered. David E. assigned the photography to the late, and much missed, Humphrey Sutton. Humphrey and I met at a midtown Manhattan restaurant to sketch our route. Just as we were entering the restaurant a taxi came to an abrupt halt, and a motorcyclist behind it came to a halt that was not quite abrupt enough. Rider and bike slid up under the Checker. Considering what publication Tom Sargent was the publisher of, Humphrey and I should have taken this event as an omen rather than an excuse to drink at lunch.

The Buick Special had been stored for the previous few years in a hangar at Sargent's father's home in Crescent City, Florida. Humphrey and I flew to Daytona Beach where Mr. Sargent, senior, picked us up in his Cessna 180. He took us thirty-five or forty miles northwest and landed on a grass strip, coming to a stop right in front of where he'd rolled the Buick onto his lawn. Rolled, not driven. Tom had neglected, until the night before, to inform his dad that we were coming to fetch the car. We almost got the Buick started a number of times before we removed the mouse nest, and the mice, from the carburetor.

Due to Tom's tardy phone call and Humphrey's and my vineous lunch in New York, not much forethought had gone into this expedition. We drove away from Crescent City with an ancient set of filed-down points in the distributor, no tools, no manual, not even a flashlight, and a map of America showing only railroad lines. We did have a Styrofoam cooler full of beer.

"For obvious reasons we called the Buick 'Sergeant Dynaflo,'" I wrote in my original *Car and Driver* piece. But the obvious may need explaining to anyone under forty. Buick was noted for its unique automatic transmission of the Dynaflo name. This was a hydraulic-fluid-filled device with variable pitch blades that delivered power from the 322-cubic-inch V-8 to the rear wheels smoothly, quietly, and, most of all, very, very slowly.

For other obvious reasons it became clear that the Buick was going to have to be driven from coast to coast on two-lane roads. I no longer remember what became obvious first —the Shake 'n' Bake front-wheel shimmy at fifty miles per hour, the Dynaflo acceleration that meant an inability to reach freeway speed without using a mile of shoulder as part of the merge lane, or the temperature gauge's slow but relentless minute hand movement toward hell.

It's odd to think back and realize that this Buick was only twenty-one years old at the time. A twenty-one-year-old car was an awful lot older then than it is now. Just as, to my mind, a twenty-one-year-old boy is an awful lot younger. At least in the matter of cars, this is not merely old-guy perception. As noted in Chapter 2, I have a garage full of daily drivers bearing about two decades of vintage. My Porsche 911 will be twenty next year—a few tire and brake pad changes and one valve job and it's as reliable as it was new. (Never mind that the valve job cost more than my first three cars.) My wife's 1989 BMW 3-Series convertible is the same way. The top was replaced in the midnineties and I had a little suspension work done to take out some bumps and clunks. A 1984 Jeep Scrambler, bought new, is still my year-round farm vehicle. All its knobs and switches have fallen off, and it leaves grease patches on the garage floor, but you'd have to drop a thirty-foot oak on it to kill the thing. I've done that too, and it's still running. Next time Al Gore complains about the wasteful and unprogressive nature of the automobile industry, tell him to go find the car from his daddy's days in the Senate and drive it to . . . I can think of several places.

Saturday, June 25, 1977
Crescent City to Nowhere

The Buick Special was, however, beautiful: two-tone turquoise and white with seat covers to match. The weather was splendid. People smiled and waved to us as we rolled through the small north Florida towns (which snowbirds had not yet pooped on.) At blue highway speeds the Buick was a big, steady pleasure to drive. We went 150 miles like that, sipping beers and returning salutes. The Buick ran perfectly right up until it didn't.

When the engine went out we were in a godforsaken stretch of piney woods on County Route 98 somewhere around about, but nowhere near, Tallahassee. All of a sudden the car was too quiet, and we weren't going as fast as we should have been. We figured it was the old set of points.

There was a shack about two hundred yards down the road with two broken gas pumps and a sign that said BEER. It was half overgrown with creepers in the front and half sunk into what, these days, would be called wetlands in the back. The scene resembled an EC horror comic *Swamp Thing* title panel, but it was the only building we'd seen for twenty miles, and it did have that sign that said BEER. We pushed the Buick there. I went inside to borrow some tools.

About a dozen hard-visaged, definitely unfriendly, and possibly cannibalistic Southern types were in there, all eyeing me suspiciously. The bartender was a big, nasty-faced old guy with an enormous paunch, a flat-top haircut four inches high, and a cigar turned backward in his mouth. (I assume, but am by no means certain, it was unlit.) I got the idea he didn't like my looks either, but he loaned me a screwdriver and an adjustable wrench.

Humphrey was all business under the hood, tinkering with this and tapping on that. I thought maybe he knew what he was doing until I realized he couldn't find the spark plugs. Buick used to put these lid things over them. After we'd pried one off and given ourselves some spark-plug-wire electrical shocks, we figured maybe it wasn't the old set of points. Maybe it was vapor lock. If you leave vapor lock alone it gets better. This was exactly the kind of mechanical problem that Humphrey and I were good at solving. We decided it was vapor lock and went to get a drink.

Humphrey was from England so he thought this bar was quaint, charming in its primitive way, a real piece of Americana. I'm from Ohio and I thought we were going to get killed.

The South was still the *South* in 1977. And the Florida piney woods weren't full of good ole boys in Ralph Lauren Polo shirts who'd made it big developing gated (and degatored) golf course communities. The Florida piney woods were full of the kind of rednecks who were beginning to fill that bar—none of them an improvement on the rednecks who had been there already. This was only five years after *Deliverance* hit the theaters and only eight years after the premiere of *Easy Rider*, which I had seen three times when I was trying to be a hippie (and which—from my present perspective of a dad with daughters, surveying the good-for-nothing young men on motorcycles who might want to date them—has a happy ending). I mean, Jimmy Carter had carried the South in '76. They were so primitive down there that they hadn't even evolved into Republicans.

And then there was Humphrey's English accent, a posh accent, one might even go so far as to say a plummy accent. It was a nice accent to have—in England. In the Florida piney woods it was an accent that might not sound, well, you know, *manly*. And Humphrey, after he'd had a few drinks, began to speak—as English speakers the world around do, especially in foreign climes—more loudly. When Humphrey started talking a little louder, people started to look at us a little funny. The louder his talk became, the funnier the looks we got. And just when I was *sure* we were going to get killed somebody asked if that was our old Buick out front with the hood up. We said yes. The room went silent. Then there was, I swear, an audible sound of cracking smiles (revealing a good number of missing teeth). Even the bartender's expression turned faintly cheerful.

"That old Buick quit on ya?" someone else asked. We said yes. There was a rush out the door. Trunk lids popped up, tool cases snapped open, and in minutes our engine compartment was packed with fearsome drunk Florida crackers undoing fuel lines, pulling off plug wires, and wrenching on things that I couldn't see while beer bottles piled up in front of the grille.

Not that any of them were able to get the car started. Humphrey and I went back in the bar and began drinking at a table with the local game warden and José, an immense half-Indian, half-Mexican who'd been the 1959 and '60 Rocky Mountain Professional Wrestling Champion and whose presence in the Florida panhandle was never adequately explained. The game warden said that he himself had had a '56 Buick. "Had one just like it," he said. Several other people said the same thing. In fact, on our entire trip, it was hard to find a man over forty-five who said he *hadn't* had a '56 Buick. And they were fondly remembered, to a car. "You couldn't break 'em with a stick," said the game warden. "That car'll run forever."

Humphrey said he'd settle for tonight.

I asked the warden what the BEER place was called. "Well," he said, "sometimes we call it the 98 Inn and sometimes we call it the 98 Tavern, but mostly we don't call it anything at all. Hell, you're thirty miles from nowhere and forty miles from nowhere else." Then he went off and got into a fight.

By midnight Humphrey and I were very drunk. We were talking to a fellow named Jack who was twenty-two and looked like he robbed gas stations to get his heart started in the morning. He had a sharp Appalachian face with various scars and a row of absent dentation. He'd recently shot himself in the stomach over something to do with an estranged wife. He showed us where the bullet had gone in and where it had come out. Now he was living in a trailer with another lady and her five kids, but they were all off at her mother's canning something, so he invited us to stay with him. We were sure he was a homicidal maniac but it was that or sleep in the car.

Jack turned out to be a perfectly amiable guy. It was all we could do to keep him from persuading us to take a little vacation and spend a week down there bait fishing for razorback hogs, or whatever it is they do on vacation in the Florida piney woods. And he did persuade us to share his quart jar of moonshine.

Sunday, June 26
Nowhere to Mobile

Ouch, we woke up. Our friends of the night before had done a fair amount of damage helping us out. There were a lot of loose hoses and wires. Fuel lines were draped over the fenders and the contact arm on the points had been bent double. Humphrey decided that he'd better work on this himself, so he squatted atop the valve covers and sweated and diddled in the distributor for the next two hours. Finally, Jack rounded up yet another local, who took a big screwdriver, jammed it once into the points, slapped on the distributor cap, and started the car first try. "Had one just like it," he said.

Humphrey and I drove south until we found the ocean. We rented a motel room for the day and had showers and a lot of Bloody Marys. And then, God knows why, we went to a water park.

Humphrey thought this was quaint, charming in its primitive way, a real piece of Americana. I thought, between our hangovers and all the Bloody Marys, we were going to drown.

Then we went to Sears and bought some tools that must have seemed at the time as though they would be useful: a large hammer, three unusual sizes of Phillips screwdrivers, a pair of tiny Japanese pliers, and a pry bar.

Just after sundown we got back in the Buick. It was running perfectly now. We drove to Mobile with no problems except that Humphrey turned out to be scared of insects they don't have in England, which is most insects. He nearly put us into a ditch when he got a June bug down his shirt. Also, we couldn't figure out how to work the instrument panel lights so the driver had to open his quarter-ton door every time he wanted to check the speedometer or the gas gauge and this would cause the driver to accidentally yank the steering wheel, sending the car careening across the road into oncoming traffic and making all the water that had leaked out of our busted Styrofoam cooler slosh into our shoes.

Monday, June 27
Mobile to Natchez

We figured that if the points weren't screwed up before, they certainly were now, after being jammed with a big screwdriver. But only one junkyard in Mobile had a '56 Buick, and it had kudzu growing up through its engine compartment, and the distributor was missing anyway. Eventually the junkyard owner found a garage that had a new set of points. We were on our way there when the car quit again. This time we *knew* it was the points. I hitched to the garage and came back with their tow truck. The driver (he'd had one just like it) unhooked the fuel line to the carburetor. There was a vicious reptilian hiss. "Vapor lock," the tow truck driver said. We had a new set of points installed anyway and spent the rest of the day battling vapor lock all across Mississippi.

Back in the 98 Tavern, José the wrestling champion had told us that the one surefire cure for vapor lock was to put wooden clothespins all along the fuel line. We thought that sounded pretty stupid, but by the time we got to Hattiesburg we'd bought two bags of them and had stuck on as many as we could fit. When we stopped for gas in a little town, the station owner opened our hood to check the oil and the half dozen loafers hanging out at his station burst into hysterics. So the clothespins had to go. I thought we should give them another chance. Maybe they'd start to work or something. But Humphrey said he drew the line at getting laughed at if we died in a wreck.

Tuesday, June 28
Natchez to Dallas

We now had the process of unhooking the fuel line and curing our vapor lock down to about one minute, but we'd quit getting vapor lock. And we were just congratulating ourselves when the water temperature hit the bad peg and wouldn't come down. We had to spend an hour and a half cooling off in Louisiana's Kisatchie National Forest. There is absolutely nothing to do in Louisiana's Kisatchie National Forest except sit around and look at the one kind of conifer that grows in the Kisatchie National Forest. Let us call it the Kisatchie cedar. Whether it is rare or endangered I do not know. I do know that after an hour and a half it cries out to be clear-cut.

The engine overheated again as soon as we started the car, and we limped into Clarence, Louisiana, where the proprietor of the sole filling station told us that the Buick's thermostat had "shit the bed." He didn't have any parts or even a garage but he gave us the phone numbers of all the local mechanics and the use of his phone. I called everyone in a thirty-mile radius but no one had a hand free to do the work. Finally, I got one fellow who said, "Hell I had a '56 Buick, and I just tore the damn thermostat out. Threw it away. If you ain't got a gasket, slap some damn cardboard in there. Damn thing'll run forever."

I was embarrassed to admit that I didn't know where thermostats made their home. But the filling station owner did. He made a gasket out of the back of my reporter's notebook and bolted it into the water hose connection where it stuck out on every side, little spiral binding holes and all.

The overheating was fixed, and while we drove toward Dallas that night Humphrey and I debated whether to have the thermostat fixed as well. Buick must have had some reason for putting a thermostat in besides cold mornings in Kansas. Even in Africa or Southeast Asia, where it's always hot, cars have thermostats. At least we thought they did. Maybe thermostats provide back pressure or something in the water pump or somewhere to prevent, you know, surge and gurgling in there. Maybe we'd really need one in the desert where surge and gurgling could be expected to be at their worst. Without a thermostat all the water might swish around too fast in the cooling system, running through over and over again at hundreds of gallons per minute and turning into superheated steam until the whole car blew up like the steamboat *Sultana*. We didn't know.

Wednesday, June 29
Dallas to Nowhere in Particular

The new thermostat—plus labor, fresh antifreeze, a radiator flush, a "water pump inspection," and several other things I couldn't make out on the bill—cost almost fifty dollars.*

Out beyond Dallas somewhere we came upon something called the Cadillac Ranch. A sculptor (soi-disant) had planted ten Cadillacs nosedown in the empty prairie. The Caddys—1951 through 1960, if I recall—pretty much covered the history of tail fins. About half of each car was sticking out of the ground, on a slant calculated so that the truly enormous fins of the '59 Coupe deVille formed an equilateral triangle with the Earth. Voila, art. Humphrey and I inspected this cultural treasure and found beer can and condom package indications that the backseats of the sculpture had been used for traditional backseat purposes. You don't see that so much with, for instance, a Rodin.

When we got up toward Wichita Falls we realized we needed a drink and, also, the engine was overheating again. So, as it turned out, was the air-conditioning unit in my motel room. And the desk clerk told us that this was a dry county, and it was fifty miles to the nearest bar or carryout.

Thursday, June 30
Wherever We Were to Tucumcari

The Texas panhandle has to be one of the most featureless landscapes on earth. They have sightseeing buses that take

*Evidence would suggest that the inflationary increase in the cost of auto repair has outstripped medical bills and college tuition combined.

you into Lubbock to see the tree. Or they should. For lack of anything better to do we stopped at a junkyard in Quanah or Goodnight or someplace where the owner had a lot of old Buicks parked in a field. He said our overheating problem had to do with the cylinder head design. "They'd all overheat," he said, "all those '56 Buicks." The next person blamed it all on hot oil in the Dynaflo transmission. Somebody else said the radiators were "too thick and not wide enough." Another said they were "plenty thick but too high." And one man in Barstow claimed that the problem was "this shitty weather we've been having for twenty years." But not one of these people was shaken in his belief that a '56 Buick would "run forever."

Actually, just then, our '56 felt like it would. The temperature gauge was strangely somnolent, and we didn't have a single major problem all day except for the hour or so when our fuel pump was spraying gas all over the hot exhaust manifold.

For thirty miles, approaching Amarillo, Humphrey and I were complaining that the city stank of gasoline. And Amarillo does have a lot of refineries. But the gas smell kept getting worse for thirty miles, leaving Amarillo.

When it eventually occurred to us to stop and look under the hood we found that the tiny rubber gasket under the bolt that holds the fuel pump cap in place had collapsed and gas was squirting out and boiling up in little spitballs on the headers. I have no clue why this didn't turn us into a miniature *Hindenburg,* not even after Humphrey gasped in dismay and let the cigarette drop out of his mouth and fall right in there. I forget what we used to stop the squirting until we'd bought a small rubber washer two cents at a Tucumcari hardware store. Very possibly it was chewing gum.

Friday, July 1
Tucumcari to Albuquerque

There's a beat-up old road, Route 104, running northwest out of Tucumcari through the desert to Conchas Lake, then up into the Cornudo Hills and across a grassland plateau to the Sangre de Cristo Mountains and Sante Fe. I'd flown to the West but I'd never driven over it. This little 150-mile byway awed me to imbecility. Humphrey said I was dangerous behind the wheel—bouncing up and down in the seat and jabbering about purple mountain majesties above the fruited plain and pointing out all the cows. We had to stop in Sante Fe to have a beer and settle me down.

Other than that it was just another day, with the engine overheating all the time and a new vapor lock problem that happened only on the edge of precipices or in the middle of blind curves. And even when the Buick was running right it was, truth be told, a very ordinary car. Once the museum-piece novelty had worn off, driving it was about as exciting as driving a new Buick. Or it was until we got lost down some lousy dirt roads south of Sante Fe and the car just sort of fell apart. The shocks and springs got Parkinson's disease, and all four wheels broke loose and headed every way but straight. At twenty miles per hour you would have thought we were racing the Baja 1000 in the Unlimited Class.

Humphrey had a theory about suspension harmonics or something and claimed that everything would be much better if he just drove faster, which made everything much worse. At least the Buick took to getting vapor lock in front of bars and taverns in all the little towns we went through, and that was good. But by the time we arrived in Albuquerque we were beginning to doubt the wisdom of this enterprise. In fact we were sick to death of the trip and the thing it rode in on.

Saturday, July 2
Drunk All Day in Albuquerque

Saturday we were drunk all day in Albuquerque.

Sunday, July 3
Albuquerque to Somewhere, Utah

Up in the Nacimiento Mountains we had a truly perplexing mechanical problem. We'd stopped for lunch in Cuba, New Mexico. When we came out of the restaurant the car wouldn't start and there was no vapor lock hiss when we opened the fuel line. Humphrey thought maybe the fuel pump had lost prime and was pumping backward. This seemed as likely a story as any to me. When we took the top off the fuel pump it was blowing bubbles in there. That, Humphrey told me, was a contraindication of backward fuel pumping. I took his word for it. Humphrey tried to suck some gas up the fuel line. That didn't work so I tried until I began to giggle from the fumes and get sick.

Speaking of which, the restaurant where we were stalled was halfway along a mile of road between an Apache reservation and a liquor store. The Apaches coming from the reservation paid no attention to us. But the Apaches returning from the liquor store found our huffing and puffing of gasoline fascinating. After an hour we had a John Wayne movie's worth of Apaches surrounding us. Whether they considered us harmless lunatics or thought the opportunity to sniff Mobil premium was a prize worth capturing we could not determine. In fact, we couldn't get much dialogue going with the Apaches at all. Every now and then one would come from the liquor store to our engine bay and announce, "Me, Indian." Then he would act like I had and giggle and get sick. (I realize that "Indian" was, even in 1977, not the sensitive term of ethnic description. But my code of journalistic ethics forbids me from reporting that any Apache said, "Me, Native American.")

Humphrey found a length of radiator hose, which he put over the fuel filler neck and blew into. What this was supposed to do I don't know, but it certainly made him look funny. More Apaches giggled and got sick. After that Humphrey insisted on taking the fuel pump apart. I'd never seen the inside of a fuel pump. (It isn't wildly interesting.) Humphrey claimed that the fuel pump was doing all a fuel pump should. He put it back together. Giggling, sick Apaches were closing in. I tried the starter and the engine caught and ran like nothing had happened, thank God.

We got out of Cuba, over the continental divide, and into the huge Navajo reservation that takes up almost a quarter of Arizona. The landscape opened up, impossibly vast and void, and it dawned on us, for the first time really, that when the next thing broke we might be in serious trouble. We'd go forty or fifty miles without seeing another car and the Buick was overheating worse than ever. We'd bought a five-gallon jerry can in Tucumcari and whenever the gauge went all red we'd stop and one of us would get out and splash down the radiator while the driver gunned the engine. This would hold us for two hours, or one hour in the midday heat, or ten minutes on an uphill grade. We had no business being away from the amenities and attentions of the interstate in this car. We knew that. But we'd started out driving on the back roads because the Buick couldn't make turnpike speed, and these little bypaths had been so quaint and charming in their primitive way, and with such quaint, charming people and so many quaint, charming places to break down in front of and buy beer in that we'd forgotten ourselves and now we were in a real piece of Americana indeed.

Between Kayenta and the Grand Canyon we went a hundred miles without seeing any sign of human life besides each other—and the signs of life in these two humans seemed precarious. Then the sun went down and for the first time since we'd left Florida the temperature fell below seventy degrees. All of a sudden the Buick was a different car. It seemed to exude an aura of strength and dependability, almost as if it might run forever. I was driving, so I put my foot down and—in a Dynaflo way—we took off. If I pushed the old Buick enough past fifty mph all the jitterbug and hootchie-kootchie in the front end went away. Maybe Humphrey was right about "suspension harmonics" (whatever they may be), at least on smooth pavement. And upon smooth pavement we were. We went 65, 75, 80 miles an hour down these twisting roads, whipping along for all the world like a freshly minted Mercedes-Benz.

We were pulling out onto Route 89 just over the Utah border when some fellow in a Datsun Fairlady, of all things, buzzed by doing eighty-five or so, and I lit out, lumbering after him. It was wholly dark by then, and a misty night, and I wonder what the guy thought when he saw that wall of chrome well up in his rearview mirror. He was being overtaken by the past. And the past went by at a hundred miles per hour with door handles higher than his head and two inches of travel left under the accelerator. For me it was a truly exhilarating moment of rapport between man and machine. Then we got vapor lock and the engine conked out.

Monday, July 4
Utah to Las Vegas

We had to go almost a hundred miles up into Utah to find motel rooms. I celebrated America's birthday by awakening in a condition that those who've spent much of their lives on the road in America will recognize. I had no idea where I was. I looked around the anonymous room and there was nothing—no note pad, no matches, no phone book, no area code on the phone—to indicate my location. I turned on the TV. It wasn't working. Usually such disorientation is momentary, or, at worst, you just can't remember the name of the woman snoring next to you. But there was no woman in this case, and my amnesia lasted through shit, shower, and shave. I was beginning to suspect I'd died in my sleep and gone to motel purgatory when I thought to open the door. There was the Buick. Purgatory was not an option.

It was raining. The Buick wouldn't start for a while. Something had gotten wet under the hood and we had to wait for the showers to let up and mop around under there with a motel towel before we got it going. Ten miles down the road it began to rain again and we discovered that we didn't have any windshield wipers. We'd been hearing obscene sucking noises from the brake pedal for a couple of days and we knew there was a problem somewhere in all the tubes and hoses of the Buick's Medusa-head vacuum assist mechanism. But everything seemed to work and we didn't realize that the windshield wipers ran off this system too. I could get the blades to move a little when we were headed uphill and acceleration increased the vacuum pressure. But downhill deceleration did the opposite. The only way to maintain any vacuum pressure at all was to keep my right foot pressed on the accelerator while using my left foot to try to slow down. Since the drum brakes on a '56 Buick are about three times more effective in front than they are in the rear, the back wheels began to slip around. It was not a recipe for safe driving. And, naturally, we were treated to clearing skies up every incline and drenching squalls down every slope until we got back into the desert and began to overheat.

We played it safe through Arizona and Nevada, sticking to Interstate 15 almost to Las Vegas. Then Humphrey insisted that he had to see the Valley of Fire. So we filled the jerry can and headed down a maze of gravel roads into that red sandstone wasteland. I suppose it's very beautiful, if you think you're going to live to tell anybody about it. We were completely alone, and it was 110 degrees in the shade. I was sure that when they found us—our bones picked clean by whatever it is that bothers to live out here—they'd think we were left over from some 1956 Vegas mob slaying. And we did manage to get lost. To add irony to probable death, we'd had a CB radio with us all along. But we'd kept forgetting to have it installed. It was a glum moment out there in the desert when Humphrey and I realized we would not be able to figure out how to connect that radio. Not, literally, for the life of us.

Fortunately we got unlost. Then I decided there was a quicker way to get to Las Vegas than the interstate and we got lost again for a while. Quite a while, actually, so that when we pulled over the top of one more hill and saw the city glistening below us we were almost out of gas, completely out of water, and totally out of patience with each other.

Dirty, half-naked, and our car covered with dust and grit, we weren't sure they'd take us in at the Sands. But the doorman had "had one just like it" and bent our ears for twenty minutes about how nothing ever went wrong with a '56 Buick.

Humphrey and I drank a few drinks in the lobby bar. I went to my room, exhausted. Humphrey ordered a nightcap. This apparently turned into a morning sombrero. (He *was* drinking tequila sunrises.) I came out of my room early in the A.M. and there was Humphrey, more or less where I'd left him, but now accompanied by two scantily sequined young ladies of the type who may be said to have "a rich and varied social life." I must say they were quaint and charming in their primitive way, and each was a real piece of Americana.*

Tuesday, July 5
Las Vegas to Los Angeles

There's a 2,400-foot climb up the Barstow incline on the California-Nevada border, and we knew that if we didn't make it before ten in the morning we wouldn't make it at all. So I had to pry Humphrey away from his bosom buddies and pour him into the car. Besides, we were three days overdue in LA and practically broke. (Humphrey had been luckier in love than at craps.)

Somehow we made it to Barstow without seizing up. The temperature gauge was half in the red at exactly fifty miles per hour and if I went even two miles per hour faster the radiator began to boil from engine heat while if I went two miles per hour slower the radiator began to boil from lack of cooling air.

*In fairness to Humphrey Sutton's memory, this was years before he married Nancy Grimes and fathered Courtney. In fact, he had not yet even been introduced to Nancy. And this is a good thing since she would have given him a swift kick.

Humphrey was flopping all over in his sleep, flailing at me and falling against the steering wheel. Once, when we were completely boxed in—trucks fore and aft and a car in the left lane—his leg shot out and he stamped on my accelerator foot. We would have crashed if I hadn't given him a swift kick and caused him to curl up on the seat.

Tom Sargent lived in Bel Air, and Humphrey knew his way around Los Angeles (a city with a street plan and a freeway system that baffle me to this day). So, in San Bernardino, Humphrey sobered himself enough to drive. He did this, much as I had done at the Utah motel door, simply by standing back and taking a long look at the Buick. Then we ran it through a car wash.

It had taken eleven days to cross the country, and we'd had some kind of breakdown every one of those days except this last one. When we got to Bel Air Humphrey passed Sargent's house, went to turn around, and reverse gear gave out. Gave out completely—the Buick couldn't even be pushed backward in neutral. We had to make a circle through Bel Air, go out onto Sunset Boulevard again, and come back to Sargent's address.

I suppose I still love old Buicks. I remember thinking I probably wouldn't try to drive another across the whole grocery store, A&P, Atlantic to Pacific. And I never have. And I never have found out how Tom Sargent got that car out of his driveway.

4

NASCAR Was Discovered By Me

NASCAR was discovered by me. I did a piece for *Rolling Stone* in the early 1980s. I was the first feature journalist from north of the Mason-Dixon line to write about NASCAR for a general interest magazine.

The foregoing is a fair sample of the kind of lie that car journalists tell each other late at night in bars. In the first place there is the small matter of Tom Wolfe writing about Junior Johnson in *Esquire* a full twenty years earlier. Wolfe's article (inept echoes of which can be heard below) was called "The Last American Hero." In 1973 it was turned into an excellent movie starring the best American actor, Jeff Bridges.

In the second place, *Rolling Stone* is not a general interest magazine. Corporal interest, maybe. But the *Stone* never made it to the Pentagon of publications. Not even back then when it was being edited, with brilliance, by my friend Terry McDonell, who somewhat resembles Jeff Bridges and is nowadays more sensibly installed as head of *Sports Illustrated*. Terry, I mean, not Jeff. Although I'm sure Jeff would do a fine job.

Thus I cannot claim in any way to have debarked from the *Mayflower* of journalistic NASCAR colonization, landing at (or in a) Plymouth. However, the pocket of every falsehood contains the small change of truth, or some truth lint, or something. One mustn't measure oneself against genius such as Tom Wolfe's, or how would one feel? Like me, probably. (By the way, Tom Wolfe is not *technically* from north of the Mason-Dixon line.) And the fact of the matter is that in the early 1980s if you'd said "NASCAR" to urban, trendsetting *Rolling Stone* readers, they'd have said, "Gesundheit."

So, in the early 1980s, I said I'd discovered the best spectator sport in the world and changed my mind about half of America in one weekend.

I went to Charlotte, North Carolina, to a National Association of Stock Car Automobile Racing (NASCAR) Grand National race and had more fun than is generally allowed unless you turn Buddhist and get another lifetime. I'm something of a car race fan but I always looked down my nose at circle track, just as I always took a rhinal line of sight at the South. I thought stock cars lacked sophistication, and I thought the South did too. Plus I got beat up down there in 1967 for trying to wear my hair like Roger Daltrey.

But I have an old friend, Don Hunter, who lives in Charlotte and is one of the country's top stock car photographers. He got me to come down, picked me up at the airport on Friday, and took me on a cocktail-punctuated whirlwind tour of the local stock car team HQs.

A stock car isn't just one car and maybe a backup, as I'd thought. Each driver needs at least four and, if possible, as many as seven fully prepared race cars to keep him on the circuit from February to November. Even learning that didn't prepare me for the garages. They were so clean you could deliver babies in the grease pits. And the engine-tuning bays, the machine shops, and the dyno rooms were so crammed with electronics and technical equipment they looked like a George Lucas peyote vision.

These are merely the places where the cars are tweaked and maintained. Then we visited an awesome shop where the things are actually built, using just seven pieces of sheet metal from the original Detroit cars and everything else from scratch. There was one ole boy there, hunkered down with all manner of folksy verb tenses. I asked him something about what kind of steel the tube frames are made from. He launched into a Nobel Prize lecture on metallurgy in which "molybdenum" was the smallest word I noticed.

I love machinery and if you'd made me nine again and gave me a speaking part in *Return of the Jedi* I wouldn't have had a happier day. Plus, by ten o'clock that night I was knee-walking drunk, something I wouldn't have appreciated when I was nine, any more than I would have appreciated the terrific French food I was eating in a terrific fancy restaurant on top of a building a terrific lot taller than you'd think they made them in Charlotte.

Saturday, Hunter fixed me up with every sort of pit/press/photog credential and dragged me around everywhere to meet everyone who had anything to do with anything. And I kept dragging him back to the fabulous Union Oil VIP lounge, one of thirty glassed and soundproof boxes across the top of the grandstands at Charlotte Motor Speedway. Each of these boxes is fitted with a bar, closed circuit TV, and half a dozen tiers of armchairs with programs, press kits, pens, ashtrays, and fresh packs of Winstons arrayed on tables in front of them. The prettiest women in America were on hand to ask, "What can I get you-all?" The answer being a new career covering NASCAR.

Not that I was qualified. Yes, reporters are famous instant experts. And with any ordinarily arcane sport—cricket, for example—a weekend would have sufficed for me to argue all the fine points of the game in every pub in England. But there was something about that mechanic's molybdenum tutorial that made me think I wasn't anywhere near smart enough to play dumb, down South NASCAR–style.

Maybe the drivers would be more on my level. Braver than I am, of course. But maybe no smarter. How smart can you be, going out to get yourself killed once a week for a living?

Pretty damn smart, it turns out, to judge by the business empires these guys build with their pay. Furthermore, the NASCAR drivers were models of courtesy and charm. Richard Petty, Harry Gant, and Darrell Waltrip all seemed glad to stop for a moment and do a little storytelling in the inimitable fashion of their sport's home ground. Not that all stock car drivers are Southern any more. And none of them are hicks. Not even the legendary former whiskey-running, present chicken-farming-and-raceteam-owning Last American Hero Junior Johnson. He is about as much dumb redneck as Henry Cabot Lodge.

Courtesy and charm prevailed. The track officials and the security guards and the people in the crowd were nice as hell. I had to get back up to the VIP suite for more to drink because I'd lived in New York for ten years, and the only people who are nice to New Yorkers turn out to be Jews for Jesus.

There's more hoopla to one NASCAR weekend than Paris in the '20s managed to pack into a whole decade. There was a go-kart race, a midget-car race, an opening act three-hundred-mile race for the older-bodied "Sportsman" class stock cars, a gigantic pit barbecue in the infield, a boxing match, a mock dogfight by World War II fighter planes, appearances by Miss Charlotte Motor Speedway, Miss National 500, Miss This, and Miss That, a 'Vette Club parade, an Air National Guard flyover, a landing by the U.S. Army's precision sky-diving team, and some young fool named "Jimmy the Flying Greek" jumped a school bus at seventy miles an hour. I don't mean he jumped over the school bus. The lumpy yellow behemoth itself was doing seventy miles an hour when it hit a ramp and sailed an honest 225 feet through the air and landed in a pile of junk cars and Jimmy was hauled away to the hospital with a standing ovation from the crowd.

Corporations were carpet-bombing the place with money. Union 76, Winston, Coca-Cola, Champion spark plugs, and Goodyear tires had their names on everything. Miller beer was sponsoring the Sportsman race. Valvoline, Gatorade, STP, Mountain Dew, Wrangler jeans, and the Hardee's fast-food chain were all sponsoring cars tricked out in their product colors. U.S. Tobacco, which backs a team owned by Burt Reynolds and director Hal Needham, put out a sitdown dinner for fifty at the Hilton, with the mayor and half the dignitaries in the state in attendance, and afterward Needham threw a giant dance full of beach music and shag dancing.

And when we tired of that we hied ourselves over to the local swell watering hole at the Radisson Plaza hotel with Billy Hagan, the longtime Le Mans racer who was possessed of all that sophistication I had thought stock cars lacked and who is sponsoring a NASCAR team now. We were just getting very sophisticated indeed with a bottle of Jack Daniel's when in walked Texas oilman J. D. Steel who had a car of his own in the next day's race. J.D. faced the bar full of two hundred–some revelers and shouted, "It's all on me!" The Jack Daniel's led to champagne and the champagne led to French '75s (which is where you put brandy and sugar in the Froggy pop to get an effect like being hit with a seventy-five millimeter artillery shell), and something else led to another thing and the next thing I knew I was following Billy Hagan out of the bar on a dare, walking across the tops of little cocktail tables the length of the room, with drinks and cut flowers and purses and ashtrays stepped upon, broken, and knocked everywhere. That is, Billy walked the whole length of the room. I crashed and burned in turn one, and I'm told it was a spectacular one-point landing. I noticed an attractive girl into whose lap I had plunged, and I don't know but that something even more interesting might have happened if a corporate executive who will go unnamed hadn't handed me a Corona-sized joint right there in front of God and everybody and I took a pull and passed out.

The next noon I was down in Billy Hagan's pit with a hangover the size of Billy's tip to the Radisson Plaza cocktail waitresses. But it all went away when the engines started.

Oh, Jesus, that stupendous noise, that beautiful and astounding sound—not the flatulent blasting of the drag strip or the bucket of puppies squeal of tiny Grand Prix engines, but a full-bore iron block, stroked-out American symphony of monster pandemonium. Exhaust notes so low they shake the lungs like rubber bell clappers in the rib cage and shrieks of valves and gears and pushrods wailing in the clear and terrifying soprano of the banshee's wail—I could not leave my ear plugs in, it was too beautiful. And the pit crews with their jetés and glissades, refueling the car and changing four tires in less than half a minute like five hulking Baryshnikovs in fast forward. And the cars themselves: words flunk description.

Grand National is the most extreme, precise, elegant, and exhilarating racing I've ever seen. Unlike road racing there is no "line" to take through the turns. At Charlotte they go into the big banked turns sometimes three abreast—unthinkable in a Grand Prix. A driver charts his course around a NASCAR oval a hundred different ways depending on traffic and track conditions, excellence of his car and himself, and, of course, most of all on bravery. Which last seems taken so much for granted by these people that it forms an unmentioned basic fact of life, like shit. And these guys knock the shit out of each other, slap sides and crack bumpers at 140 miles an hour if they get crowded or mad enough.

It's racing everyone can see and understand. Up in the bleachers you can glim every inch of the track. And I met people who did not know from cars, who thought car racing was a nihilistic type of teenage dopery, and I saw them sit riveted by four hours of action, unwilling to take a leak for fear of missing a nuance, a crazy pass, a wild spin. This is the stuff for any sports fan. It makes the NFL look as boring as baseball, renders baseball as dull as carp fishing.

It set me to thinking about the South. I was having a better time there than I'd ever had in New York. What was the difference between the South and the rest of America? It was a while before I figured out there wasn't any. The South *is* the rest of America. In fact, there really is no South in the old sense. The racism, the class system, the agrarian idiocy is almost gone. The only talk I even heard about skin color was the president of Charlotte Speedway "Humpy" Wheeler's happy statement that 15 percent of his spectators were black—up from practically none a few years ago. And I have it on good authority that NASCAR is itching to get black drivers and Hispanic drivers too, to give some healthy partisan rooting to the full spectrum of the nation's residents. (Humpy Wheeler is called Humpy Wheeler after his father, Humpy Wheeler, who was called Humpy because the football coach at UNC caught him smoking a Camel between scrimmages.)

The South is what we've had all along in this bizarre, slightly troubling, basically wonderful country—fun, danger, real friendliness, energy, enthusiasm, and brave, crazy, tough people. After all, America is where the toughest crazy people on the planet came to do anything they damn pleased. And a NASCAR weekend pretty much covers all the everything. America's original Indians were themselves tough and crazy. Put us all together and we're the biggest, baddest, best sons of bitches anywhere, and the hell with foreign countries because that's where all the sane wimps stayed.

In the South you can still feel that loony American hybrid vigor and special USA camaraderie. The place is devoid of narcissistic personality disorders. It may be the "Me Generation" up north, but it's the "How You-All?" generation in the South. Nobody's eating roughage, running marathons, and taking yoga classes down there. People still drink, still smoke, still have guns, and still believe in a personal God who listens to *them*. They're not worried about the future. This country didn't come from people who worried about the future. It came from people who *whipped the future's ass*.

I think all of us who live in New York and suchlike places had better quick have a drink and do something loud. Otherwise this country might turn into Europe, and then there wouldn't be anybody left to beat sense into us when we try to wear our hair like Roger Daltrey.

5

The Rolling Organ Donors Motorcycle Club

In the fall of 1979 I went on a motorcycle trip with *Car and Driver* boss David E. Davis Jr. David E. invited Bill Baker, chief of public relations for Fiat of America, and former motorcycle racer Trant Jarman, who'd become a crash test engineering consultant and spent his days happily dropping cars from crane hoists, nose first, onto concrete garage floors. (This is the kind of thing that men used to do for a living before computers began simulating all the enjoyment in life.)

We obtained three clunky, awkward, and mechanically primitive Harley-Davidson motorcycles and, by way of comparison, one Suzuki GS1100—probably the fastest and most sophisticated retail bike of the time. We spent a weekend riding seven-hundred miles through Michigan and Indiana for the purpose of . . .

During the heyday of the glossy magazines the purpose of everything was *fun*—to provide the readers with some fun. And you can't give what you haven't got. The fun began Friday after work, at Brew's on Thirty-fourth Street in Manhattan around the corner from the *Car and Driver* offices. The fun adjourned to the bar at LaGuardia airport from which it was transported (with the aid of those libation-pouring stewardesses of yore) to David and Jeannie Davis's house in Ann Arbor, Michigan. And the fun, when last seen at about three A.M. Saturday morning, was drinking toasts out of the salad bowl and singing:

There once was a Spanish nobilio,
Who lived in an ancient castillio.
He was proud of his tra-la-la-lillio
And the works of his tweedle-dum dee.

I thought, in a college town like Ann Arbor, illegal drugs were supposed to be readily available, to go with the Bloody Mary, the brandy-laced coffee, and the aspirin and gin on the rocks that I needed to face the day. Also, it was raining, and I'd lost the face shield for my old Buco helmet, and I hadn't been on a motorcycle in almost ten years. (It's difficult to practice for motorcycle riding if you don't have a motorcycle around. You can try operating the throttle and the brake with your hand while shifting gears with your foot, but it's hard to do this in your pickup truck and see where you're going.)

The others looked as bad as I felt. Even Mrs. Davis and photographer Humphrey Sutton were queasy at the prospect of this journey, and they were getting to ride in a proper automobile. It had all seemed like such a good idea just hours before. Jarman and Baker were experienced riders but rusty. David E. and I were trying to remember which way you face on a motorcycle. None of us had a valid motorcycle license. The bikes themselves presented a daunting spectacle, dripping wet and tippy-looking in the Davis driveway.

The Harley-Davidson FLT-C-80 Tour Glide Classic was supplied with windshield, fairing, running boards, saddlebags, dual headlights, a complete instrument panel, and a lockable trunk with more luggage space than a vacation condominium bedroom closet. We nicknamed it the "Two-Wheel Time Share." If its kickstand ever gave way we'd have to call the National Guard to get it upright again.

The Harley XLS-1000 Roadster was a slightly smaller, slightly less accessorized version of the full-dress garbage can FLT-C-80.

And (with H-D's perennially confusing model nomenclature) the FXE-80 Super Glide, stripped to its frame and a seat, was the honest-to-Nazi-helmet, nude-tattooed, sleeveless jean jacket *Harley* of a Harley-Davidson—the Hog. It set movies running in your head: *Easy Rider, Hell's Angels on Wheels, The Wild One* (never mind that Brando rode a Triumph).

And then there was the Suzuki GS1100, with its docile looks and dulcet exhaust note. Yet it had a top speed of 140 mph and did the quarter mile in eleven seconds. Any twist of the throttle put you in danger of being left there with empty bowlegs, like a Roy Rogers figurine after the dog ate the plastic Trigger.

Off we splashed into the Irish Hills. We were Heck's Republicans (leaving the pillage and rapine to our money managers). The sun emerged about the same time that we emerged—from a bowling alley in Coldwater, Michigan, where we'd been having breakfast beers. In a scene that was *not* straight out of an early Jack Nicholson biker flick, we'd been terrorized by a Saturday morning Cub Scout tenpin league. Their squeaks of childish glee and the thump of their gutter balls had made our heads pound.

We chose a secondary road, Route 1, that ran due south. We rolled through the cornfields and then other cornfields for a hundred miles, trading bikes as we went.

I started out on the XLS-1000 Roadster, which was more civilized than the Harley-Davidsons of my youth. For one thing, I was surrounded by a nagging, matronly clutter of government-mandated mirrors, reflectors, and turn signals. Then there was the Department of Transportation–required noise pollution equipment—the half-quiet exhaust system and the valve clatter of V-twin combustion chambers silenced by a big plastic air cleaner in place of the old Harley chrome candy dish. It used to be you couldn't hear yourself think on a Harley. This was a good thing. When you came home with a used one and your mother screamed at you, "What were you thinking?" you could honestly say you didn't know. Also, all our Harleys had electric starters so that in the course of the weekend not one of us did a Nadia Comaneci over the handlebars as the result of a midkick backfire. The Roadster was still powerful, however, with the torque of a locomotive and approximately the same weight.

Which weight was as a Vespa compared to the Tour Glide Classic. This was a motorcycle that hollered, "Get a car!" In fact, it drove like nothing so much as a Honda Civic with handlebars. The fairing was so complete and envelop-ing that I was too warm in there even on this chilly fall day.

The fairing also produced a kind of aerodynamic undertow that made my hair blow forward toward the windshield. I discovered that by spreading my knees I could create an updraft that would then cause my hair to stand on end. I would pass the slow-moving family Chevys on Route 1, wiggle my legs, and my hair would act like an animated fright wig. Humphrey took some photographs of this in case, later in life, I was tempted to run for public office.

The Suzuki seemed to come from another motorcyclical planet. It was a large bike but tidy and compact in its largeness and positively dainty in its precision of control. The gearshift was a little metal nipple operated by the merest flick of a toe. The brakes were telepathic. There was no tremor or mechanical palsy at any point in getting up to (a blindingly fast) speed or coming down to (a shockingly abrupt) halt. Response to every maneuver was quick to the point of déjà vu—you were already laying over, deep into the corner that you thought you were getting ready to turn. I hadn't known it was possible to build a motorcycle that was, all at once, so powerful, fast, smooth, and sweet.

No doubt about it, only one of our motorcycles would really stir your blood. Only one cried out to be begged, borrowed, or stolen, then ridden like a proton in a particle accelerator down all the roads in the land until bugs covered every tooth in your grin. That motorcycle, however, was not the Suzuki.

We would pull into a gas station, a fast-food joint, a 7-Eleven, and there we were with the GS1100, one of the most glorious pieces of speed demon engineering in the world: sixteen valves, dual overhead cams, six gears, and a ten-grand redline. And every bystander would rush to see the stripped-down Super Glide FXE. That Harley had the smell. It exuded the aroma of which all the great old bikes—the Indians, the Vincents, the BSAs—reeked, the wiff of danger. And on this particular FXE the dual straight pipes and original air filter had been restored so that the Harley exhaust rumble said what a Harley rumble is supposed to say: "Lock up your daughters and wives."

Unlike the GS1100 the FXE was not a modern motorcycle with crisp, quiet lines that reminded you of an appliance, a microwave on tires, the safety of your kitchen at home. Motorcycles *are* dangerous. You *should* be scared of them and of the people who ride on them. Well, not of David E. Davis, Trant Jarman, Bill Baker, and me in particular. But in general people who ride motorcycles are doing something that's so scary in the first place that they are statistically unlikely to be scared of you. That is, unless you are as much above the statistical average of scariness as David E., Trant, Bill, and me in particular are below it.

This notion reoccurred to me years later when first the book and then the movie *Schindler's List* came out. I thought there was a great missing of the point by author Thomas Keneally and director Steven Spielberg. Oskar Schindler had been a successful motorcycle racer. There's no mystery about why he did what he did at his factory. He felt like it. And there's no mystery about why he wasn't afraid of the Gestapo. He wasn't afraid of anything. Pencil-necked punks in fake leather raincoats—Gestapo, *geslopo*. To put it in two of the historically most-used words in the biker lexicon, "Fuck you."

Or, to put it motion, there was Trant Jarman on the GS1100 flying down Route 1 at three times the legal speed limit.

Let's face it, the appeal of the motorcycle is not rational. And let's not mince words about the Freudian nature of the psychological message—big, throbbing, steel-hard thing between your legs. Not exactly hard to decode, symbolically speaking. And "Harley-Davidson" sounds more like it means business than D. H. Lawrence's "John Thomas" or Elvis Presley's "Little Elvis" or, for that matter, "Suzuki." Women gaze upon a Harley with a look combining mild trepidation with . . . "*He was proud of his tra-la-la-lillio / and the works of his tweedle-dum dee.*"

The farm girls and the small town teen angels standing in the parking lots of the Laundromats and feed stores as we rode south through Yoder and Ossian and Bluffton and Reiffsburg, Pennville, Redkey, Modoc—standing there on the verge of a lifetime of expanding hips and contracting dress budgets—their eyes said, "Take me!"

In Connersville we dismounted at a mean-looking bar. I was having flashbacks to Humphrey's and my Buick trip across the panhandle of Florida. I said to Humphrey, "Don't you dare tell the people in here that they're quaint and charming in their primitive way."

Indeed, we had no more than ordered our drinks when a red-faced drunk wove toward our table. His intentions were unfriendly, as were his pals at the other end of the bar. We were just wondering if we should slip a sawbuck under the ashtray and skedaddle when the formidable granny of a barmaid intervened.

"Don't you let ole Leroy here"—she gestured toward the drunk—"or none of the rest of them"—she gestured toward Leroy's friends—"bother you none. They don't mean no trouble." Leroy meekly returned to his bar stool. And we, with some amazement, realized that the barmaid hadn't been protecting us from her clientele; she'd been protecting her clientele from *us*. The Harley-riding terror and its posse had descended on Connersville—the editor of the *National Lampoon,* the editor of *Car and Driver* and his wife, an English photographer, a PR executive, and an engineer. (Actually, Trant, although a little guy, might have—being an ex-motorcycle racer like Oskar Schindler—wreaked some havoc if annoyed. But the rest of us would have skedaddled and left him there.)

Thirty years on the vignettes above must seem—to use Humphrey's word—quaint. The real swastika-wearing one percenters in the never-washed jeans are on Medicare now, their beard braids grizzled, the hair under their Wehrmacht headgear mostly gone. Today, the rice-burning crotch rockets have Power Ranger styling to go with their power. And the kids aboard them are more likely to stomp themselves against phone poles than to stomp rival gang members or innocent citizens or Leroy. Harley-Davidson has gone from being a mechanized dinosaur that somehow survived the Wisconsin ice age to being the last solvent motor vehicle company in America.

Yet in these scenes from long ago you can detect the first germs of what would become a raging infection of senior management flabby guys trying to ride out their midlife crises on Harleys. They want to recapture the bar fear and farm girl yearning. They've forgotten that they never provoked that fear or yearning because they were pasty geeks who drove Pintos and were studying like mad to get into business school. Sorry, you chubby renters of *Wild Hogs,* the bars in rural Indiana now have bare brick walls, hanging fern planters, and wine lists. The farm girls sold the farms and are managing successful ethanol operations. The small town teen angels are worried real estate agents and mothers of three who are still upset by Sarah Palin's defeat and don't even listen to John Cougar Mellencamp CDs anymore.

I hope that this ancient article in *Car and Driver* was not in any way responsible for the embarrassment that modern motorcycling has become. I'm willing to take the blame for popularizing NASCAR, but not for this. And memo to the "Wheezy Riders" and the "Mild Ones": If your old lady is wider than the gap between your mortgage debt and your house value, please do not seat her pillion and make us look at this on the highway.

From Connersville we went west on Route 44. Despite the heartland's reputation for bland scenery, this is as pretty a road as you will find from Smokies to Rockies. Route 44 has hills and curves and sudden right-angle county line jogs, dips, dells, one-lane wooden bridges, and occasional sprinkles of sand and gravel to get your attention in the tight bends. We went down this stretch hellbent-for-Naugahyde, leaving the chase car to trail behind in a wake of tire squeals and brake-light panic blinks. Bill Baker was out front on the Suzuki. It may not have had the below-the-belt appeal of the Milwaukee pig iron, but it was a beautiful thing to see as Bill tipped it over in the acute spots and popped it up in the straights. Trant, on the XLS-1000 tricked-out Roadster, and David E., on the FXE-80 pure Harley, were making somewhat more ponderous charges at the curves. I lagged, my hands full with the FLT-C-80 Tour Glide Classic the size of an Elks hall. Taking this at sixty miles per hour through the bendies and over the culvert humps was like flying Howard Hughes's

Spruce Goose in the Reno Air Races. Yet the behemoth would do everything I could summon the nerve to ask it to do. Coming into a sharp turn, I'd press the opposite bar, point my head at the apex, and the son-of-a-gun would keel over like an America's Cup yacht and hang there at a forty-five-degree angle, close hauled. All it needed was someone blonde in a bikini bottom and Top-Siders hiked out over the lifelines shouting at me to reef the main sail. Or something like that. I know even less about sailing than I know about motorcycle riding. What I mean to say is that the Tour Glide handled better than you'd think a barge like this would. It was not, however, a motorcycle for the indecisive or the changeable-minded. Once you had committed yourself to a particular line of attack, you were—if I may indulge in the umpteenth change of metaphor in this paragraph alone—permanently out of radio contact with central command.

It was fun. I recalled then, after a decade spent driving—as bikers would say—"in a cage," how fun riding a motorcycle is. And I'm recalling now, three decades later, how fun fun is. And how important. Fun saves us from political dictatorship. Perhaps the midlife crisis Harley riders should be forgiven or even exalted. Motorcycles strike at the very foundation of authoritarian politics, because they are so much fun. (And let us ignore, as the act of ignoramuses, the Iron Crosses worn by biker gangs.) How can you oppress and collectivize a people who are having fun? You have to catch them first, while they're rollicking around with bottles in hand, sexing each other in the shrubbery, making heaps of money and blowing it on whatever they like. How can you bureaucratize such a people or organize them into armies to fight other people they've never heard of? How can you even get them to be quiet for a moment and listen to a public service announcement about wearing seat belts? (Seat belts on motorcycles?) You can't. That's what makes America a mess—a wonderful, glorious, hilarious, fun-filled mess.

We're an ungovernable bunch of fun-loving hooligans looking for kicks. And what do you do for kicks in America? You get on a machine—a truck, a tractor, a snowmobile, a Jet Ski, a riding mower, an RV, a car, even a bus, and especially a motorcycle. Machines have given us common folk the ways and means to run around all over the place doing whatever we want. Before machines, thirty miles was a day's journey if you had a horse, and you didn't. We were in thrall to shank's mare, to the vagaries of weather and of our betters who owned the railroads. Without personal, private machines there was no freedom. And what's freedom for? Freedom is for fun.

Any mom knows this. Not that moms are necessarily in favor of fun. As we roared toward Bloomington and the home of that very fun institution (and alma mater of my dear future wife) Indiana University, we passed a mom and dad snailing along in their Dodge Bluegill with a six- or seven-year-old son in the back. The kid got a look at our motorcycles and began to bounce around like Tigger. And then his mother—a Democrat, I'm sure—did a remarkable thing. She reached around and put a hand over the boy's eyes.

In Bloomington we had a dinner planned with Bob Tyrrell and Ron Burr, the editor and publisher, respectively, of the *American Spectator*. In those days the *American Spectator* was the (loud) voice of unrepentant conservatism. It had just published a cover showing a proposed presidential portrait of Jimmy

Carter, a frame with nothing in it. The *Spectator*'s original publisher, John von Kannon, had been diagnosed with leukemia. (He recovered and is now the vice president and treasurer of the Heritage Foundation, the [quiet] voice of unrepentant conservatism). When John got out of the hospital and returned to the *Spectator's* office near the IU campus, he was bald, carrying about ninety-eight pounds on his six-foot-plus frame, and walking with two canes. He had a T-shirt made for himself—size XXL—printed with six-inch letters: "I Am a Vegetarian."

David E., Trant, Bill, and I got out of our leathers and into our dinner clothes while Jeannie Davis mixed cocktails and Humphrey sampled them extensively for purposes of quality control. We arrived at a restaurant called the Cork and Cleaver. And I believe that to this day, if you're in Bloomington and go to the Cork and Cleaver, it would be unwise to mention *Car and Driver*. There's something about 350 middle-aged miles of motorcycle riding that doesn't burnish the finer points of politesse. I noticed it at the Cork and Cleaver bar when the normally mild-mannered Baker growled an order for "a pig trough full of bourbon."

The hostess said there'd be a short wait and asked, "Can I have a name?"

"Christ," said Trant, "didn't your parents give you one when you were born?"

Our waitress wore a Kappa Kappa Gamma pin but she was not responsive to our inquiries about the secret lesbian initiation rites at her sorority. I think it was David E. who asked if he could use one of the Cork and Cleaver's bedpost–sized pepper mills to go out back and kill a cow so our steaks would be extra fresh. And I'm not going to say who it was that suggested to the waitress a possible alternative use for the pepper grinder.

We went through three dinner waitresses in fifteen minutes. David E. decided that the second one, a handsome olive-skinned brunette in pigtails, was particularly healthy looking and that I had been single (as I then was) too long. He offered to arrange a marriage to be performed on the table after the soup course and consummated under the table during dessert. "How many rifles and blankets does your father want for you?" asked Jarman.

Bob Tyrrell and Ron Burr—loud voices of unrepentant conservatism though they may have been—were starting to get a "For gosh sakes, we have to live here" look on their faces. The *American Spectator* was and remains committed to fun, but maybe not quite as committed as we motorcyclists.

We motorcyclists who should have been committed to a twelve-step program. Rereading these various tales of transportation misadventure I notice that, as certain pompous English professors used to say, "a subtle pattern begins to emerge." We were drunk all the time. Our generation drank a lot more than the current generation does. And we still would if we could, but our prostates are shot and one beer means going to the john every five minutes for the rest of the journey. In fairness to ourselves we didn't have Prozac and hadn't discovered Valium. Plus, the generation before us was even worse. We, at least, didn't indulge ourselves with martinis during the day. We stuck to vodkas on the rocks.

The man for whom I worked at my day job, Julian Weber, president of National Lampoon Inc., was a member of that generation before us. A lawyer by trade, Julian said that he always knew it was time to stop talking business at lunch with his Irish colleagues when they started putting their cigarettes out in the butter. Is there such a thing as retroactive AA meetings?

The next morning suicide seemed like an attractive alternative. So we had breakfast at Denny's. When that didn't work we rode back to Ann Arbor. Being too hungover to safely ride motorcycles, we thought the answer might be to have someone who didn't know how to ride a motorcycle ride a motorcycle so that we would look competent by comparison. Jeannie Davis acquitted herself well behind the handlebars of the XLS-1000 Harley Roadster. Humphrey wanted to ride a motorcycle as well, but he wanted to take photographs of us and himself while he was riding. Which didn't sound very safe, and it wasn't. Trant had to be kept informed of the score in the ongoing Lions game. This was accomplished by the chase car's driver making a variety of hand signals that Trant kept misinterpreting to mean that we should stop for gas. I actually dozed off for a moment in the wombish fairing of the FLT-C-80 Tour Glide. That was scary. We all pegged the speedometer on each of the bikes. That wasn't so scary because, in that era of the Carter administration double-nickel speed limit, speedometers were calibrated only to eighty mph. However, using a highway measured mile, I tested how fast the GS1100 really would go. It really would go faster than I would. I ran out of nerve at what Jeannie Davis clocked as 130 miles per hour, well before the Suzuki's sixth gear ran out of revolutions per minute. The odd thing was there was no odd thing. Other than keeping from wetting myself, nothing about riding the GS1100 at 130 was difficult. It was the same as riding the bike at 70 or at 50 or at 30.

Near Muncie, or a place like Muncie, the oil pressure in the XLS-1000 disappeared. And the XLS disappeared too. No amount of shouting for oil pressure would get the oil pressure to return and no amount of Trant's tinkering with the engine would either. So the XLS had to be left behind. As my *Car and Driver* story went to press, a Harley-Davidson employee was still questioning David E., trying to get David to remember where near Muncie—or a place like Muncie—the motorcycle had wound up.

Only one thought occurred to me the whole day, and, considering my headache, even that was overdoing it. But I did wonder what the political and cultural response would be, in those dark days at the end of the 1970s, if motorcycles had never been thought of and someone just invented them. "You see, it's sort of like a car, but you sit on the engine, with the gas tank between your knees, and it has only two wheels."

The powers that be would have had a fit, from the head of the National Highway Traffic Safety Administration (at that time an evil witch named Joan Claybrook) on down through the insurance companies, the state police, the local police, the school crossing guards, and the Mothers Against Everything. You can still hear their hypothetical shrieks echoing in the halls of suppositional history: "Sitting on an engine! Gas tank between your knees! *Only two wheels!* You'll fall over! You'll explode! You'll burn! You'll die!"

It was sad to think that America, a nation founded on danger (not to mention biker-type pillage and rapine), had come to such a pass. And, sadly, this particular form of 1970s darkness never did lift. There was no morning in America for our idea of fun. The nation remains obscenely intrigued with safety in all its forms (including, now, investment risk).

My children cannot so much as pedal their bicycles around the paved apron in front of our garage door without being suited up and padded out like NFL linebackers. I await with dread the "Dear Parents" note from school announcing that students will not be allowed to go outside at recess, walk in the halls, eat lunch, or sit in classrooms without safety helmets. (Particularly annoying to my family—you can't hurt O'Rourkes by hitting them on the head.)

However, I was wrong to believe in 1979 that no newly invented two-wheeled vehicle could be accepted by post-perilous American society. A number of years after our (somewhat) wild ride, the Segway would be conceived, with all the inconvenience and impracticality of the motorcycle and none of the motorcycle's cool and injury-prone appeal. I can imagine what the farm girls and small town teen angels who looked so longingly at the Harley-Davidson FXE-80 Super Glide would have thought if I'd been riding a Segway: "Dork."

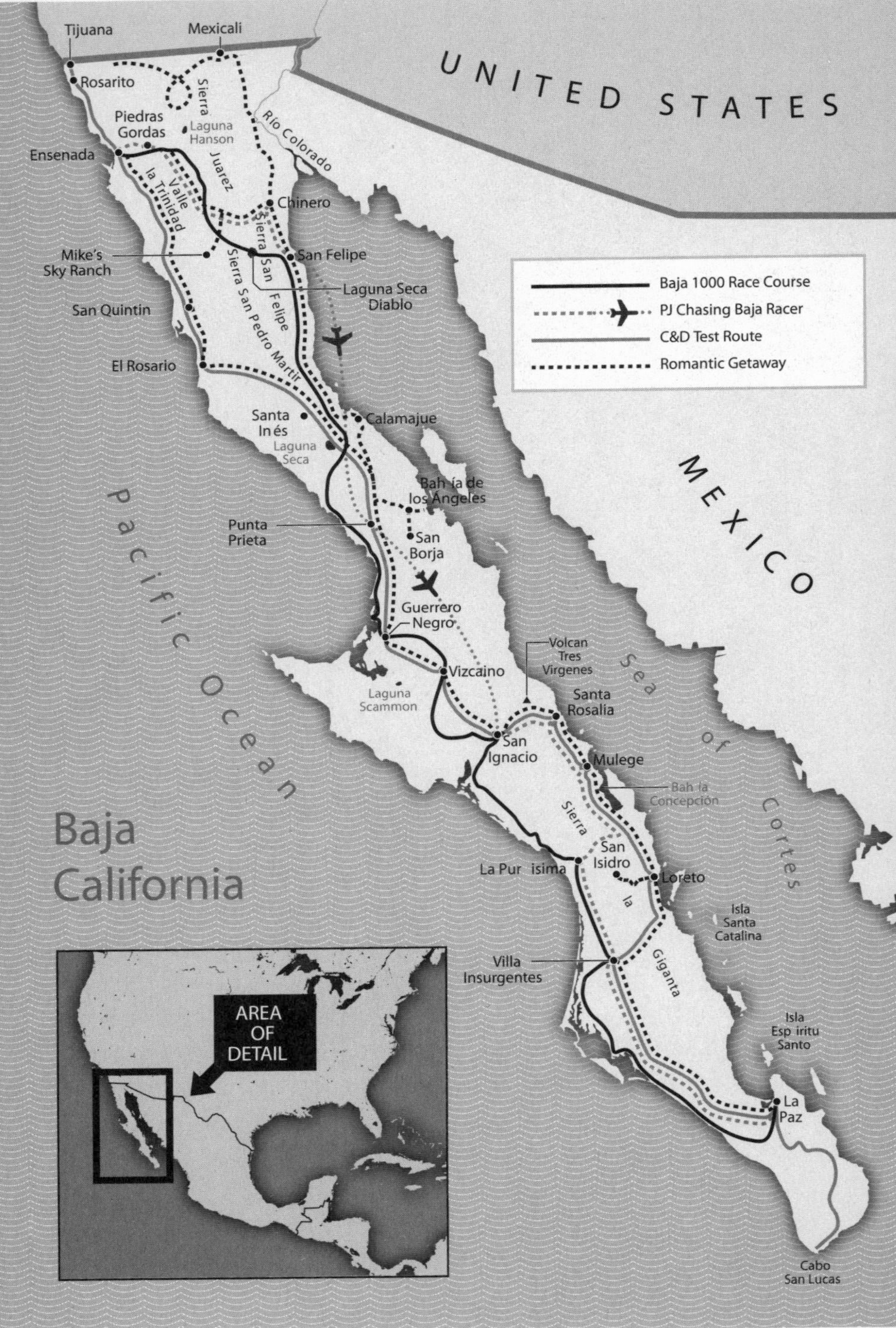
UNITED STATES
MEXICO
Pacific Ocean
Sea of Cortes
Baja California
Baja 1000 Race Course
PJ Chasing Baja Racer
C&D Test Route
Romantic Getaway
Tijuana
Mexicali
Rosarito
Sierra Juarez
Laguna Hanson
Piedras Gordas
Ensenada
Río Colorado
Valle la Trinidad
Chinero
Sierra San Felipe
San Felipe
Mike's Sky Ranch
Sierra San Pedro Martir
Laguna Seca Diablo
San Quintin
El Rosario
Santa Inés
Laguna Seca
Calamajue
Bahía de los Ángeles
Punta Prieta
San Borja
Guerrero Negro
Vizcaino
Laguna Scammon
Volcan Tres Virgenes
Santa Rosalia
San Ignacio
Mulege
Bahía Concepción
Sierra San Isidro
La Purísima
Loreto
Sierra la Giganta
Isla Santa Catalina
Villa Insurgentes
Isla Espiritu Santo
La Paz
Cabo San Lucas
AREA OF DETAIL

6

"Come On Over to My House—We're Gonna Jump Off the Roof!"

Torrid, rocky, thorny, maddening, it was a desperate love affair—and filled with snakes and scorpions too—when I met Mexico's Baja peninsula in the 1980s.

It began with a phone call from Michael Nesmith. Nesmith was one of the creators of MTV. He's a musician and songwriter; a movie, TV, and record producer; a successful businessman and a philanthropist. But such is the careless nature of fame that he's still best known as a Monkee—the tall one in the knit hat, the one who could actually play his instrument. Contrary to normal rock star eschatology, Michael saved his money and invested it sensibly. At least he invested some of it sensibly. He also bought an off-road race truck and raced it.

Michael called to see if I'd like to come along with his race team on the 1983 Baja 1000. He was using the race to promote a movie he'd just produced called *Timerider*. (Motocross competitor accidentally gets sent back in time to the Wild West. Ignore Leonard Maltin's review in *Movie and Video Guide*, it's a perfectly good flick.) I guess Nesmith's thinking was that when *Timerider* got projected on bedsheets in the dirt piazzas of the mission towns in Baja California the audience would be presold and that, plus the readership of *Car and Driver* (which will watch anything on wheels), would guarantee an international hit.

The Baja is that long turkey wattle hanging off the Pacific chin of North America. It is a thousand-mile drive from Tijuana on the border to Cabo San Lucas at the tip. There's only one paved road, and not taking it is the point of the Baja 1000.

The Baja is mountains, lava fields, arid barrens, sand flats, cactus forests, and leviathan rock piles. It contains the most precipitous precipices, the most desiccated deserts, and the least inhabited uninhabitable terrain between Tierra del Fuego and Nome. And a quarter of a century ago Cabo San Lucas had not yet brought forth its eructation of luxury resorts, so there wasn't even any topless starlet trash at the end of the journey.

The Baja 1000 was, in those days, run right through the middle of what, these days, is doubtless a UN World Heritage Biodiversity Site of endangered habitat necessary for the sustainability of threatened plant (with vicious prickers) and (poisonous) animal (that bites) species. You started in the streets of Ensenada, just south of Tijuana, and ended in the streets of La Paz, north of Cabo. In between were dry washes and cattle trails at best, except for the roads through occasional villages where the campesinos threw empty beer cans at you.

The race was conducted under the auspices of a somewhat catch-as-catch-can sanctioning body called Southern California Off-Road Enterprises, or SCORE. There were twenty-four competition classes including motorcycles, trucks, three-wheeled all-terrain vehicles (Remember those? So lethal that motorcycle companies, sworn purveyors of lethality, quit making them.), and cars ranging from stock VW bugs to unlimited single-seat dune buggies that looked like something in which a Wookie would cruise the drive-in.

Michael Nesmith was running in Class 8, defined by SCORE as "full-sized two-wheel-drive utility vehicles." Michael had a '79 Chevy short-bed step-side pickup—named "Timerider"—with a 350 big-block V-8. It was heavily modified, so much so that it was able to do things that TV truck commercials show trucks doing.

We took Timerider on a shakedown run in the high desert near Edwards Air Force Base outside LA. The exterior of the Chevy looked tame enough, like the big-wheel boonie wagons that, in the '80s, every Sam and his girlfriend Dixie was turning hairy-side-to-the-sky on weekends across America.

It went differently, however—like a rocket goat. We popped down into a ditch and Jupiterean g-forces squashed me to oompa loompa proportions. Then we went through a series of road corrugations or whoop-dee-doos. The little ones were like Larry Bird dribbling my eyeballs. The big ones put my liver in my mouth. After that we did a carrier-deck landing, a roller-coaster turn, an inside-a-U-boat depth charge attack movie scene, and something that caused a view of rocks coming toward the windshield as if in a video game played by Paleolithic teen man.

Until I'd strapped myself into the codriver's seat, I hadn't known whether Nesmith was really any good at this or just fooling around. In a minute I wished he was just fooling around. A skillful driver can beat the crap out of a passenger in an off-road race vehicle better than he can do it with a baseball bat.

"The trouble with this truck," Nesmith said, driving off the lip of a ditch at a hundred miles an hour, "is . . . *OOF* . . . it's so good it makes you feel invincible."

Is "vincible" a word? I was feeling that. Easterner that I am, I'd worn a pair of cowboy boots into the desert. I thought that was what you were supposed to wear. But the stupid boot heels were banging up and down and sliding around on the steel floor.

"You need rubber-soled shoes," Michael said. You also need a jock strap. The testicles in my boxer shorts were whapping against the Recaro seat like little bowling balls being dropped out fourth-story windows. And every time we went airborne the shoulder harness gave me emergency cardiac defibulation. I had to give the harness the slip and try to ride it out with the lap belt over bladder muscles I developed going to college in a state with 3.2 beer.

All the same there was a smile across my face as big as Jimmy Carter's—a raccoon-eating-shit-out-of-a-wire-brush smile. Michael plopped the truck down on the El Mirage dry lake and stood on it—100, 120, 130 mph across the expanse of dead-level clay, racing toward ever-receding mountains through a featureless space so vast all sense of movement was lost.

God on a drunk couldn't find something more fun to do. Except drive it Himself. Michael let me do that without my even asking. And then I got a surprise. This hot dog, hypertuned, race-ready dynamo was more civilized than a Chrysler Imperial. Power steering, lock-proof brakes, and automatic transmission—Timerider had none of the limited, balky, quirk-ridden feel of a racer. The engine was smooth, timed, and cam-supplied for a broad range of power. You wouldn't hesitate to drive it from Des Moines to visit your sister in Orlando. Though you might wish for side windows. Nesmith did. He was too busy to run the whole SCORE circuit but, he said, "If I raced full-time, I'd air-condition the thing. I really would." For additional pleasure, Timerider had NASCAR mufflers that made such a pretty noise it was like having a happy tomcat stuck in each ear.

Being a passenger was an unbelievably bone-yanking experience, but when I was driving what I couldn't believe was the small effect that came from the giant holes and foolishnesses that I hit. Blasting down an arroyo-creased, sand-plastered, boulder-lumped Mojave trail, rocks and ruts and looming road tumors just disappeared into the enormous shock travel. I skipped from tip to top of humps and ridges, the gentle rise of well-calculated spring rates bringing me level and steady after every dip. The truck punched over or through everything I aimed it at, with no loss of power, traction, or control.

My technique left something—in fact, everything—to be desired. It was necessary to keep the left foot on the brake to mash the suspension down for cornering (much the same as the "trail braking" taught at the race car driving school where I'd done so well—on paper). I kept forgetting. I also kept forgetting Timerider was an automatic, and I hit the wide brake pedal with jabs from my left foot several times while shifting. I also had to use the brake pedal (on purpose) in the whoop-dee-doos to keep the truck's polar momentum from building in a way that would cause an end-o after the third or fourth whoop. I didn't know how to do that either. But the truck was too good to make me look stupid. Well, except for when I hit the brake pedal while shifting. I did look stupid then.

Shakedown was an unqualified success. Timerider went for a final tweaking, first to the shop of Mike Burke, who built the engine and would codrive the second leg of the 1000 with championship motorcycle racer Keith Crisco. Then Timerider went to Bruce Eikelberger, who made the chassis and would codrive the first leg with Nesmith.

Burke had been a member of the legendary Checkers motorcycle club. In the early 1960s the Checkers—membership limited to twenty-five tough-ass sons of bitches—were the pioneers of American off-road racing. (And of cheating at it, or so their rivals said.) But you can't cheat death, and the Checkers set some death-defying times through the southern California deserts on great, ungainly Triumph bikes.

Eikelberger was a veteran of off-road racing in several competition classes, with 186 top three finishes to his credit. He and Burke had taken exquisite pains with Timerider. Every weld was like a row of dimes. Every bolt showed a dozen threads above its nut. Every edge of metal was filed smooth as a Gucci belt buckle and painted more carefully than a thing in the Louvre.

Timerider's stock bodywork enclosed a custom chassis more sophisticated than a Grand National car's. SCORE rules required that the original frame be kept and that no material be removed. Therefore, in order to make something that wouldn't bend in the middle like a sucker ace in a game of three-card monte, it had been necessary to weave a system of strut and brace metal tubing over, under, and through the original frame. This had to increase strength, create a roll cage and shock towers, and yet not add weight while also shifting the weight that was not being added to the rear wheels—a neat trick. The real element of genius in this frame tubing, however, was its joints. The major component connections were made with bolts, not welds, and they were cushioned with polyurethane pads that allowed the entire truck to flex, bend, absorb energy, and spring back into shape. Eikelberger was one of the geniuses who created these joints, which were what gave Timerider its mellowness when driven across stray cattle-sized rocks.

Timerider's design was sophisticated but, unlike most modern car technology, it was comprehensible to the likes of me, who can't fix a can of tuna. There were no black boxes, no triple gerbil exercise wheel turbos, none of the stuff that can't be understood without having a desktop computer monitor on your lap as you race. "Simplicity is the sharpest trick," Eikelberger said. He told me about someone running a VW-powered dune buggy in the Baja 1000, who blew up halfway to La Paz, flagged down a Mexican family, bought the engine out of their Bug, bolted it in, and won his class.

From what I could tell about our fellow off-road racers in Ensenada, they were crazy. But it wasn't the hardships of Baja racing or the brushes with death that had driven them nuts. It was the logistics. Timerider's crew alone nearly filled a motel. There were people and vehicles, car parts and cans of race gas spilling out of windows, and the number of beer coolers, burritos, and bottles of Lomotil pills needed to keep this act together was legion.

I made a list of the bigger things that were required for Timerider's Baja run: the race truck itself, its trailer, a GMC crew cab to pull it, a forty-four-foot travel trailer, a Blazer to pull that, a used utility company lineman's truck and another trailer, both filled with pit-stop supplies, a Baja Bug and two dirt bikes for scouting duty, an Econoline van, a Mitsubishi 4WD pickup, a single-engine Cessna 210, and a twin-engine Cessna 411.

We still ran short of vehicles. Eikelberger had to rent another pickup in LA. In those days (or these days either) most rental companies wouldn't let you take their renters to Mexico. Eikelberger said he was headed to Lake Tahoe. "But will it run on cheap Mexican gas?" he asked. "Just in case I run into any for sale in that neck of the woods?"

In addition to all that, a Baja 1000 effort had to have a whole other race machine, a prerunner. This was supposed to be almost as good as the real thing in order to try the course ahead of time at about 80 percent speed. Nesmith was using his retired Class 8 race truck, a mid-'70s Ford with another of Burke's engines in it, a 351 Windsor.

All told, the Timerider team had eighteen wheeled and winged vehicles and people beyond counting in Ensenada. To be a Baja racer you need courage, endurance, and more friends than Bill Clinton and Facebook combined, and in 1983 neither of those last two had been invented. Plus these friends had to be willing to work for beer, refried beans, and motel rooms with suspect bedsheets.

* * *

The second-leg drivers, Crisco and Burke, were already in the southern Baja, having spent the previous three days checking the course, sleeping in the prerunner, and heating up cans of food by sticking them in the air cleaner and running the truck around until the Beanie Weenies were warm.

In Ensenada Nesmith and Eikelberger were making last-minute checks on Timerider while Michael's wife, Katherine, and Bruce's wife, Anne, were doing quartermaster duty.

The travel trailer had been hauled to San Ignacio, a little oasis town that was the crew-change point for the race. San Ignacio is a puddle of palms in an empty volcanic landscape, about equidistant between Ensenada and La Paz, north-south, and between the Sea of Cortés and the Pacific, east-west.

A fellow named Al Alcorn, who'd been instrumental in developing Pong, would ferry parts down the Baja in his Cessna 210. Accompanying Alcorn was Dr. Victor Lopez, who had the Lomotil and an ability to speak Spanish. The Cessna 411 would take mechanics and wives from Ensenada to San Ignacio and on to La Paz.

Then there was the matter of the nine pits and their pit crews scattered along the thousand-mile route, many in places visited by English-speaking people only during International Geophysical Years and the Baja race. The organization and crewing of the pits were of a complexity beyond my powers of understanding or expression.

The race would start when the sun came up. And Timerider would, we hoped, reach San Ignacio by midnight. When that happened Nesmith would fly to La Paz and an exhausted Eikelberger would get out of the race truck and into the prerunner with me. The prerunner would now have become the chase vehicle.

While Crisco and Burke bounced through the wilderness, Eikelberger and I would drive like hell on the Baja's sole highway (fittingly named Route 1) east to Santa Rosalia on the Sea of Cortés and south to Mulegé, then along the Bahia de la Conception until we picked up a back road across the ominously ycelpt Sierra de la Giganta west to the checkpoint at La Purisima. We hoped to get there before Timerider did. If everything was going well—a ridiculous "if"—we'd follow Timerider on the course itself, a sand track south to Villa Insurgentes, located about three-quarters of the way down the Baja. Then the racer would return to the trackless wastes, and Eikelberger and I would reintercept Route 1 and continue 145 miles to La Paz.

Before any of that could happen, though, Timerider had to make it to San Ignacio. I would drive the rented pickup carrying spare parts southeast out of Ensenada on a semi-paved road. I would drive at the rental rate of speed—much faster than a truck I personally owned could go. I hoped to beat Nesmith and Eikelberger to the first pit stop in the Sierra de Juárez highlands, then to the second pit stop in the Sea of Cortés resort town of San Felipe.

If the spare parts weren't needed, Alcorn and Dr. Lopez would pick up myself, a drive shaft, a master cylinder, a power steering unit, half a dozen universal joints, and a milk crate full of odds and ends. We'd make a cramped and overweight flight in the Cessna 210, from San Felipe's dirt strip to a dry lake near another pit stop in El Crucero on the straggled neck of northern Baja. Then, if we lived, we'd continue on to San Ignacio.

* * *

In Ensenada the forty-five motorcycle entries buzzed away at first light, making the soundtrack for an Excedrin commercial. Four-wheeled vehicles were scheduled to start one hour after the last bike was out of the gate. The course followed a dry wash to Piedras Gordas, a town so small it turned out not to exist. I waited until the bikes were gone and drove to Piedras Gordas—or, rather, to where Piedras Gordas was supposed to be. As far as I could tell, with my bar Spanish, Piedras Gordas meant "fat feet," or maybe, more appropriately to Baja racing, it meant "heavy foot." [Piedras Gordas translates as "big rocks"—ed.] I was there early enough to see Timerider go by. Nesmith was driving conservatively, at the back of the pack.

I then went down the pavement, so called, to the number one pit at Valle de Trinidad. Off to my left I could see the bikes kicking up rooster tails of dirt. It was open country there, notched with half-lush valleys and with no visible habitations. Yet locals came out of nowhere and stood patiently along the course.

Timerider came through, in midpack now. The only problem seemed to be radio communication. Timerider could send but not receive.

I had to drive at eighty to beat Timerider to San Felipe. A *federale* in a patrol car gave me a cheery wave. I headed east across a featureless plain until white salt marshes rose on the horizon. This was the delta of the Colorado River, where it empties into the Sea of Cortés. The marshes stretched for fifteen miles to the water, blank and glaring, an empty movie screen across the skyline, my first hint of the Baja's eeriness.

I came into town, scattering spectators, burros, etc., looking frantically for the pits. Timerider, to judge by Eikelberger's wild radio calls, was having the same problem. They'd had a flat and were running behind most of Class 8. But two early leaders had already blown up, and there was plenty of yardage left for recovery. Timerider's spare had had something wrong with it. The pit crew put on a new wheel. Alcorn, Dr. Lopez, and I packed the spare parts into the Cessna.

Alcorn flew along the east coast of the Baja, parallel to the race course. We could see trucks and bikes struggling along the cliffs south of San Felipe, but turbulence kept us from getting low enough to pick out Timerider.

At Bahia Gonzaga we headed inland, over the Sierra de Calamajue. There was an almost embarrassing expanse of naked geography. The world looked newly made, not painted or decorated or ready to be occupied by people. I felt creeps of fear and isolation not helped by crackling radio transmissions from the El Crucero pits. Winds were gusting over forty miles per hour on the dry lake. Alcorn located a little airstrip twenty miles to the south at Punta Prieta and put the plane down through skittering buffets.

Punta Prieta was as much in the middle of nowhere as anywhere could get. It sat on the level valley bottom of a vanished river. Machete peaks encircled the flats, shimmering in the heat. The ground was as hard and bare as tarmac so that the airstrip was distinguishable only because no cactus grew there, no horrible humanoid cholla cactus or bizarre boojum trees that rise to a point, straight up fifty feet or more without a leaf or branch.

We had just deplaned on this stage set for *Don Juan in Hell* when soldiers, M-16s pointed at our bellies, appeared from concealment in flora too sparse to conceal them and surrounded us. Dr. Lopez had a long, grave discussion with their lieutenant, who looked sixteen. The soldiers lowered their guns and trudged back into oblivion. "He says they do this every time a plane lands," said Dr. Lopez. Perhaps it was part of the freshly launched war on drugs. But which side were the soldiers on?

The pit crew came and got the parts and we flew south.

In San Ignacio that night Crisco and Burke were ready to take the Timerider wheel. All they were missing was Timerider. Generators were running and lights shone on crowds of townspeople as we gathered around SCORE's static-filled ham radio receiver. There was no report of Timerider passing through El Crucero. On the other hand, there was no report of Timerider *not* passing through El Crucero. The ham radio network was sketchy. We went out to dinner at a place on the edge of town. It was a typical adobe house except it lacked a roof. Rain comes only every several years here. We were served a delicious yellowfin tuna in white wine sauce.

Meanwhile, in the race truck, everything had been going to hell. Nesmith and Eikelberger hadn't had time to prerun all of the race course. They hadn't bothered with the very first part, figuring there was only one way out of Ensenada. Not true. They'd just entered the dry wash when they took a wrong turn into the cactus. When I saw Timerider at Piedras Gordas, Nesmith wasn't at the back of the pack because he was driving conservatively. He was at the back of the pack because he'd gotten lost. Then he was further slowed in the pine forest at the top of the Juárez mountains because some of the locals—getting into the spirit of the race, perhaps—had felled trees across the road.

Between the Sierra Juárez and San Felipe, coming down a sandy wash into Diablo dry lake, Timerider had slipped sideways and stabbed a rear tire on a rock. The truck had different-sized wheels front and back. Fronts were what usually blew and, being smaller, they'd fit either end. So the truck carried only front spares. But when Eikelberger and Nesmith had started to fix the flat they'd discovered that their front wheel center holes had been mis-drilled by a fraction of an inch. Neither spare would slide all the way in over the rear axle spline. They'd bolted the wheel on as best they could and driven the fifteen-mile high-speed run across Diablo with their heads going like bobble dolls.

When they'd gotten a good wheel at the pit in San Felipe, they'd taken off at top speed, and so had Alcorn, Dr. Lopez, and I with their truck parts. But we stayed gone. Timerider went four or five miles down the coast road, headed into a curve doing about 120, and came up with no brakes. Nesmith did some very fancy Soap Box Derby driving and coasted Timerider to a safe stop. A can of brake fluid was poured in. That lasted forty feet. They had to turn around and creep back to the San Felipe pits. By then the spare master cylinder was in the air, halfway to El Crucero.

Eikelberger managed to adapt a salvaged Jeep brake cylinder to the Chevy, but by the time he finished Timerider was an hour and a half off pace.

From San Felipe to Gonzaga Bay, the course went over a set of mountains called Tres Hermanas, or Three Sisters, known as the three ugliest sisters in Mexico. It's only a sixteen-mile stretch across the mountains proper, but it took Timerider an hour and a half to negotiate it. The road was steep and apparently had been graded by titans using basketball hoops as gravel screens. The only way through was to get on the accelerator until you "make it up or break it up."

Because of the time lost to brake failure, all the little cars—the Class 11 VWs and Class 6 two-wheel-drive production cars and anemic Class 7 mini-pickups—were in the Three Sisters before Timerider. The road was littered with parts and pieces of them and some whole ones too, helplessly stuck. Nesmith and Eikelberger got caught in back of a huge Swede in a stalled Saab. The Swede refused to reverse out of the way and was too big to argue with. And when they got out to give him a push, he yelled, "Not dere! Dot's fiberglass! Yu'll break it if you push it dere, yah!"

When they got the Swede out of the way they ran up behind a stuck Class 7, and while pushing it uphill they got stuck themselves. When they tried to back down they were blocked by a stalled Blazer. "Just go ahead and back into the goddamned thing," said the Blazer's purple-faced, Blazer-kicking driver. They did and bounced and got some speed up and made it over. Then Eikelberger looked back and saw that Timerider's bed was rippling in a manner more like a waterbed than a pickup bed.

The tubular cage that formed the shock mounts for four of the six rear shocks had begun to break up. Shock absorbers were prodding the truck bed from beneath. Timerider made it the rest of the way over the Three Sisters with only two shocks locating the rear axle, and these at an almost horizontal angle. Also, when they'd reached the top of the third sister, the water gauge was at 280 degrees and the transmission temperature was over three hundred degrees.

Eikelberger found an unused set of shock mounts on the frame, left over from some previous rear suspension experiment. He added another set of shock absorbers, but these too were almost horizontal. The loose and flexing suspension cage was beginning to tear the back end of the truck apart. They bungeed and cabled and wired Timerider's aft until it looked like the victim of a drunk spider the size of an elk.

By then, Nesmith said later, they'd gone "from race face to finish face." But tangled-in-a-ball-of-twine-Timerider worked surprisingly well through the valleys southwest to El Crucero. So Nesmith sped up and a seam opened in the oil cooler.

The pit crew at El Crucero rerouted the oil lines and threw away the oil cooler. Fifty miles later there was a flat stretch that looked easy on the suspension. Nesmith pushed the accelerator again and the oil pressure went to zero. When they opened the hood there was oil everywhere. A new length of braided steel hose had split. To replace the hose the oil pump had to be removed. Solid walls of cactus blocked both sides of the narrow path. The only thing to do was to push Timerider into this thicket. Eikelberger lay on his back and pulled the pump and hoses. He was still sleeping on his stomach weeks later.

Timerider's flashlight was missing too. Eikelberger did the work by braille with help from just a faint glow of headlights reflecting on the needled plant life.

And yet Timerider was *still* fast. Nesmith and Eikelberger went, at nearly full speed, down the Pacific coast above Scammon's Lagoon, where the gray whales breed each winter. (Not that they stopped to watch.) If they could make San Ignacio by two-thirty A.M., they'd still be in the running for maybe second or maybe third place in their class. Then they hit the silt beds.

A silt bed looks like a dry lake but is actually an accumulation of clay dust that's one, two, or even three feet deep. Huge ruts lurked beneath that dust. The only way across the silt beds was to go like hell and hope like heaven. This didn't work. Timerider got high-centered. Eikelberger and Nesmith spent an hour shoveling dust and piling brush under the rear wheels. In that hour they went thirty feet. They got to San Ignacio at four A.M.

We had begun to worry. SCORE's ham radio communications went from bad to none. Nobody knew where anybody's car was. The generator kept going out. Every time the lights came back on I noted that the large crowd of not entirely sober Mexicans had closed in tighter. They weren't hostile, but whenever a car came into the pits the crowd rushed to help, scattering parts and tools everywhere. A Mexican entry arrived to popular acclaim. But he had a broken frame member. While the driver's back was turned several onlookers grabbed welding equipment and came to the aid of their countryman, sending showers of sparks over the cans of race gas.

Rumors began circulating in the pits. Everyone was lost. Everyone was in La Paz already. There'd been a terrible accident. There'd been a riot. There'd been a huge explosion at Villa Insurgentes. (Actually a ham operator had bumped his radio antenna into a high-tension wire, burning himself on the leg and knocking himself off the top of a truck.) The best rumor was about Mark Thatcher, the British prime minister's son, who was driving a Class 3 4WD Dodge pickup. We heard he'd been kidnapped by political terrorists. In fact, though no kid, he was napped—asleep in the back of a Lincoln Continental behind the San Ignacio pits after having been stuck in Tres Hermanas like everybody else.

Finally, at three A.M., an entrant came in with the news that Timerider was sitting just off the road forty miles north, where the course crossed Route 1. One of the pit crewmen and I got in the preracer and went, at ninety, up the highway. It wasn't Timerider sitting just off the road. It was more of our own crew in the Baja Bug, looking for Timerider too.

We got the preracer back to San Ignacio moments before the busted-looking Nesmith and Eikelberger and their busted truck arrived.

Eikelberger leaped out and grabbed the arc welder. He didn't have the right welding rods or any reinforcing material. It was a freestyle welding spree and anything hanging loose got a bead on it.

"We're going to get fifty miles down the road, and it's going to break," said Burke.

"No, it won't," said Nesmith, "everything's broken already."

About four-thirty in the morning, Crisco and Burke took off.

Eikelberger and I waited for an hour to make sure Timerider didn't come gimping back. Then we left to try to beat the truck to the checkpoint in La Purisima.

Out of San Ignacio the race course turned west to the tidal marshes along the Pacific, then down the coast for 150 miles. The only way Eikelberger and I could catch Timerider was to turn east, and then south on Route 1 and take the supposedly decent dirt road back across the peninsula. After five hundred miles and twenty-four hours of natural and mechanical agony, Eikelberger insisted on driving the prerunner himself.

We headed out of San Ignacio at 115 mph, cows all over the place. I swear Mexican cattle come out like chickens to gravel along the roadside in the early morning. We missed every Bossy and drove toward the biggest, reddest sunrise ever. We'd liberated some race gas from the pits and the Windsor was singing like a whiskey-throated Mormon Tabernacle Choir—down through the mountain passes above Santa Rosalia and by the palm jungles of Mulegé and along the cliffs above Bahia Conception.

The road west to La Purisima, when we found it, was nothing but a wander of dog tracks. Our only means of navigation was to keep the sun at our backs as we headed into the awesome (and not always in a good way) Baja interior.

In forty miles I saw a dozen things that would be national monuments, federal parks, or huge tourist attractions if they existed in the States—nameless buttes the size of Manhattan with sheer pink cliff faces as high as the Chrysler Building, whole Mount Shastas made up of loose boulders the size of houses, a cactus forest with the cactus growing thick as lawn grass and big as bridge abutments, and places where the land itself seemed to have been incarnated in horrid lifeforms by the forces of wind erosion. What there was of road bumbled through this, two-thirds wide enough for our truck. One door scraped against a topless rock wall while the other door opened on a bottomless abyss. Eikelberger never took his foot off the gas. "We went through some of this easy stuff on the way to San Felipe," he said.

We went down into a grove of cactus. On top of every plant for hundreds of yards around was a vulture, five hundred vultures at the very least. We went up into highlands deserted by all of life, plant and animal alike. If there is a Valley of the Shadow of Death (which would be where the vultures were) then these are the hills that cast it into shade.

We came upon a gravel road up there, well maintained but steep and treacherous. We descended on it into what seemed to be a giant quarry until we came around a curve and almost drowned in a lake. Palm trees were waving on its banks. Amid the palms was a village with an ancient mission church at its center. All around were pin-neat grass huts with thatched roofs. Each had a vegetable garden, a woven-stick corral full of fat pigs, and a yard where plump cows wandered and sleek goats strained at tethers.

People waved as we skidded through their town. They were smiling and healthy-looking and wore clean, white clothes. We drove past a great aqueduct built from hand-hewn stone and appearing to date back to the conquistadores if not before. This was San Isidro. I meant to go live there forever. But before I got around to it the village was gone, and we were up another hill and back in the rocks with no living thing visible for miles in any direction.

When we arrived at the checkpoint in La Purisima, we found that Crisco and Burke had been and gone an hour before. We thought they must be doing okay.

They weren't. About forty-five miles out of San Ignacio Crisco launched Timerider into a set of steep downhill switchbacks and the brakes failed again. Timerider slipped over the berm and slid sideways down a forty-five-degree incline, riding on the rocker panel and the tire sidewalls for hundreds of yards, nearly rolling every second. But they were back on the course when they got to the bottom. They pried open a crushed exhaust pipe, pulled the fenders away from the tires, and poured some fluid in the ex-Jeep master cylinder.

Another forty miles or so and they got a flat, using up their only remaining spare. They borrowed some likely looking wheels from a DNF at a place I can find on no map called Ejido Candejo. And seeing that they couldn't stop very well anyway they decided to go full-speed to Villa Insurgentes.

There's a rug-flat coastal plain bordering the Pacific from La Purisima eighty miles south to Insurgentes. The road is deep sand and perfectly straight. Eikelberger gave me the wheel of the prerunner and showed me the technique for deep sand driving. You put your foot in it and go like stink. This, you'll recall, is the same technique used for steep rocky trails and for silt beds and, as far as I can tell, for every other eventuality that Baja racers encounter.

The Mexican highway department had put culverts under this sand road, one every three hundred meters, to keep the road from washing out. The road washed out anyway, leaving each culvert two feet high athwart the road. The ride to Villa Insurgentes was like having four-hundred-horsepower hiccups. We knocked the top off the toolbox and wrenches went flying. We cracked a shock mount and we broke a gas tank strap.

On Timerider they had busted the whole rear suspension cage repair and, at Villa Insurgentes, they'd had to weld it together again. By the time Eikelberger and I arrived, Timerider was gone again.

Crisco and Burke were out on the beach in the penultimate leg of the race, with 170 miles left to La Paz. We took Route 1, filled with Mexican gas now and pinging like a sheet metal harpsichord. We had to stop every thirty miles and pour toluene in the tank to jack the octane. But the prerunner managed a hundred miles per hour just the same.

We got to La Paz about noon. Nesmith et al had arrived that morning in the Cessna 411. Crisco and Burke, however, had halted at the last pit stop—just before the course turned east toward La Paz—and found Timerider's rear suspension had come apart for the third time. There was nothing left to weld. They jury-rigged the back end with more bungee cords and a nylon strap come-along and kept moving. High tides forced them up into a cactus patch where they got two flats. Timerider was out of tires once more. The truck quit—out of gas. It was a long walk to get any, and when they came back and opened the gas cap the tank was full. A loose strut had been rubbing against the fuel filter, had worn a hole in it, and the engine (and apparently the gas gauge) was sucking air.

Burke bypassed the fuel filter. They drove on. But a few miles later a float stuck in one of the carburetor bowls. Burke put a screwdriver blade against the carb and whacked the screwdriver handle with a rock, meaning to jar the float loose but driving the screwdriver right through the bowl instead. Fortunately it was the bowl for the four-barrel's secondaries and he was able to seal these with duct tape and run on the primary barrels. But as Crisco opened the door to get behind the wheel he stepped into a big cactus apple that lodged in the center of his forehead.

There is no way to touch a cactus apple without embedding its barbed thorns in your flesh. And it was tangled in Crisco's hair as well. Burke had to give him a haircut with a pair of tin snips and remove the cactus apple with pliers.

Crisco and Burke finally nursed Timerider across the finish line at three-thirty in the afternoon. Elapsed time: 31 hours, 5 minutes, and 57 seconds.

* * *

They won. That is, as far as I was concerned, they won. Technically they were fifth in their class and more than thirteen and a half hours off the overall winning time, which was set on a 500cc motorcycle. But from what I'd seen there was only one opponent in the Baja 1000 and that was the Baja, and if you beat that you won.

Motor racing in the 1980s had come to mean watching a skinny Frenchman in a bathtub full of gasoline run two hundred miles an hour straight at a wall to see if his airfoils worked. So I couldn't say enough good about the Baja 1000. It harkened back to an era when skill, ingenuity, friends, cooperation, guts, and riding mechanics meant more than sponsorship by a jeans company. I'd had as much fun as I'd had at the NASCAR race, in a more tiring, scary, and less hungover way. I stood convinced that the Baja 1000 was flat-out the best kind of racing on earth.

The only thing I couldn't understand was why anyone would do it. "Well," Nesmith said, "I like the big trucks and I like the people. But there's something else. I don't know if you'll know what I'm talking about. But I grew up poor in west Texas. There wasn't much to do. Sometimes one kid would say to another, 'Come on over to my house—we're gonna jump off the roof!'"

7

A Test of Men and Machines That We Flunked

So many interesting and entertaining disasters had resulted from running a fully prepared race machine the length of the Baja that I lobbied *Car and Driver* to do the same with eight wholly unprepared new sport sedans.

Everyone at the magazine thought this was a great idea. And it *was* a great idea. It was not, mind you, a good idea. But it was a large thought-provoking notion and perfectly suited to the times.

The early 1980s was the era of the genius car journalist. The cars were so stupid that the car journalist considered himself a genius by comparison. This explains why some of us geniuses thought we could drive, at a rate of more than five hundred miles a day, in box stock vehicles to Cabo San

Lucas and back over a long weekend. Among the brainiacs involved: David E. Davis Jr.; Csaba Csere (later to become editor of *Car and Driver* when David left to start *Automobile*); Jean Jennings (later to become editor of *Automobile* when David left to start a consulting firm); Rich Ceppos (later to become publisher of *Autoweek*); me (later to become . . . um . . . more me-like); virtuoso tech editor Don Sherman; crack photog Aaron Kiley; and legendary genius car journalist Brock Yates.

Brock was arrested while extending his legend, so to speak, and improving the sanitation of the parking lot at Hussong's Cantina in Ensenada. The cop didn't understand English or what Brock was saying about his mother. Fortunately Jean Jennings had taught herself to speak Spanish by adding *o*'s to the end of every word. She explained that Brock was a genius—or something. Unfortunately for Brock, instead of getting material for a best-selling book about his years in Mexican prison he got a small fine for public urination.

DUI was not yet a sin on the level of smoking or raising children with low self-esteem. Lunch at Hussong's had been long and hilarious. When we changed cars fifty miles later, two were left by the roadside—a Datsun Maxima from the Triumph-Herald-stretch-limo school of Japanese design and a Volkswagen Quantum automatic (three little words say it all).

We found them. And a good thing we did. When we were arrested the next day—for driving a hundred miles per hour through La Paz with wallets—Jean gathered the police around the Maxima. Then, by leaving a door ajar, she made it talk. We were let off with a small fine. Maybe they were awed by our powers. Maybe we were too pathetic for jail.

We decided that driving at night was dangerous. Unfortunately it was night when we decided this. Csaba Csere promptly hit a cow. It did a flip, leaving two pointy horn dents in the roof of a Dodge 600ES. (Remember Dodge's attempt to turn the K-car into a sport sedan with a Jim Carrey Cable Guy cable shift? Neither does anyone else.) Also, the radiator was crushed. We pushed the Dodge sixty miles to Cabo with an Audi 5000S, soon to garner *Sixty Minutes* fame for "unintended acceleration." It should have done such a good job on the back walls of old farts' garages.

Then we all got sick.

After a restful day sitting on toilets between brief stints of radiator repair we headed back. Jean and Don Sherman were in the Dodge, with styling improved by lack of ugly hood and bumper. They were arrested in Loreto for not reporting an accident. "Thieves stole the hood," they explained. They were rearrested for not reporting a theft. We did what you'd expect of the brotherhood of car journalists and went on to San Ignacio, leaving them in custody. Jean gave the cop's girlfriend a manicure. Don fixed the police station's copying machine. They were let off with a small fine. But they ran out of gas. They used a length of "Tijuana credit card" plastic tubing on a tourist motor home, choosing the Winnebago with the worst bumper sticker: "Children Need to Pray, Too."

We hadn't counted on rain in the Baja's rainy season. In the morning Don took off at his customary top speed in the Maxima. The tires of the period were prone to aquaplaning, but not in a gully wash three feet deep. The Maxima's UNIVAC-sized onboard computer drowned. We attempted repair with hair dryers. (It was 1983, we *all* had hair dryers.)

Waters rose. Tempers rose. We were trapped. Drink was taken. Brock and I blew up at Csaba because he wouldn't stop talking about throttle body fuel injection. "That's not what cars are about!" we yelled. "Cars are about beauty, women, sex!" Csaba said that if we didn't understand the problems of throttle body fuel injection we were probably having sex several feet away from the women. Don blew up at the Maxima. David Davis blew up at everybody. Sinking cars! Hitting cows! Being jerks! It was Jean—the only one who hadn't been crazy, useless, or drunk all week—who began to cry. There weren't many women in car journalism back then. Did she feel excluded from our collective genius? We'd done our best to let her go to jail like Leona Helmsley. What more could feminism ask of us?

We found a back road on high ground above the flooding, albeit going in the wrong direction. We abandoned the Maxima, headed back south to La Paz, and got arrested. We were traveling in an illegal convoy at three times the speed limit, had failed to register our cars with Mexican customs, and were badly groomed due to burned-out hair dryers. Luckily we had official papers—with Lincoln, Jefferson, and Jackson on the front. We left the remaining cars in someone's backyard and flew home.

The stupid 1980s cars had, in fact, done nothing stupid except what we made them do. I heard they all eventually got back to the United States. But I prefer to believe they didn't. I like to think of them still down in Mexico—the Quantum, the 600ES, the Maxima et al—converted into the oddest of lowriders. And under the Audi's dash is a special switch that, instead of causing the car to hop, makes it unintentionally accelerate into a pack of genius car journalists. Anyway, Brock wrote the main car-test report, using his genius to find a few nice things to say about the sport sedans so that our advertisers wouldn't have a cow and cause *Car and Driver* to go the way of the Dodge. And I wrote the following travel guide.

* * *

So you're going to the Baja? You're buzzing with happy anticipation, boning up on the Berlitz, learning "*Buenas noches*" and "Excuse me, but I think this sandwich is made of dog." What to pack? Take lots of cheerful resort clothes (handy for spreading on the desert floor to signal airborne rescue parties). Take plenty of American money. Take a powder. Take Interstate 15 back north and stay in Palm Springs.

¿No, gracias? Then cross the border into Tijuana—adventure, here comes you! Total immersion in a different culture, different values . . . Don't be an ugly American and throw up. In Tijuana, garbage collection means displaying your collection of garbage in the street. But this is no excuse for forgetting the "good neighbor" policy the way some Americans did in 1848 when we stole half the country (the half with all the money and jobs).

Moving right along, let's zip down the beautiful four-lane, sometimes two-lane, occasionally no-lane highway to Ensenada with its breathtaking view of where the ocean would be if a lot of American recreational vehicles weren't parked in the way. On the road we see the quaint Mexican toll booths where they'll accept *anything*—yes, a button, an Oreo, a child's gym sneaker. This is the result of Mexico's interesting new currency system: each peso is worth one hundred centavos, and the centavo is worth nothing at all. We gringos, we'll probably never get how this works. But it's fun galore when you're bargaining for an entire miniature mariachi band made of dead stuffed frogs. (Memo to U.S. Customs, re. smuggling of rare, endangered, dead stuffed frog species: they were planted in my luggage by a jealous *Road & Track* correspondent.)

Don't miss the Museum of Third World Toilets (on display in Ensenada and *everywhere* else). Cheerful, fun-loving tour member Brock Yates did miss it. The fun-loving, happy-go-lucky local police were not amused. "You have made the violation of a laws," they said (Spanish for "Give me ten dollars"). The Mexicans have an interesting method of paying their police: they don't. Just "free guns and all you can eat." Maybe some of our stateside big-city budget balancers should take a tip from this useful idea.

By the way, don't forget to stop at the checkpoint south of Ensenada and get your tourist permit stamped. Otherwise it's illegal to go more than one hundred kilometers south of the border. The checkpoint is closed weekends, holidays, nights, mornings, and siestas. Also, it doesn't exist. And remember, Mexico's traffic laws are different from ours. They're made up on the spot. Mexican roads are different too. The Mexican Highway Department is known as the "Miracle of the Sierra Madre" because the entire national road system was built without surveyors' instruments, rulers, T-squares, or any of the sticky stuff that holds asphalt together. The roads are a little narrow by U.S. standards—just room enough for a large truck in the oncoming lane and a large accident in yours.

Sun's down, ready for some fun? Night life is *muy bueno* in little desert towns like San Ignacio. Wade to your car. Drive half a mile through water up to the doorsills, then a couple more miles to the restaurant with no roof, because it rains here only every three years and this is the year. Your soaking wet hosts will try to trick you into eating a jalepeño that will allow you to levitate above the third world toilet seat in the morning. Plus your hosts will fill your headache with memories of home by playing their one American country-and-western tape over and over again at top volume. Yes, when night falls in old Mexico, anything goes. And everything was gone—especially the electricity—by the time we got back to our motel.

The Baja has plenty of beautiful scenery. Or maybe it doesn't. Who can tell? Cheerful (well, sort of) tour guide Don Sherman loves to go hippity-hop quick as a bunny down Mexico's amusing roads—terrific view of white knuckles clenching sweat-drenched steering wheel. And for extra fun at a hundred-plus, be sure you have a front-wheel-drive car with wildly excessive understeer, which doesn't give any tedious old advance warning when it goes for a closer look at the Baja's flora and fauna.

Speaking of flora and fauna, everything that's more than three feet from the highway is poisonous, has thorns, or is armed with a .45—a naturalist's paradise! (Keep car doors locked and beep horn until the Marines arrive.)

Some stick-in-the-muds say you shouldn't drive at night south of the border. You might hit a cow or something. A lot of malarkey, say we. (Write care of this magazine for good deals on Mexican beefsteak and a Dodge 600ES front end, used hard only once.)

The rest of the food in Mexico is fabulous too—broiled *langostino,* succulent yellowfin tuna, tasty *carne asada,* beautiful salads, and fresh vegetables. And here's a surefire hint for avoiding tummy troubles: don't eat any of it. Fun-imbibing tour member David E. Davis Jr. has a great method for finding all the best Mexican restaurants: stop where the flies do! Eleven million insects can't be wrong.

Did someone say sickness and danger? Mexican officialdom was eager to give us a tour of the country's penal facilities—their way of saying thanks for our speeding, traveling in an illegal convoy, speeding again, being so fun-filled, having cow accidents, and speeding some more.

But worldly wise veteran traveler Jean Lindamood Jennings turns out to be fluent in . . . we'll call it "Spic-n-Spanish" because her happy patter let us make a clean getaway.

Watch Jean get directly involved in native life! She's siphoning gas from American automobiles in Santa Rosalia, stealing the *federale*'s squad car in Loreto, and driving around town with his girlfriend. Maybe we got special treatment because the Mexicans believed that if they detained us they might have to keep Jean too.

Yes, you'll want to stay in Baja forever, the way we almost did. Ah, the sights, the smells, the vistas, the stronger smells, and the wonderful, beautiful weather. The weather in Baja is incomparable, glorious year-round. Don't call it rain, call it liquid sunshine. Why, the climate is so warm and dry that the Mexicans don't even bother to build bridges. They just pave right across the bottom of arid river beds and never have any problems at all with . . . WHERE'S SHERMAN? JESUS CHRIST, GET ROPE! GET SANDBAGS! Happy touring, *amigos*, and *adiós* for now to the cheerful, fun-filled . . . BAIL, FOR GOD'S SAKE! BAIL! MAYDAY! MAYDAY! MAYDAY!

8

A Better Land Than This

There is a thing known as car nut logic. It's misnamed insofar as ratiocination is implied. But having your brain on "auto" is a dominant mode of thought for many American men and for no few American women, although not for the two American women who accompanied me and Michael Nesmith on one more Baja adventure in 1984.

The Baja was a bad place to race and a worse place to test sport sedans. Therefore, Michael and I reasoned, it would be a swell place for a romantic getaway. Michael invited his then-wife Kathryn and I invited my then-girlfriend Elena to go on an "off-road road trip." We would take two four-wheel-drive vehicles down the Baja, for fun, attempting to avoid all pavement while camping out along the way. I'm not *blaming* the Baja for Michael's divorce or my breakup. But . . .

I talked the then extant American Motors Corporation (I'm not *blaming* the Baja . . .) into loaning us a pair of their products—a newly introduced SUV model, the Cherokee, and a CJ with a pickup bed, the Scrambler.

We took these to Michael's race garage in LA. We (by "we" I mean Michael and his mechanics) reinforced the suspensions, bolted in extra spares, fitted the Cherokee with a safari-style roof rack and an electric winch, and wired each Jeep with a set of four auxiliary lights. When the lights were switched on they lit the garage like a Los Alamos A-bomb test.

Mexico has only one brand of gasoline, Pemex, owned by the government. Quality and supply are the same as they would be if the U.S. Post Office was also the gas station. We installed thirty-gallon gas tanks, added backup fuel filters, and packed a case of octane booster.

We also packed oil, coolant, extra radiator hoses and fan belts, a tow strap, jumper cables, fire extinguishers, several sets of wrenches, a shovel, and an air compressor; plus tents, sleeping bags, coolers, twenty gallons of American water, a camp stove, dried food, a compass, two-way radios, piles of maps and guidebooks, and four snake-bite kits.

In retrospect this strikes me as three snake-bite kits too many. I mean, once I've had to use one snake-bite kit I'm out of there. Hello medevac, good-bye me. On the other hand there was no medevac in the Baja. While you're treating yourself with the first snake-bite kit, I guess the same snake could sneak up and bite you three more times. Even so, for the sake of our love lives, Michael and I would have been better off replacing a couple of the snake-bite kits with a pair of small blue boxes from Tiffany & Co.

Larger gifts from Tiffany wouldn't have fit. The Jeeps were so full that we had to leave a lot of things behind, but only the things we'd be needing. It took us from morning until late afternoon to pack the Jeeps with the other things. On the first day of our journey we made it to Huntington Beach.

On the second day, Tuesday May 8, we entered Mexico at Tecate and took Route 2 east along the border to the Mesa del Pinal, the pine forests on the western slope of the Juárez mountains. Here we turned off the road. Forty miles south was Laguna Hanson, the Baja's only lake.

We were lost two hundred yards from the pavement. Lumber is scarce in Baja, and Mesa del Pinal is webbed with woodcutters' roads. Once a way is cleared in the desert it stays clear. The woodcutters' roads overlaid four centuries of cattle trails, mining cuts, Indian paths, and missionary pack routes—all still open to passage, mainly by us. We'd left the compass behind.

Still, it was a beautiful afternoon, sun lighting up the stands of trees, air redolent with incense cedar, piñon pine, sage, and gasoline. I stopped the Scrambler. Gas was pouring out of our custom-fitted tank. A little nest of vent tubes designed to meet some U.S. air pollution regulation had come undone. We would dribble gas the rest of the trip.

Michael got under the car. Elena walked off to photograph the scenery. These uplands look inviting, like Devonshire pastures, but the flapjack-shaped nopal cactus has tiny spines that must be removed by depilatory waxing. Cholla cactus spines are large, barbed, and nearly unextractable. And cholla branches detach so easily they're said to throw themselves at people. Elena was back in a minute.

We kept driving around in the pines. The sun was setting. We got out all our maps. No two agreed on anything. "Laguna Hanson," I read aloud from one of the guidebooks, "is named for an American ranch manager who was murdered there."

We got back in the Jeeps and Elena confessed she'd never spent a night outdoors. I looked over and saw her knuckles gleaming white on the grab handle. I explained that there was nothing to worry about. We had enough food and water to spend weeks lost in the piney woods. Furthermore, Elena had been born in Havana. "You speak the local lingo," I said.

"Are we going to die?" she asked.

We couldn't find any place to pitch camp except the dry washes. These are poor campsites because livestock wander up and down them all night except during flash floods. A stake bed truck passed by full of drunk and yelling ranch hands. "You see," I told Elena, "we're not that far from civilization. What are they yelling?"

"You don't want to know," she said.

We found the highway again about eleven P.M. We'd penetrated maybe twenty miles into the wilderness.

The Juárez range had climbed gradually from the Pacific, but to the east the descent was immediate. The road peeled down a giant bluff in frenetic switchbacks. There were no shoulders on the highway. Cliffs rose without preamble from one edge of the asphalt and dropped like ruined stockbrokers from the other. Guardrails were few and there were no dents in them, just large holes punched straight through. The only traffic at midnight was enormous diesel trucks doing eighteen-wheel drifts through the turns at seventy miles an hour or, worse, going ten miles an hour in both lanes with their lights out. Clusters of memorial crosses decorated every curve. Sweat greased my palms. My knees shook. I looked at Elena. She lived in New York. Apparently she equated being back on pavement with urban security. Lulled by the familiar noise of honking horns and squealing brakes, she was asleep.

We reached flat land at Mexicali and drove into a fog of chemical spray and fertilizer stink rising from the irrigation canals. We rushed across the border and checked into an American motel.

We were ashamed of ourselves in the morning and returned to Mexico immediately, driving south on the San Felipe road into the delta of the Colorado River. For years Mexico had been arguing with the United States about Colorado water rights. During the Carter administration a treaty had been signed and the United States agreed to divert less of the Colorado's flow. But the Mexican government hadn't completed its channel dredging operations in time. The land Mexico was eager to irrigate was now under four feet of water.

Farther south was El Desierto de los Chinos, the desert of the Chinamen, where nothing grew at all. To the east was the wide salt flat, as eerie as it had been when I'd seen it on the way to San Felipe a year before. To the west was sand as bright as the salt, rising to shining hills that merged with brilliant sky, which arched back to the salt's glare until the whole landscape pinwheeled. The temperature was 120 degrees.

About 1900 a group of Chinese immigrants set out across this desert, hoping to find work in the United States. They paid a Mexican guide $100 to lead them. He said he knew where the water holes were. Halfway between San Felipe and the delta the guide admitted he didn't. They all died, including the Mexican. (Leaving us to wonder how we know the story.)

At El Chinero, where the bodies were buried, we turned west up the San Matias pass, which divided the Sierra Juárez from the Sierra San Pedro Mártir, the highest range in the Baja. Six thousand feet up in these peaks, a hundred miles from any city, and separated from the road by twenty miles of crag and gorge was a hacienda with a dirt air strip and guest rooms: Mike's Sky Ranch.

Michael and I had been eager to get into bad terrain. We were anxious to try our expensive car modifications. The handcrafted dual-front shock-absorber mounts on the Cherokee came loose immediately. Then there was an ugly noise from the Scrambler. I stopped. Water was pouring out of the radiator. One fan blade had bent double and sliced an arc out of the radiator core.

In the Baja 1000 race they attribute such accidents to a special gremlin, the Baja Monster. They say the Baja Monster makes things go wrong no one ever heard of going wrong before. I'd certainly never seen this happen to a fan blade. Actually, like most remote places, the Baja was supposed to have a monster. Tibet had the Yeti. The Rockies had Sasquatch. And the monster reported by early travelers in Baja was, rather sadly, Zorillo the rabid skunk.

We towed the Scrambler over the now less attractive rocks and gullies to Mike's.

Mike's Sky Ranch sat in the large valley by a small stream that contained its own species of trout. Wonderful cooking smells came from the sprawl of white adobe buildings. The sun went down between mountains as if into rifle sights and threw a violet cast across the sky. In the last moments of light, hundreds of birds flew out. Kathryn and Elena were delighted by their lambent, darting turns. Michael took me aside. "Those are bats," he said.

On Thursday Michael pinched the radiator tubes shut as well as he could. I straightened the fan blade on a rock. There was supposed to be a man with a soldering iron thirty miles away in Valle de Trinidad. He wasn't there. We now had to drive either eighty miles northwest to Ensenada and have the radiator boil from mountain grades or drive eighty miles southeast to San Felipe and have the radiator boil from desert heat. Kathryn and Elena thought we'd be better off in Ensenada. "They have more jewelry stores there."

The Ensenada radiator shop fixed the Scrambler in ten minutes and charged us eight dollars. You could get anything fixed in the Baja, which was good because everything broke there.

That night we stayed at a new hotel on the Pacific coast at San Quintin. Beach dunes had already destroyed the landscaping.

Below San Quintin Route 1 turned inland and there was a sudden change in scenery. Mesas and granite mountains were replaced by boat-sized sandstone boulders. Wind erosion had ground and drilled these into scary caricatures. The scruffy Sonoran desert foliage gave way to unearthly growths. There were dense spreads of Cardón cactus, something like the saguaros in Arizona but more anthropomorphic and much larger. Once again, as on the drive to San Isidro, flocks of vultures perched in the cactus. Sometimes five acres of Cardón would have a carrion bird on every arm. There were also forests of boojum—more properly, cirio. The tall, unbranched trees looked like air carrots from Mars. Scattered in the cirio and Cardón were Copalquins, or elephant trees, whose fat spare-leafed limbs make agonized prehensile shapes. Every child has imagined such a thing under the bed.

Rough weather, rougher geography, and protecting seas have turned the Baja into a set of biological atolls. There are hundreds of plants and animals that live nowhere else. More than eighty species of cactus are endemic to the Baja. Cirio trees are found only within a 125-mile radius. The Baja has flowers pollinated not by insects but by bats, and bats that eat fish instead of insects. Isla Santa Catalina in the Sea of Cortés has a rattlesnake species with no rattles. And on Isla Espiritu Santo a race of black jack rabbits has developed. The black fur does not provide protective coloration, much less comfort in the sun. The mutation seems entirely pointless.

Our awe of nature was dulled, however, by garbage all over the place. And the shapely rocks were spray-painted with political party symbols, advertisements, and messages of love. Nature was at its worst here and man wasn't much good either.

There were also, everywhere in the Baja, wrecked cars, hundreds of them, mostly upside down and burned. One guidebook tried to pass these off gaily: "Don't be bugged by those wrecked vehicles here and there along the highway—they're just jalopies abandoned by road construction workers." We stopped for lunch at a little landing strip called Santa Ines. A collection of crashed airplanes was piled behind the cantina.

After 180 miles of living and dead grotesques, Route 1 curved back toward the Pacific and ran along empty beaches through land that looked like the land around Los Angeles would if vanity plates were fatal and bulldozers were free. The beaches end at the town of Guerrero Negro next to Scammon's Lagoon, the largest of several Baja inlets where all the world's gray whales mate and calve. Whaling ships discovered the lagoon in 1857 and hunted it until grays were thought to be extinct.

Guerrero Negro also had an enormous sea salt harvesting operation. There have been many attempts to get something out of the Baja. The first expedition in 1533 was sent by Cortés to gather pearls at La Paz. The captain was murdered by the pilot, and the pilot was murdered by the Indians. Cortés tried again in 1535. Pearls were found but the pearl divers starved. Agricultural settlements failed in 1603, 1636, 1649, and 1685. Silver mines have been sunk in a hundred places, also mines for gold and lead. In 1868 J. Ross Browne, a reporter for *Harper's Magazine,* wrote that no mine had yet repaid its investment. In 1866 an American land company received a grant of eighteen million acres from the Mexican government and colonization was attempted. The colonists left. There have been onyx quarries at El Marmol, a French copper concession at Santa Rosalia, an attempt to breed pearl oysters on Isla Espiritu Santo, et cetera. They're all gone.

On the outskirts of Guerrero Negro, where the twenty-eighth parallel divides the Mexican states of Baja California and Baja California Sur, was an immense gawky steel constructivist sculpture of a landing eagle. There was a museum at the base with rows of flagpoles and a large amphitheater. All this was built to commemorate the opening of Route 1 in 1973. It was abandoned, its windows broken, the sculpture rusty, and sand filled the arena seats. An osprey and his mate had made a nest in the broken road sign beside the steel eagle.

Inland at midpeninsula the country changed again, turning to fields of black lava. Tres Virgenes, three perfect volcanic cones, rose in the eastern distance. We traveled eighty miles in this unrelieved scene, then crested a hill and were confronted by the startling tropical luxury of San Ignacia. The oasis occupied a theatrical cleft in the rocks. A lagoon filled the bottom, surrounded by magnificent date palms. Thatch-roofed houses with thick flower gardens were set among the trees. Behind them pale blue and pink adobe buildings faced a broad plaza sheltered by giant Indian laurels. San Ignacio was heaven with bugs.

A colonial baroque mission church filled one side of the plaza. The walls were four feet thick, built from lava rubble, and carefully plastered and painted to imitate dressed stone. The mammoth gilt wood altar and huge murky paintings of Ignatius of Loyola were imported from Spain. Crude local carvings of angel faces decorated the vault above.

The mission was founded in 1728, one of thirty-three missions built by Jesuits, Franciscans, and Dominicans to convert the Baja Indians. The Indians' language had no words for "marriage" or "honesty." They went around naked and did not know how to make pots, weave cloth, or build a hut. They ate insects and lizards and anything else. If a particularly good thing to eat was discovered, they would tie a string around it, swallow the morsel, pull it back up, and pass it to the next person.

In June, when pitahaya cactus fruit were ripe, the Indians gorged themselves, stopping only for naps and to fornicate with everyone, regardless of family ties. During pitahaya season the tribe defecated on large flat rocks so the undigested fruit seeds could be picked out and ground into flour. Father Francisco Maria Piccolo, who in 1716 was the first European to visit San Ignacio, was given some bread baked from this flour. He ate it before discovering its source and was the target of jokes from his fellow missionaries for the rest of his life.

The Indians were not interested in Christianity. It took heroic efforts to gather them into irrigated settlements, introduce them to agriculture and other benefits of civilization, and give them the blessed sacraments. But the missionaries did it. The Indians promptly died. Between the founding of the first Baja mission in 1697 and the expulsion of the Jesuit order from Spanish territories in 1767 the Indian population—with its utter lack of immunity to European, or even new world, diseases—decreased from 50,000 to 7,000. In 1984 only a couple hundred were left near Mexicali.

On the morning of Saturday, May 12, we left San Ignacio by the back way, driving up to the most spectacular view of the oasis, which is from the dump. Then we went across the remaining volcanic highlands to Santa Rosalia, the old French mining concession by the Sea of Cortés. On the town square was a sheet iron church designed by Gustave Eiffel. It was created for the 1889 Universal Exposition in Paris as an example of a "manufactured building." It won second prize and was shipped to Baja by mistake.

Twenty miles south, on the lip of Bahia Concepción, was Rio Mulegé, one of the few Baja rivers that reaches the sea. Mulegé canyon was filled with palms and mangroves backed by naked hills. Man-o'-war birds, whose shape in flight mimicked a pterodactyl's, hung on the thermals. The effect was a museum diorama of the Mesozoic era blown up to horrifying size. The beauty, like so much of Baja's beauty, was hard to bear, a physical assault. It was a relief to look down the highway and see litter and more burned-out, overturned cars.

Under the cliffs along the Bahia Concepción the surf was police-flasher blue. The bay was twenty-five miles long and five miles wide and didn't have a single home on its shores. At the foot of the escarpments, though, if your car would make it, there are campsites on small parabolas of beach.

The water was the temperature of love. The breeze was the temperature of beer. Two kids in a dinghy sold us a kilo of big, perfectly round scallops—the best scallops I've ever tasted. The sun lit the cliff tops purple. Cormorants dove in formation. Pelicans skimmed the tide. It was a moment to justify the whole trip. And a moment was how long it lasted, followed by biting gnats, a soaking dew, and me kicking over the camp stove and setting fire to the beach towels.

Quests and challenges never seem to have a middle until you're in it. Everyone likes to address a challenge. Everyone likes to return from a quest. But the middle is another matter. We were tired, filthy, brilliantly sunburned, and queasy from the constant jolting ride and smell of gasoline. Elena had to be on a plane to New York via Mexico City on Monday, leaving no one to translate. The Baja highway was coming up in chunks from heat and traffic, and during the previous two years winter storms had corrugated whole miles of it. All the oil seals on the cars were weeping, every screw and bolt seemed to be working free, and our gear had shaken loose and was rattling maniacally. No amount of octane booster could help the Pemex gasoline, and each hill climb was accompanied by a wrecking clatter of predetonation in the engines.

A little after dawn on Sunday we stopped in Loreto where the Baja's first mission was built. Hanging in the church were excellent, astonishing seventeenth-century paintings of the disciples, the style just a little short of El Greco's. They were pulling from their frames and the canvas was rotting beneath the oil. Elena could find out nothing about them. "They are just anonymous," a shopkeeper told her. "There's supposed to be a Michelangelo under one. But we haven't scraped the paint off yet."

We drove two hours to a mountain oasis to see cave paintings, but they had been defaced. No one knows who did the cave paintings either. The Indians told the Spanish they were done by giants.

Back on the highway we climbed the terrible face of the Sierra de la Giganta, the mountains named for those artists, and drove 350 miles to La Paz through an unrelenting span of yuccas and bare grit.

Government and business had been working hard to make La Paz a famous resort though the town has no excuse for existence. Even the oysters John Steinbeck wrote about in *The Pearl* have died off. We checked into the new big concrete hotel. It seemed to have been jolted too. All the fittings were broken, the carpet was coming untacked, and there were holes in the bedclothes. On the mirror over the bathroom sinks were insincere-looking decals that read "agua potable."

Elena began to get sick at the airport. Kathryn and I were sick an hour later. I looked out my window and saw the hotel's sewage treatment plant in the same enclosure and nearly indistinguishable from the water purification equipment.

We managed to go out to dinner that night. The special was endangered, Mexican government–protected sea turtle.

Sea turtle steaks are the color of those school chalkboards that are supposed to ease eye strain. "It is like beef," the waiter said, "but with a different smell."

We were sicker yet on Tuesday. La Paz was hosting an International Rotary Club convention. Vendors were out in herds on the paseo along the harbor. Taped mariachi music barked from loudspeakers. La Paz was filling with Americans complaining that the town wasn't authentic enough. We tried to leave.

Three blocks from the hotel Kathryn called me on the radio. "There's something wrong with our car." I asked her if it was engine trouble. "I don't know that much about automobiles," she said. "It's hopping up and down." I looked in the rearview mirror. The Cherokee was hopping up and down.

The front axle assembly where we'd attached our double shock absorber modification had disintegrated. The nearest Cherokee axle was in San Diego. We bobbed slowly back to the hotel.

We'd set out to travel in places uninhabited and nearly unexplored, to see land unchanged since the first Europeans saw it, to tread where even aboriginal man had barely trod. And we'd wound up with diarrhea at a third-rate luxury hotel in the middle of a Rotary Club convention. Baja California was geography with a sense of humor. And geography always has the last laugh. It would take a Lear jet, a twin-engine Cessna, two race drivers, six Mexican welders, and the American Motors corporate public relations department to get us home.

An early missionary, Father Juan de Ugarte, once preached to the natives on the agonies of hell. His congregation began to laugh. Father Ugarte asked them what was funny, and an old Indian replied, "There must be no lack of firewood in hell. So hell is a better land than this. We would be wise to go there."

It was Baja that was first called "California." The name was a joke. Califia was an Amazon queen in *Las Sergas de Esplandián*, a romance popular in Spain when Mexico was being conquered. California, the island Califia ruled, was "at the right hand of the Indies very close to that part of terrestrial paradise and inhabited by women without a single man among them." Baja too, was thought to be an island and Spanish sailors named it "California" after encountering Indian matrons who washed themselves in urine.

It takes imagination to travel in a land like this. First you must imagine there's a reason to go there. Then you must imagine there's a reason to stay. Our disbelief had come unsuspended. Michael got on the phone and began hectoring the switchboard operator with hopelessly polite guidebook phrases. It took an hour to get the hotel's one long-distance line.

American Motors sent Clay Bintz, fleet manager for its West Coast PR office, to the Orange County airport with two new shock absorbers. The Lear jet owned by Michael's company, Pacific Arts, picked up Clay and Randy Salmont, Michael's new race truck codriver, and brought them to La Paz that night.

By nine the next morning Clay had found a man with an arc welder who worked under a tin-roofed ramada in a back alley. Clay held up the shock absorbers and began to mime. Then he stooped and drew pictures in the dirt. The welder and his five assistants clustered around. One peeked under the Cherokee. "Ay, que fucked!" he said. Michael and Kathryn and I went off to find beer and some bathrooms.

The welding crew pushed the Cherokee over a trench. By noon they'd built a new suspension out of scrap metal. An English-speaking neighbor told me, "You found the best welder. There is nothing he cannot repair." The neighbor inspected the discarded custom shocks. "However," he said, "much trouble in life comes from fixing things that are not broken."

Clay and Randy drove us to the airport. The two of them would try to nurse the Jeeps back to the States on Route 1. The Lear was fueled, gleaming, and ready on the crumbly tarmac. Kathryn scampered on board and Michael and I were about to follow. Michael stared wistfully into the desert. "I bet these cars won't make it," he said. He was wavering. He was chickening out on chickening out. "Especially if we went up the Gulf side and into San Felipe on the really bad roads."

Then Barry Connelly, the jet pilot, volunteered to return and fly air support, as he'd done for Michael's '83 Baja 1000 effort. "Just in case you die out there," Barry said. Kathryn stayed on the plane.

If the Cherokee was going to break we wanted it to break as soon as possible. Michael and I drove it hard out of La Paz on Route 1, slamming into ruts and holes and pounding our heads on the roof liner. Clay and Randy followed in the Scrambler. We made it to Loreto in six hours.

The next morning Barry flew back in Michael's Cessna 411 and landed at Bahia Los Angeles on the Sea of Cortés coast. The rest of us drove another three hundred miles up the highway past Guerrero Negro, then turned east into the wormy rocks and cirio forests on a forty-mile cutoff to the bay.

Bahia de Los Ángeles was a perfectly sheltered blonde sand cove about five miles across. Jagged arroyos radiated from it like a circle of dog mouths—bloodred granite pointed with veins of white quartz. This had been the site of a failed silver mine, a dead Indian tribe, and a massive resort development that never happened. There was a small motel there, some houses, and a shack of a gas station. The road built for the resort had come apart so badly that in places we got off and drove through the desert beside it.

The motel was all right. It was too hot to mind the cold showers and we only found one scorpion in the rooms.

Before dawn on Friday we headed back out the cutoff. We planned to take Route 1 north a few miles then get off road northeast along the Calamajué riverbed. We thought we could reach another cove, Bahia San Luis Gonzaga, by nightfall. Barry would stand by until noon and then fly over our dust trail.

Clay and I took the Scrambler. The ruts and pavement gashes seem to have grown in the night. The thing to do was to go fast, get "on top" so the Jeep's wheels would hit the far side of the holes before they had time to drop in. At sixty, if you have the nerve, this works on all but the biggest holes. And it was a very big hole we hit. We were tossed out against our shoulder harnesses, dropped back into our seats, and bounced up into the roof. Then there was an ugly noise. Water was pouring out of the radiator again. The same fan blade had bent the same way and cut a second arc through the radiator core.

We pushed and coasted the boiling Scrambler back to Bahia de Los Ángeles and woke Barry. He and Clay loaded the radiator into the Cessna and flew three hundred miles to Ensenada, to the same radiator shop. The shop owner had a good laugh, they said. Randy and Michael and I went down to the beach and drank.

It was four in the afternoon when we got the radiator back. Bored and half drunk, we drove a dozen miles out the cutoff and went south on a road into wide broken valleys full of Cardón. "Road," in such cases, meant just a place someone else had taken a vehicle. And brought it back, we hoped.

It took us two hours to go twenty-one miles to the ruins of the Mission San Borja. The mission was founded in 1759 to serve the spiritual needs of three thousand Indians. It was named "Saint Borgia" because that appalling family's contributions to the Jesuits financed it. By the time the granite church was complete in 1801 only four hundred Indians were left alive. The settlement was abandoned seventeen years later.

The ruins were not ruins at all. The church stood with huge futility almost perfectly preserved. The nave, at least thirty feet high and maybe seventy feet long, was roofed by an arch built without mortar from oval streambed rocks. Someone had put a color magazine illustration of the Virgin of Guadalupe on the dusty altar.

Here was an enormous monument to blindness and folly, built with the lucre of swine and causing the death of thousands of people. Yet there was a feeling of sanctity to the place. Maybe God likes a good joke too. I crossed myself and put a couple hundred pesos under a devotional candle.

The sun went down. We raced the cars back to the Bay of LA, sliding sideways into the cactus and getting airborne over piles of rocks. Our ten headlights lit a pantheon dome of roiled silt above the desert floor.

At our motel they'd prepared an enormous meal, sea bass so large that it was cut into porterhouse steaks. All the food in Baja was splendid. The local lobsters were split and grilled slowly over mesquite fires. Delicate flour tortillas and fresh goat cheese were made into quesadillas. There was no refrigeration so everything was exactly fresh (or obviously otherwise). Chickens were, of course, free range and necessarily organic. Steaks were lean, from grass-fed cattle, but well flavored, especially when served ranchero style with peppers so hot they made your nose run and the top of your head itch. And the AstroTurf colored, odorous sea turtle turned out to be—one might say—endangerously good.

We sat with the motel owner after dinner and had too much to drink. That afternoon out on the long sand spit closing the mouth of the cove there'd been hundreds of shark heads—blue sharks, sand sharks, hammerheads. I asked the proprietor about this. "The local boys cut the sharks up," he said, "and sell them to tourists as scallops. You can always tell the fake scallops. They are so big and perfectly round."

We tried for the Calamajué River again in the morning. This river bottom may be the best road in Mexico—a crown of natural crushed gravel on a level base of sand. The canyon walls cut through six hundred million years of freshman geology. There were cliffs of igneous and metamorphic rock, sandstone escarpments, walls of conglomerate, towers of ocean sediment, and upended fields of slate in fracture patterns.

About ten miles from the mouth of the river we turned north to climb over a nameless mountain into Gonzaga Bay.

The track here had been graded once and made a fairly good road except it was the wrong one. We were lost for hours, but we didn't mind. We saw two bighorn sheep right beside us by the road, looking indeed like sheep yet in such unsheepish postures, grand as elk and silly as a hamster fight. The correct road was lousy, but we didn't mind about that either. In most places the road was sand with shards of slate embedded like broken bottles on top of a wall. We blew out two of the Scrambler's tires. In other places the road was almost impassable. Alongside one of the most difficult stretches was a 1949 Cadillac coupe, charred and lying on its roof, a Baja version of the frozen leopard in "The Snows of Kilimanjaro."

Gonzaga was a blue eclipse on a beach of moonlight-colored sand ruffed with mangroves. A few American sport fishermen had ramshackle casas on the shore. There was no telephone, no mail, and all the water had to be carried in. There was one electric generator hooked to two lightbulbs and the beer cooler. And there was no street in front of the houses, just a landing strip a bit too short for safety.

At the little beach shack restaurant, Alfonsina's, they served us abalone. The restaurant owner unmounted one of the Scrambler's huge, rigid tires with the handle of a lug wrench and the blunt side of a hatchet. Then he patched the tire with an old air mattress repair kit. We slept on the beach just above the high-tide line. The sand was so soft, the air so benign that we needed neither cushions nor blankets.

At sunrise we drove along the coast, up the famously difficult Tres Hermanas road. The going was steep to the limits of adhesion and too narrow for the bodywork, some of which we lost. What seemed to be boulders in the road was, in fact, the roadbed. There were places in these big, loose stones where to lift from the accelerator would be to slide backward, fall over the side, and die.

Randy Salmont took the Scrambler and Michael drove the Cherokee. It took them four and a half hours to go sixteen miles. They picked their way over things neither Jeep had the clearance to pass. This took an exact sense of where each wheel was. The tires had to be carefully put on top of the largest rocks. At some point the Cherokee's undercarriage rolled one stone up atop another and the transmission casing was rammed into the chassis. The drive line's slip shaft was pulled halfway out of the transmission but there was nothing to do except go on, with the gearbox whacking against the floor. The ascents were granite but the downward slopes were slate, cereal box–shaped rocks that made a sound like driving across dinner plates. The temptation was to hit the brakes, but the motor needed to be left in gear to keep any control over the half-accidental slide.

Fear improves the weather. We'd finished the last downhill grade before we realized it was one hundred degrees. Ten feet from us, under a shelf of rock, sat a yellow coyote. He was watching us carefully, but he wasn't going to be spooked away from the only shade in miles. We looked under the cars. It was as if someone had gotten down in the arc welder's trench and gone at them with a sledgehammer from below. Mighty dents appeared in floorboards, oil pans, and gas tanks. Fluids dripped from everything. Edges of fresh-torn metal glittered in the shadows.

But there was nothing tough ahead of us, just fifty miles of good sand road into San Felipe, then 130 miles of pavement to the United States, to working telephones, superhighways, real gasoline, clean drinking water, and successful business enterprises—an orderly, serious, law-abiding society with air-conditioning. The Jeeps would get us back in three hours.

"Let's flip them upside down," Michael said, "and burn them."

9

Getting Wrecked

No man is a traffic island, as the poet almost said. But I met a fellow named Dave Schwartz who was a green and pleasant median strip. (As the other poet almost said, and before "green" was a malediction like "organic.") Schwartz was the founder of Rent-A-Wreck. He presided over his franchise's original car lot. The place and the man were quiet, calm, refreshing breaks between the endless lanes of Los Angeles traffic cacophony and chaos.

In 1981 I was living in LA, for my sins. The din of Angelino motor vehicles was unlike the noise of New York's. There wasn't much horn honking or many fender crunches, and certainly there were no bellowed recitations of *Illiad*-long poetic invective such as old-time New York cabbies could produce. What deafened you on LA streets was the roar of, "LOOK AT ME!"

Contrary to received wisdom, Los Angeles was a tiresome place for an automotive enthusiast to be. Not because of a lack of wonderful automobiles but because of an excess. The city was full of desirable, arousing, priapism-inducing cars of every kind: Bugattis, Facel Vegas, Cords, three-wheeled Morgans, SS100 Jaguars, Testarossa Ferraris, Lancia Aurelias, not to mention bevies of MG TCs and TDs, slews of bug-eyed Sprites, more bathtub Porsches than Germany had bathtubs, and ranks and files of plain, vanilla cars-you'd-love-to-own.

Every one of these automobiles was tuned to perfection, washed, waxed, and maintained in a state of preservation that was positively Egyptoid. To say that the fine cars of Los Angeles were merely in "concours condition" would have been to slander the poor Mexicans who daily cleaned each wire wheel spoke with Q-tips dipped in Brasso and dental-flossed every crenellation of tire tread. The scenery was fabulous in LA, as it was in the South Africa of that time. The problem was with the folks who owned the view.

A Sargasso Sea of car-buff slime weed were the people who held the pink slips to LA's auto treasures. Less charitably they could have been called chrome lampreys sucking the main bearings out of Maseratis, eels on mag wheels, ditch carp with driver's licenses. No, carp have backbones. Such an invertebrate, sucker-bearing, cephalopodan crowd the city's car fanciers were—heading backward with eight arms aflutter, spewing clouds of murk—that it was a wonder they could drive at all. But drive they did, to the parking spaces with their names stenciled on the curbs at the movie studios where I was working for them, which was like sitting naked in a washtub full of live squid.

The Hollywooden heads would buy a car for almost any purpose except a worthy one. Many automobiles were purchased to attract members of LA's eight or ten opposite sexes. Since the denizens of America's Gomorrah were incapable of verbalizing any idea more complex than "box office gross," the expensive car served as a substitute for witty come-on and seductive chat. (It should be noted that the pursuit of libidinous satisfaction was such a mania in '80s LA that if the local citizens had ever performed any normal acts of copulation our country would now be three fathoms deep in twenty-eight-year-olds named after astrological signs.)

Of course there was nothing wrong with owning an expensive car that possessed sex appeal. But "expensive," not "car," was the operative word in Los Angeles. The LA woman (a species that resembled a more attractive version of a real woman but acted like Ebenezer Scrooge on cocaine in panty hose) could be hooked only by chumming with large amounts of cash. Probably a few of the shrewder men in town saved on garage and detailing expenses by padding their underpants with hundred-dollar bills. But most of the trollop-trollers relied on a car for bait. Therefore it was imperative that the car be expensive in an obvious manner. A Tatra T87, rare as it was, wouldn't have done because it looked like a VW beetle with a bolt-on shark fin. On the other hand if LA women knew how many times they'd been bedded by fiberglass kit cars built from actual VW beetles . . .

The sheikhs of Shakeytown bought cars not just to screw people literally but also to impress people and screw them metaphorically. They could have impressed people with a teenage lover or a Lucien Piccard wristwatch, but they couldn't lock these and leave them in front of their houses.

Impressing people was, as far as I could determine, how everyone made a living in LA. Doubtless, in the less fashionable neighborhoods, there were people with jobs (washing expensive cars, for instance). But in Beverly Hills and Bel Air you didn't have a job. You had a deal. You made a deal by impressing someone who used that deal to impress someone else who, in turn, impressed you. The way to get this chain of impressiveness started was with an expensive car. Thus Range Rovers that had seen dirt only in plant store windows, 1940s Chrysler Town and Country convertibles with tops down and aftermarket A/C units going full blast, Shelby Cobras owing their racing pedigrees to Ma Maison parking attendants, and Lamborghini Countaches that had had their highest speeds clocked by repo men on their way back to the dealership. Something as bog slow and dog-ass ugly as a '58 T-Bird was preferable to something as fast and pretty (and cheap) as a Datsun 240-Z.

The Santa Monica Stirling Mosses would tell you their cars were "well engineered" when they had never looked under the hood and had to take the things to the dealership to get them shifted from first to second. Surely this was the place where the Porsche engine joke originated: "Don't worry dear, I've got a spare one in the trunk." The Malibu Mario Andrettis would tell you their cars were "beautiful," which they may well have been. But how could men in orange Gucci loafers with shirts unbuttoned to the location of their ulcers *know*? And all of the Beverly Phil Hills would tell you they loved cars.

Dave Schwartz said he did not love cars. He said he didn't give a damn about them. Fibs, I'm sure, but the sort of fibs a loyal Democrat might have told about politics at the embarrassing end of the Carter administration. I like to think what Dave Schwartz didn't give a damn about was rolling padded expense accounts and four-wheeled siren songs to would-be whores of stage and screen. Schwartz's Rent-A-Wreck lot on Bundy was filled with the kind of cars that the Rodeo Drive Alfas-aren't-good-enough Romeos wouldn't own if their triple-bypass operations depended on it. Here were the scruffed, the dented, the banged-up, the beaters, jalopies, junk heaps, go-to-work specials, mechanics' delights, rattletraps, crates, and sputterbuses. Prominent among them were the Tin Lizzies of the era: Ford Mustangs 126 of them, every one of which could be parked by sonar with equanimity.

Dave Schwartz was originally a used-car dealer. He set up business in 1959, specializing in very used cars. He did well, he said, because he always told people what was wrong with the cars he sold. In 1970, Dave sold a car to a young lady for $200 and it self-destructed with even greater alacrity than $200 cars usually do, the same day in fact. Dave returned the young lady's money and offered to sell her something else. But she said she was going to be in Los Angeles for only a few weeks. She hadn't wanted to buy a car in the first place. It was just cheaper to buy a used car than to rent a new one from Hertz or Avis. A lightbulb appeared over Dave Schwartz's head.

Rent-A-Wreck was an immediate success. Its rates were, in 1981, less than half what the major car rental companies charged. But there were other reasons for R-A-W's popularity. Dave and all of his employees were fun. Dave told me that he wouldn't hire anyone who didn't think the job was fun. He was having fun himself. By the time I met Dave he had more than 150 Rent-A-Wreck franchises nationwide. He continued to run the Bundy operation, for fun. When I arrived in Los Angeles it was Dave, in T-shirt and baseball cap, who met me at the airport.

Dave liked to make sure that people got the car that was right for them. He had me pegged for a '57 Fairlane 500 two-door coupe. I was flattered, but I had to drive to San Diego that weekend and Dave—true to form—had already told me the Fairlane was not a long-distance runner. So he put me into something even better, a 1967 289 Mustang hardtop with almost all its lime green paint worn away by beach party sand, salt spray, and spilled beer.

Dave and his crew had to move half the cars on the lot to get to the Mustang. They did it with the bravado and good cheer of Kookie, the maestro of valet parking on *77 Sunset Strip*. (If anyone reading this is old enough to know what I'm talking about, Kookie was played by Edd Byrnes, my second favorite actor after Jeff Bridges.)

Good cheer was endemic at Rent-A-Wreck, and bravado too. Dave's head counterman, Ray Tigner, could deliver good cheer with bravado even when he wanted to know when the hell somebody was going to pay his bill. The Bundy lot was a Seven Dwarfs diamond mine place of employment. Dave's chief mechanic, Elihu Dunbar, was cast in the role of Grumpy. But Elihu wasn't so much grumpy as he was hard at work fixing cars—something not every mechanic does.

I asked Dave about all this whistle-while-you-work. He credited his two entrepreneurial principles: 1. Fun workers 2. Fun customers. Dave said, "I won't deal with a customer who isn't any fun. I can spot them fifty yards away, by posture. And I can weed them out from a single phrase on the telephone. I refer them elsewhere—cheerfully."

I stayed in Los Angeles for as long as I could stand it, which was four months (or, to put it in actress years, half a career). During that period my '67 Mustang had only one mechanical glitch. The fuel pump gave out at the corner of Mulholland and Beverly Glen, causing me to roll backward into the San Fernando valley. Dave sent a tow truck and gave me a purple 1968 Cadillac with one side caved in and something interesting dragging underneath.

Elihu Dunbar had the Mustang fixed the next morning. But I was busy for a few days sitting around in producers' offices listening to their suggestions for making my lousy screenplay much worse. I couldn't get to Rent-A-Wreck during business hours. I called to apologize. "Don't worry," said Dave. "I'll drive the Mustang home and you can come over tonight and trade me." I did so and wound up drinking beer and watching a UCLA basketball game, a rare occurrence with the president of Hertz.

The Mustang was pre-dinged and bongo-drummed all over its body, so much so as to make cosmetic harm almost impossible. Driving up Topanga Canyon I was forced off the road by some aromatherapy evangelist in a drug-colored microbus. I drove over several hamster cage–sized rocks, reducing them to pea stone with the right rocker panel. Visible damage to the Mustang: none. The house I was renting had a driveway with the width and angle of ascent of a small-gauge cog railway. My girlfriend misjudged this while trying to back out using the mirror in her compact or something. It took a two-man wrecker crew three hours to extradite the Mustang from a row of Lombardy poplars. Damage: strictly to my reputation with AAA. And there were scores of times when I was able to make extraordinary traffic maneuvers simply on the strength of ugly. No local was going to hazard the Corinthian grille and flying lady of his Holby Hills Halftrack in a dispute over a lane change with my repugnant pony car.

The Mustang had some 120,000 miles on it. The shocks might as well have been toilet plungers. Everything that loosens on a car had long since come unloosed. The transmission slipped around like an Ice Capades performing bear. But damn, the thing would drive. It leapt from stoplights. Amazing what a little V-8 and a four-barrel could do absent antipollution emphysema. On an expressway I could whistle along in the young hundreds. But my specialty was the wonderful stretch of road in Benedict Canyon from Mulholland to the Beverly Hills Hotel. My runs up and down this in the middle of the night were things of terror to the wildlife, the neighbors, my girlfriend, and, for that matter, me.

Downhill was the best. I'd roll off the edge of Mulholland Drive into Benedict Canyon like a dive-bomber. The outside turns on the switchbacks appeared daunting. The land dropped from the road so steeply that the car seemed half-suspended over the pit of doom. In fact, I knew there was a ten-inch-high asphalt curb rendered invisible by color identical to the roadbed's. So it wasn't as bad as it looked although, when the Mustang's full and brutal oversteer was summoned, it was plenty bad enough. Courage for even greater speed was gained on the inside curves where walls of rock rose reassuringly ready to scrub off excess enthusiasm. Nighttime reduced the chances of blind driveway surprises or unannounced head-ons. Which saint is it that protects against burned-out bulbs in car lights?

I'd go down the switchbacks and the S-bends for about a mile of steadily increasing momentum and alarm. Then there was one of the best corners in America—a banked hairpin with high-crowned pavement where, if I set myself just right between curb and crown, it was a bobsled run and I could go through the hairpin as fast as I could make myself.

The Mustang's body lean was so severe that the tires rubbed against the wheel wells and acrid blue smoke filled the interior. Coming out of the hairpin there was a swerve to the left, a swerve to the right, a slam dunk off a one-lane culvert bridge, and another hairpin—the antithesis of the first—with decreasing radius and off-camber bank. The technique for getting through this turn was to aim straight at a phone pole until my whole life had passed before my eyes up to the day after John F. Kennedy's assassination. Then, just when word came on the radio that Lee Harvey Oswald had been captured in a Dallas movie theater, I'd crank the wheel full left, stand on the gas, and pray the tires caught. (Of course this worked only for someone born in 1947. I don't know how anyone else got through the turn.) After that it was almost a straight shot to my house, just a couple of easy sweepers with only a few deep depressions concealing storm sewer drains. And even these weren't fatal unless I was going over ninety.

The chief pleasure of my sojourn in LA was to find a smooth dude with a Corvette or a Porsche 924 or anything else the dude mistakenly thought was a sports car and trail him off Mulholland and into my canyon. He'd take the first couple of turns in high style, fancying himself A. J. Foyt in $200 blue jeans and an Armani jacket. Then he would look into his rearview mirror and see a full nine yards of ruptured Mustang grille with one headlight pointed at Voyager 2 and the other searching for nightcrawlers. Mr. Open-knuckled-driving-gloves would then put his Bally'd foot down a little harder, smirk in self-satisfaction, look in his mirror again, and find the Mustang nibbling his tail pipe in an all-out NASCAR draft. After that I'd ease up and let him get half a curve ahead until we came to the bobsled hairpin where I'd start tapping shave-and-a-haircut on his bumper until we reached the second, off-camber, hairpin where—if he dared turn his head—he'd see what I looked like sideways in a power slide. I'd take the lead in the sweepers because, just when the dude thought he could get me on pure speed, he'd hit a storm sewer drain.

I was beaten only once—by a Mexican in a Chevy pickup full of yard-care tools and cheering children. But the truth was I didn't get to race much. Typically the locals drove like the garden slugs that the Mexican had spent his day eradicating. The gentlemen of Los Angeles might as well have put wheels on their drug-sodden wives and rolled bottle blondes up and down Sunset Boulevard.

The Mustang, however, served its purpose even when sitting still. It was a personal litmus test. Wince at it and screw you. The car was beloved by the head of valet parking at the Beverly Hills Hotel. This important arbiter of status bore a striking resemblance to Edd Byrnes. (Come to think of it, for all I know, he *was* Edd Byrnes.) Anyway, he'd park the Mustang right in front of the hotel, along with the Bentleys and gull-wing Mercs.

Aside from Byrnes and the folks at Rent-A-Wreck, I didn't care much for Los Angeles, as you may have gathered. Looking for some way to make a sensible sow's ear out of this vulgar and garish silk purse, I asked Dave Schwartz if I could do a story about R-A-W for *Car and Driver*. He shrugged. "I chose the name in the first place to discourage business," he said. "But you're welcome to hang around."

It greatly increased my respect for Robin Williams when I learned that he had rented a 1970 Pontiac LeMans while he was trying out for the lead in *Mork and Mindy*. He decided the car was good luck. He went on to drive something fancier but kept the Rent-A-Wreck LeMans parked at the TV studio. In 1981 you could have rented that same car, if Dave Schwartz liked you. Maybe you would have started making funny noises and a lot of money.

Despite my dislike of Hollywood—or, maybe, as an expression of the hypocrisy behind all professed hatred of popular culture—I'm a sucker for a celeb. Others who had Rented-A-Wreck included Paul Newman, Judge John Sirica, Alan Alda, Garry Trudeau, Jill St. John, Tony Perkins, and Henry Fonda. Each of these people, Dave said, got a car exactly suited to his or her nature.

"What did Henry Fonda get?" I asked.

"A great big flatbed truck," Dave said. I'm still pondering that.

One other Rent-A-Wreck customer was Jeff Bridges! And when *Car and Driver* sent a photographer to illustrate my story, the photographer turned out to be Susan Geston, Jeff Bridges's wife! She's a good photographer. She took the picture of me, sprawled across the Mustang's hood, which graces the cover of this book. It is the most . . . no . . . *the* flattering picture of me. She's a really good photographer.

Susan was about nine and a half months pregnant with her and Jeff's first child. This piqued the interest of Camilla, an extremely beautiful young lady who was working the Rent-A-Wreck counter with Ray Tigner. Camilla's boyfriend and later husband (and another loyal R-A-W customer) was Roger McGuinn. Roger stopped by, and Dave and the rest of us spent a cheerful afternoon in this least likely of salons—even

Elihu Dunbar put down his wrench for a bit—discussing the things least likely to be discussed in Los Angeles such as babies, Christianity (Roger and Camilla are devout), and very used cars. Later I went back to Susan's house. Jeff was building a loft to accommodate their about-to-be-expanded family. We had a beer and talked about used cars. In thirty-some years of going to Los Angeles, that was the best day I've had.

The next day was the second-best. I returned to Rent-A-Wreck and asked Dave Schwartz to name the most excellent car in the world. Being that I was a car journalist of sorts I'd asked the question before. In those days the answer was usually the 450-Series Mercedes. I didn't expect that to be Dave's answer. But I wasn't prepared to hear "The 1969 Buick Skylark."

"That can't possibly be true," I said.

"I swear it is," Dave said.

"Why?" I asked.

"The Skylark's pretty reliable," he said. "The next best are the '67 and '68 Mustangs with automatic transmissions, then sixties Plymouths with the 318 V-8, Dodge Darts with the Slant Six, and Ford Pintos. Although I don't have any Pintos for the business. They got a lot of bad press because their gas tanks blew up once or twice. Mavericks are great, Oldsmobile Cutlasses, most 1970 through '74 full-sized American cars, anything from American Motors, and Mustang IIs."

The list was beginning to sound like every ten-year-old boy's nightmare about what Dad was going to buy Mom for a second car. I was fond of old buckets-of-bolts myself, but Dave had reached some plane of automotive enlightenment that I could not attain. He claimed his opinions were based on reliability and ease of repair. I suspected him of a Buddha-like love of all carkind, a vehicular agape, a satori of the wheels. I knew Dave Schwartz owned a 1967 Mercedes 250SE convertible, a mint 1950 Mercury coupe, and a 1965 Porsche 356C. But he went home that evening in a 1960 Valiant.

10

Keep Your Eyes Off the Road

Michael Nesmith and I were on another long-distance trip in a Jeep. (And anyone who says, "Hey, hey, it's the Grease Monkees," go to the back of the room and sit down.) I don't remember exactly when this trip occurred—sometime in the early '80s. The journey must have come before Michael's and my attempt at romantic adventure in the Baja. Steven J. Harris was AMC/Jeep's director of product public relations and John McCandless was the manager of sales and marketing communication. Steve and John were two of the nicest men in the car business. But, nice as they were, they weren't giving me and Michael any more Jeeps after what we did to the Scrambler and the Cherokee in Mexico. (I ran into Steve a couple of years ago. He's forgiven us. Forgiven but not forgotten.)

Anyway, Renault had bought into American Motors using the same economic theory that's behind the current automobile industry bailout: what a business that's losing money needs most is more money to lose. The Jeep Cherokee SUV, designed with Renault's help, had just been introduced.

Steve and John came up with a brilliant press junket. Give Cherokees to eight teams of car journalists and put the journalists in a contest to see who could drive down America's west coast, from the border of Canada to the border of Mexico, using the *least* amount of pavement. The winner would be determined by a point system.

0 points per mile of interstate
1 point per mile of two-lane highway
2 points per mile of gravel road
3 points per mile of dirt road
4 points per mile of no road at all

Final score = points/mileage

We had five days to make our way from Bellingham, Washington, to San Diego, California. An AMC/Jeep referee would be sent with each team to keep score and prevent anyone from cheating by, for example, airlifting a car to the Coronado Hotel, driving one mile on the beach, and scoring a perfect 4. (Expense accounts were lavish in those days.)

In addition to Michael and me representing *Car and Driver*, there were teams from *Autoweek, Four Wheeler, Off-Road*, *Popular Mechanics, Road & Track, 4Wheel and Off Road,* and the *Toronto Star*. Competitive attitudes ranged from very serious to Michael and me. The *Autoweek* team was led by Bill Neale, one of motor journalism's greats and the coauthor, with Bob Ottum, of the best (also only) comic novel about car racing, *Stand On It.* Neale had brought along a rally driver, a complete set of U.S. Geological Survey maps and a geologist to read them, plus a support vehicle with a crew that had professional search-and-rescue training. On the other hand, the *Off-Road* team, Coutland Van Tune and Jeff MacPherson, had plotted a course involving hippie ex-girlfriends who lived in Oregon's and California's remote cannabis agribusiness regions.

Michael and I did not know what to do about this contest. Except not win it; we were firm on that point. Michael's race truck campaigns gave him all the off-road experiences he had any use for, and I'm something of an indoorsman at heart. We met with our ride-along score keeper, Jacques Poisson, Renault's manager of international public relations. Jacques was a man of refinement and taste who evinced no great desire to see Michael and me become Lewis and Clark with him as Sacagawea.

We decided to go *culturally* off-road. We'd leave the beaten track of beauty, intellect, and bon ton and show Jacques the truly untamed parts of America. The genuine uncharted territory is not found high upon mountain peaks or deep in woodland valleys. America's real wilderness is back at our Holiday Inn cocktail waitress's trailer park with her crazy biker boyfriend on pills waving a .38. We summoned her and ordered Jacques a couple of those mixed drinks that all motel bars seem to have had wished on them by a dying curse from Trader Vic. Jacques had a Samoan Wahine Bender—two parts Curaçao and three parts tequila served in a Styrofoam monkey skull with hollyhocks floating on top—and a plastic scale model of the HMS Bounty filled with burning rum.

"*Mon dieu,*" Jacques said.

His eyes widened further as we told him stories of terrifying art on Nevada motel room walls, of horrible women Winnebago drivers, and of grisly road food.

Some of which we were served that very night at the Cherokee contest going-away dinner. The beef seemed not so much to have been cooked by microwaves as killed on the hoof by them. We were each given a sherbet glass stuffed with one enormous shrimp. To judge by my shrimp's gross deformity, death must have been a mercy to it. The wine—Château Yakima—was American wine as the French would have American wine be. "Save some of that bottle for me, Jacques. I forgot to fill my Zippo." There may have been vegetables but the healing power of time has erased them from my memory.

The next morning we headed down I-5 racking up no points and stopped at the first Jack in the Box to show Jacques what passes for a croissant in Seattle. Jack in the Box really did serve croissants—of a kind. This was, I thought at the time, an ugly trend. Imagine McPâté McFoie McGras.

Jacques was polite about his meal. Nesmith tried to explain the intellectual principle of American food. "It's really pretty good if you don't think of it as a croissant. It's like Franco-American spaghetti, you know." (Jacques did not know.) "I mean it's terrible spaghetti, but if you think of it as tomato soup with noodles it's not bad. It's all how you think about it."

I agreed. The appetizer back at the Holiday Inn for instance—pour some vodka in there with the cocktail sauce and you'd have had an interesting Bloody Mary. Not good but interesting.

From Seattle we took I-90 east across the Cascade Range. Jacques had never been in this part of the United States. Michael and I pointed out the sights. Not the beautiful mountains, the French have those. Not the towering pine forests, the French have those too. We pointed out Piggly Wiggly stores, Taco Bells, 7-Elevens, Col. Sanders Kentucky Fried Chicken outlets, and the various important architectural periods of gas stations: early enameled steel Bauhaus, classic "free drinking glass" International style, and self-serve postmodern.

Car journalists perforce spend a lot of time in cars. When you do that, the great sprawl of the American roadside becomes the single main fact of your existence. Yet car journalism doesn't pay any attention to it. This time I paid attention. And now I know why my coworkers don't.

Noted architectural theorist Robert Venturi claimed there was a lot to be learned from roadside sprawl. Maybe. As the first duke of Marlborough did *not* say when Sir John Vanbrugh presented him with the design for Blenheim Palace, "It needs a Fotomat booth and a fifty-foot-high bank sign giving time, temperature, and interest rates on six-month certificates of deposit. And pave the deer park."

However, this is America, and that's freedom for you—freedom to make everything look like shit, perhaps, but freedom nonetheless. Are we going to bulldoze every Kmart and create a federal agency to design something in its place? That was how East Berlin became the charming place it was. Dairy Queens, water slides, flea markets, Cinema 1 2 3 4 5 6s, they are our family. They may be ugly and embarrassing but we wouldn't be here without them. And that's why Americans just love this stuff.

"Yes?" said Jacques.

Up on the Snoqualmie Pass in the Cascades it was too steep to build a Dairy Queen. Here the experience of car driving was dominated by scenery. How we view scenery in America is determined by the interplay between limited-access highway design and the landscape. It's easy to criticize interstates, call them bland and sterile and say they isolate us from the world. But that's the point. Scenery is boring. You look at a beautiful vista and, all right, it's beautiful. Now what? After thirty seconds you begin to fidget. You wish you had a book, a Sony Walkman, even a Taco Bell double dog-food enchilada. Everybody is ashamed to admit this. We feel that if we were more sensitive, more spiritual, more worthy we'd love to stare for hours at Snowshoe Butte (elevation 5135 feet). But we don't. Gertrude Stein was speaking for all of us when she said, or had Alice B. Toklas say, "I like a view but I like to sit with my back turned to it." Thus the miracle of the superhighway. It's forever turning your back to the view. The scenery's beauty is half glimpsed—sad and fleeting as all true beauty is. Swivel your head to capture the beauty and you'll hit a bridge abutment.

Interstates, and their bridge abutments, deserve our love even more than A&W root beer stands and coin-operated car washes. No less a romantic than William Wordsworth said so in his sonnet "Steamboats, Viaducts, and Railways."

> Motion and Means, on land and sea, at war
> With old poetic feeling. Not for this
> Shall ye, by poets even, be judged amiss!

"Yes?" said Jacques who was beginning to wish he was up some logging road with a broken half-shaft, two days' walk from a phone.

We continued on I-90 out of the mountains and across the plateau of central Washington, then southeast down the

Yakima River to state Route 221 through the Horse Heaven Hills. Here, at least, we'd get one point per mile.

As we sped along 221 something big loomed on the horizon. It seemed to be a chemical refinery. We saw tall cracking towers, gigantic storage tanks, miles of industrial piping . . . oh, no, it was Château Yakima! This was where last nights *vin* had been *mis en bouteille. Appellation* Yakima *Contrôlée.* Jacques shuddered.

Michael and I tried to reassure him. America really is a marvelous country. Another twenty-five miles or so and we'd be in Pendleton, Oregon, home of the Pendleton shirt. Pendleton shirts were just the thing to prove that we Americans are more than economic brutes, living only in the financial instant, and cognizant of naught but temporal gain. Pendleton shirts show honesty of material, simplicity of design, and perfection of craftsmanship.

The store was closed.

We looked around Pendleton for some Americanly marvelous place for Jacques to eat lunch. We settled on the Pot o'Gold Café. Something called Special Pressure Cooked Chicken was on the menu.

Nesmith smiled at the waitress, an ample homespun type. "Now, just what," he asked, "makes pressure-cooked chicken so special?"

"It don't take long," she said and thought it over. "It's cooked with pressure."

From Pendleton we climbed into the Blue Mountains. The weather was warm and clear but the road was wet in places from snowmelt. As the shadows lengthened over these damp spots, Nesmith began warning me I was driving on "black ice."

Black ice is a molecule-thin, lard-slick coating of ice crystals that, in color and manner of reflecting light, imitates moisture exactly. I told Nesmith, "Nonsense, that's water. It's too warm outside."

"It's black ice," said Michael and flicked the Cherokee into four wheel drive for me.

"Water," I said

"Black ice."

"Water."

I pulled over on the left berm to read an important-looking historical marker. Michael opened his door and stepped out onto the pavement. "EEEEEE000000WWWW . . ." He disappeared from view. There was a loud thump and Michael became visible again, framed in the open door, sliding on his butt across the highway toward the boiling rapids of the John Day River. It was black ice.

The historical marker said at that very place we were halfway between the North Pole and somewhere else.

A bald eagle was darting between the John Day's banks, flying faster than we, on black ice, could drive. The eagle looked as big as a Piper Cub and as awesome as the price of a Concorde ticket to Paris. It made me wonder about Ben Franklin. He wanted to put a turkey on the great seal of the United States. Was Ben . . . French or something? I kept the thought to myself.

Going south from the John Day River toward Nevada we entered the Malheur National Forest. Jacques was surprised at the name. We explained to him the utilization of words from other languages in American English. It's like the Jack in the Box "croissant." The use of the French has nothing to do with the meaning of the French. Think of it as Fancy Foreign Name National Forest, not "Bunch of Unfortunate Trees."

Speaking of odd nomenclature, we passed Poison Creek then drove across the Sheepshead Mountains to the Crooked River. Have you noticed that Americans ran out of place-names after they crossed the Mississippi? Back east locales were given high-minded monikers with classical references (Syracuse, NY; Athens, GA) or heroic in memoriams (Washington, DC; Lafayette, IN) or melodious Indian words (Mississippi). Out west they just called it any old thing—Sick Headache, NM; Lost My Hat, UT; Where's This?, AZ.

They were busy people, those pioneers, going places, doing things, on their way up in the world. They didn't have time to sit around on committees and take six months deciding between "Thermopylae" and "John Paul Jonesville." There's also an honesty in Western names. The Sheepshead Mountains were doubtless filled with severed sheep's heads after the cattle ranchers got finished shooting the sheepherders in the 1880s Oregon range wars. There's something to be said for such plain speaking. "Human Garbageville" would be a good name for Los Angeles. My own native city of Toledo, Ohio, could be aptly called "Dirtyburg," and the Rev. Jesse Jackson had, not long before, made an interesting suggestion for rechristening New York.

"Yes, no doubt, I see your point," Jacques said, "but *Winnemucca*?"

We arrived in Winnemucca, Nevada, had a poisonous meal that may have come out of the aforenamed creek, and went to bed with the previously mentioned terrifying motel art staring at us from the walls.

We had a bad breakfast of silver dollar pancakes. These, incidentally, do not fit very well into slot machines. I mean, they'll go through the coin opening all right but have a tendency to crumble and gum up in there. Some people who've installed slot machines in the restaurants they own have no sense of humor about this.

Gambling is so pervasive in Nevada that maybe the state should just go the whole hog. There could be pay phones where if you dialed the right girl's number you'd hit the jackpot, but if you dialed wrong you'd have to talk to your mother in Tampa. Well, actually, that's the way pay phones operate already. But there'd be gum machines that dispensed chewing tobacco if you lost. You could gamble for the toilet paper in public bathroom stalls. And fill out Keno cards in an attempt to win cancer therapy at the hospital.

This would add human interest, something Nevada, frankly, lacked. Everywhere the trace of man was visible you wished it weren't. The entire state was obviously temporary. As soon as the locals got their cars fixed they'd be moving to California. Much as I love the roadside sprawl of freedom, Nevada was littered, ugly, vile. Nevadans, I thought, should cut it out or we'd annex the place to Utah and make them give up their coffee, cigarettes, and booze and let them gamble with the fires of hell over whether the angel Moroni was telling the truth to Joseph Smith.

We drove west to Battle Mountain, a place where the quaint old part of town was the trailer park full of pink and black house trailers from the 1950s. We turned south and at midday arrived in the Toiyabe Range, site of a major strike during the silver rush of the 1860s. This was one of many rushes that have de- and repopulated Nevada over the years—a gold rush, a zinc rush, a lead rush (really), a uranium rush, a gambling and resort development rush, and, most recently, a rush to publish coffee table books featuring photographs of pink and black house trailers from the 1950s.

Nevada did have a good deal of *inhuman* interest. The floor of Big Smoky Valley glittered with a Ginsu knife layer of snow. In perfectly dry air snowbanks grow flat, serrated crystals that send a wicked sparkle across the ground. There was a smell of sage in the air, as if from a restaurant with too-modern cuisine, and a surprisingly nonunpleasant whiff of creosote bush. The mountains towered. The sky arched. For the last place on Earth that you'd want to live it was attractive.

We had a truly bad lunch in Tonopah, the sixth straight repulsive meal. Jacques was beginning to get an attitude—not a snobby Gaullic attitude but an attitude as though he had joined the French Foreign Legion to forget something, and every time we took him to a restaurant he remembered.

A disaster had happened to American road food. It was once good/bad—fragrant greasy hamburgers, crisply greasy fries, swell milk shakes in slightly greasy glasses. Grease is an important part of the food pyramid, and the American roadside had it. Then came a gigantic nutro-chemical factory somewhere, probably South Korea, where automated machinery packed calorie-like substance units into container ships for transport to a meal slurry terminal in Bayonne, New Jersey. A distribution pipeline network served every place in America that was less than five miles from me when I was in a car and hungry. I'd go to the closest Beef 'n Bung where they'd hand me a rake and shovel and plastic trash bag and herd me into the giant salad pen where there were all sorts of things to mix with my lettuce—cough drops, Silly String, hairballs the cat had coughed up. Then they'd bring me the double-meal-sized dinner with the charcoal grill marks neatly etched in laundry marker on the reconstituted beef slab . . .

Lucky for us we had Twinkies in the car. "Twinkies! That's *real* road food!" said Nesmith.

". . ." said Jacques.

We passed the famed Cottontail Ranch legal bordello, a place that outdoes itself in crumby Nevada-ishness and a good look at which in broad daylight made even a Frenchman prefer to sit in a Jeep and consume Twinkies.

We drove along the edge of the Nellis Nuclear Testing Site for about thirty miles and didn't see any Guggenheim Museum–sized grasshoppers or six-armed mutant prospectors with giant glowing burros. In the Sarcobatus Flats we turned west on a gravel road and headed over the Grapevine Mountains into Death Valley.

Death Valley had a golf course and a resort with tennis courts. This shed new light on the TV show *Death Valley Days* and the probable lifestyle of its host Gabby Hayes. Turns out the main use for Twenty-Mule-Team Borax in the Old West was to clean the swimming pools.

What Death Valley lacked in actual death it made up for in deadly nomenclature. Devil's Canasta Pack, Satan's Johnny Mop, Hell's Patio Furniture—every stone and shrub had some such handle. We traveled with the Last Chance Range on one side and the Funeral Mountains on the other until we stopped for a lunch made of something dead in Shoshone. Then we got lost trying to avoid Las Vegas. All roads may lead to Rome in Italy, but in Nevada every cow path, motocross trail, and +6 degree of difficulty rock climb leads into the parking lot of the Sahara.

Sometime after midnight we made it to the Arizona side of the Colorado River at Bullhead City. One great thing about driving exhausted late at night is that you get all sorts of wild ideas. Michael's wild idea was Grand National U-Haul Racing. NASCAR teams would compete on oval tracks, but each car would have to pull a U-Haul trailer containing everything the race car driver possessed—bed, La-Z-Boy, kitchen table and chairs, riding mower, bass boat, etc.

Jacques was doubtful this would work with Formula One drivers. "The cars, they are too small and the girlfriends are too many."

We were still ironing out the details of Grand National U-Haul Racing when we arrived at Lake Havasu. This is the real estate development owned by the guy who bought London Bridge, took it apart, shipped it to Arizona, put it back together again, and plopped it down in the middle of Lake Havasu. The trouble with having wild ideas while driving exhausted late at night is that the ideas are rarely wild enough to compete with what you're driving past.

Jacques looked at London Bridge sitting in a man-made lake in Arizona with an expression something like Napoleon might have had if things had gone otherwise at Waterloo.

The next weekend Nesmith would be running his Class 8 pickup in the Parker 400 off-road race. He had a rented house, on the Colorado River, waiting for us in Parker, Arizona. It was a warm and starlit night. Ducks gurgled on the river. Breezes wafted through the palms. I slipped between the three-hundred-thread-count sheets, my fingers curled around a Waterford crystal old-fashioned glass full of scotch older than Formula One driver girlfriends, and, suppressing a smirk, wondered what was happening to the other teams.

Van Tune and MacPherson from *Off-Road* were sleeping in their Cherokee, mired in the Oregon snow. The *Autoweek* circus had crunched a lifter and a pushrod outside Las Vegas. The *Toronto Star* was in the middle of the Nevada desert with a Rand McNally world atlas as their only map. They were attempting stellar navigation. *4Wheel and Off Road* had a busted radiator. *Road & Track* was axle-deep in a beach. And *Four Wheeler* was just plain lost. *Popular Mechanics,* however, was ordering room service at the Mark Hopkins in San Francisco and had reservations at the Las Vegas MGM Grand for the following night. (They would place second to last, after Michael and me.)

Perhaps Jacques would like to see off-roading in the American manner? We pre-ran the Parker course in the Cherokee. We didn't get far. We sped down a ranch road through low scrubland, came around a bend into a dry wash, and found a fellow named Gary lying on a rock. His Honda three-wheeler ATV had gone on without him. Gary's thigh was broken in about half a dozen places.

Gary had been riding between his two buddies who eventually realized Gary was no longer between them. They backtracked to the dry wash. We told them to go get help. We propped Gary up and gave him a Coca-Cola. He was a stoic young man but not much of a conversationalist. All he had to say by way of discourse on the ATV-riding culture was, "Boy, this really hurts."

Medical aid didn't arrive until dinnertime. If you go to Parker's only Chinese restaurant, don't order ribs in paint or three-flavor Keds.

We drove to San Diego on Friday night and got up at noon on Saturday to watch our bruised and dirty competitors straggle in. Only one Cherokee did not make it under its own power. The transmission fell out ten miles north on I-15, and the Jeep was towed to the finish line by a taxicab.

A big awards banquet was spread. "It's chicken á la king!" exclaimed Steve Harris and John McCandless. Jacques had a triple Rémy Martin instead. Michael and I lost big—a score of .9932 versus *Autoweek*'s 2.4200.

Van Tune and MacPherson had also tried to add a little culture to their trip. They were driving along a beach when they saw a huge flock of shorebirds poking around in the surf. A beautiful photo opportunity would be had if they could drive the Cherokee through the shallows and get all the sandpipers to rise in flight around the car. With Van Tune ready behind the lens, MacPherson plunged into the flock at speed. He killed fifty birds.

After Van Tune's and MacPherson's confessional article on the Cherokee contest was printed, *Autoweek* got more hate mail about the sandpipers than it had gotten about anything since the Edsel. America's real wilderness—as the Holiday Inn cocktail waitress back in Bellingham, Washington, with the crazy biker boyfriend on pills waving a .38 could have told Van Tune and MacPherson—should be kept at arm's length.

11

Comparative Jeepology 101

It would be a violation of car nut logic to talk about what cars mean. They mean I don't have to walk home.

The car is a cultural marker within a patriarchal construct. The car must be understood to embody both a socioeconomic text and a political metatext. And if you believe that, somebody should back over you with a car.

On the other hand, if I say, "European dead white male," and you think, "Wolfgang von Trips," you're reading the right book. And yet . . . and yet . . . There is the Jeep. Jeeps do seem to carry a lot of psychological/anthropological/social science freight. Jeep does, in fact, mean more than 4WD and eyeballs-and-whalebone grille. There's the war thing, of course—Bill Mauldin's cartoon of the old cavalry sergeant covering his eyes as he puts a pistol to his Jeep's hood. But there are also places in the world where the Jeep is worshipped as a totem of plenty, where Jeeps are icons in a sort of cargo cult, and the Wrangler is the deity of good wages, medical benefits, and retirement security. That would be in Toledo, Ohio, where the Jeep has been manufactured since its World War II conception, where Shriners muster fleets of Jeepsters for each parade, and Jamie Farr rides in the lead, where every third person seems to work at the Jeep plant, which was five blocks from the house in which I grew up.

The Jeep brand has survived ownership by America's least-solvent and worst-bossed automobile companies (and that is setting the bar high): Willys, Kaiser, American Motors. I still have the 1984 Jeep Scrambler that Steve Harris and John McCandless let me buy from the Jeep press fleet. (It is not, bless Steve's and John's hearts, the same Scrambler that Nesmith and I took to the Baja.) And Jeep will survive Chrysler as well.

My personal theory about the visceral appeal of the Jeep is that it is purposeful-looking while having no clear purpose. The Jeep is inadequate as a pickup, drafty as a sedan, oversized as an ATV, and lacks sufficient cargo space to be an SUV. True, Jeeps will go almost everyplace but, if you think about it, Jeeps mostly go everyplace there's no reason to go. Thus the Jeep is very cool, letting you feel like you're on an important mission every time you get behind the wheel and, at the same time, getting you away from the annoying responsibilities and pesky goals that important missions always entail. Plus you can be cool on the cheap. Jeep makes some of the least expensive new vehicles on the market, unless you want a Kia Sportage. And you don't.

* * *

Imagine my delight when I discovered islands in the South Pacific where the natives were even more devoted to veneration of the Jeep than we natives of Toledo. It looked to me like practically every item with wheels on it in the Philippines was a Jeep. There were military Jeeps, police Jeeps, delivery Jeeps, family Jeeps, hot rod Jeeps, and, blasting through every street in the land, ubiquitous "Jeepney" Jeep buses. And you could be cool in the Philippines even cheaper than in Toledo. Because you could search these Jeeps and never find a single costly UAW-made Jeep$_{TM}$ part—not so much as one knuckle-busting hood latch, scratched-to-opacity side curtain, or transfer-case shift lever that needs two men and a boy to operate. Philippine Jeeps had all been built by hand right there in the Philippines. Their relationship to real Jeeps was spiri-tual, a transmigration of mechanical souls. Arriving in the Philippines, I had found the place where good Jeeps go when they die.

I was supposed to be a foreign correspondent. It was 1986 and I had been sent to the Philippines to cover the coming-to-bits of the Ferdinand Marcos dictatorship. I met him. He may have been dead already. It was hard to tell.

Imelda was friendly, however. So were the anti-Marcos agitators. There was sporadic violence in the streets. But I'd been living in New York for the past fifteen years so that was nothing new. What really interested me were the Jeeps.

Until the end of World War II there weren't many cars or trucks of any kind in the Philippines. Conveyance was by oxcart or *cartella* horse cab or water buffalo–drawn travois. Even the invading Japanese went mostly on bicycle or foot.

But when MacArthur returned in 1944, the Filipinos were introduced to motorized transport galore, GI style. When the war was over and American troops were gone the Jeeps remained. Jeeps were durable, available, inexpensive, and would take you anywhere at—by local standards—lightning speed. They also smelled better than water buffalos. Forty-one years later Jeeps were still synonymous with all things modern and swell.

The Filipinos made parts to repair their ex–U.S. Army Jeeps—fenders, bodies, gas tanks, leaf springs, frames. When the supply of old Willys Jeeps ran out, the Filipinos just put the spare parts together to create "Jeeps" of their own.

Manufacture took place in hundreds of little street side factories, many not large enough to hold a whole Jeep. Construction had to be completed on the sidewalk. Some people bought their Jeeps by the piece and assembled them at home. The engines, drive trains, steering gear, brakes, and electricals were from Japanese light trucks. The engines were baseline fours, either Toyota or Mitsubishi gas engines or Isuzu diesels. Everything was bought used, shipped in from Japanese wrecking yards, and rebuilt in the Philippines. The Filipinos referred to these secondhand parts as "surplus," in loyal memory of World War II. Tires, lights, and a few wires and gauges were the only new equipment on a Philippine jeep. Even the batteries were reconditioned.

There was no four-wheel drive on a Philippine Jeep and no interest in getting it. In the dry season a fluff-light vehicle would take you every place a reasonable person would want to go. In the rainy season nothing except a water buffalo would take you anywhere, no matter how many drive wheels it had. And Filipinos, like most citizens of the third world, weren't yet silly enough to understand off-roading for the fun of it.

Body styles on these "owner Jeeps," as they were called, came mostly from the original Willys MB/GPW, the Korean War–era M38, and the early fifties CJ3B. Some had bogus WILLYS stamped on the tailgate or across the bottom of the windshield frame. The accuracy of the body panel reproductions was a shock. I didn't realize these Jeeps were new until I saw one made of stainless steel. There was Roy Rogers's Nellie Bell dressed in the shining armor of Joan of Arc—a vision of Jeep beatification. (The tropical climate played hell with anything corrodible.) The Filipinos excelled at metal working. They executed the tricky stainless welds and fabricated the alloy so it didn't look like a used dog dish, Mom's sink, or a DeLorean.

Southern Californians, whose dim minds love all bright objects, were crying out to own these silver dazzlers. Or they would have been if they'd known about them. A stainless body could be purchased for under $500 in Manila. I could have bolted it to the chassis of a half-pint rice rocket pickup and sold it to Vanna White for thirty big ones. I should have looked around for venture capital. I could have been a chrome Jeep millionaire.

The less expensive owner Jeeps were made with galvanized steel. The bodies for these cost only $150, the chassis another $130. You could buy the whole shebang, fully assembled with a Toyota gas engine, for $2,500.

Sometimes the galvanized bodies were left unpainted for a low-tech washtub effect. And sometimes the paint schemes would knock a hippie senseless. But metal and paint were only the beginning of what Filipinos had done with the Jeep.

Philippine society is an odd mix—inscrutable Asian and melodramatic Latin with a big splash of loony Yank thrown in. The archipelago's Spanish-American history, as summarized by its residents, is "three hundred years in a convent and fifty years in a whorehouse."

Filipinos were fully American, however, in that they could not leave a mechanical device alone. They had to improve it even if they ended up improving it so much that it wasn't good for anything. And the Filipinos liked to put their own stamp on international car design trends. Thus the simple owner Jeeps were turned into vinyl-roofed formal sedans, dune buggies, monster trucks, or funny cars. This was aided by Philippine vehicle inspection laws, of which there were none.

My favorite Jeep was owned by Dindo Ramos, a local-hire sound man for the ABC-TV news team that was covering the Marcos ouster. Dindo had turned his Jeep into what looked like the world's only U.S. military specification Bucket T roadster. It was also one of the world's few Toyota-powered dragsters. Engine-wise there wasn't much to work with in the Philippines, so Dindo used a rebuilt 1600 twin cam, fitted it with dual Solex double-barreled carbs and thirty-six-inch equal-length headers, and shaved the tread off some radials to create thirteen-inch street slicks on the back. It would lay rubber from one end of the line for green cards at the U.S. embassy to the other (and that was a long way).

But I didn't come to grips with the full significance of the Jeep in Philippine society until I encountered the Jeepney buses. As if I could have avoided encountering them. It was all I could do to keep from being run over and squashed by them.

There were thirty-six thousand fare-charging Jeepneys in Manila alone. They ran in straight-line routes along any road wide enough to kick a dog in, stopping at designated Jeepney stops, and anyplace else a policeman wasn't looking. The fare was one peso, about a nickel, for the first four kilometers and twenty-five centavos per klick thereafter. You could go all the way across Manila for a quarter.

Originally, a Jeepney was a Willys cut in half and lengthened. A pair of bench seats were installed in an open bed covered by a canvas roof. During the 1950s this evolved into an all-steel twenty-passenger people mover that served as the entire mass transportation system for the Philippine islands.

The drivers rented their Jeepneys on what was called a "boundry" (Manila Tagalog dialect corruption of "bounty") system, where they had to pay a set price to the Jeepney owner no matter how few fares they got.

The drivers bought their own diesel fuel. Although "bought" may not be the word I'm looking for, or "diesel" either. To judge by the Jeepney fumes the drivers had been swiping bunker oil from the freighters in Manila Bay. Driving shifts ran from four in the morning until midnight. On an average shift a driver would make maybe ten dollars. Competition for fares was crazed, driving doubly so.

The drivers were underfed slum kids no taller than your tie clip. They could judge traffic gaps by the c-hair, swim through the tangled rapids of the Manila rush hour like trout on the way to mate, run more red lights in an hour than the Philippines had working traffic signals, and blow you out of your argyles with a thousand-decibel electric horn that played the *Godfather* theme. They did this for twenty hours straight in a hundred percent carbon monoxide smog while simultaneously collecting fares, keeping track of passenger stops, negotiating the black-hole-in-space pavement divots, feeling the knee of the girl riding shotgun, and flirting with every woman under ninety on the street. Not only that, they did it without being able to see through the windshield.

The first rule of Jeepney decoration was that the entire windshield had to be filled with decals, stickers, saints, souvenirs, lucky charms, sun visors, ball fringe, and pinup nudes. If any glass was left unobstructed it was covered by racks of eight-track cassettes. These were played at top volume so that when you were on a street with sixty or seventy Jeepneys in earshot it sounded like the civil war in Lebanon would have if the civil war in Lebanon had been a battle of the bands.

The second rule of Jeepney decoration was to have the outside of the Jeepney embellished with, for example: a twenty-one-tone paint job complete with flames and pinstripes; a pair of custom airbrushed murals showing Jesus and the Virgin Mary singing lead for Mötley Crüe on the right side of the bus and, on the left side, the Assumption into heaven of the Other Madonna (the one then married to Sean Penn); five headlights, ten fog lights, twelve driving lights, twenty parking lights, fifty running lights, a hundred flashing green Christmas tree lights (but no brake lights); a dozen spring-mounted metal horse statuettes on the hood; a half dozen spring-mounted fighting cocks on the fenders; decorated mud flaps both behind and in front of each tire; ground-effect skirts fore, aft, and midship; colored Plexiglas silhouettes depicting wild Indians, Walt Disney characters, pirates, eagles, and naked female bodies with pistols instead of heads; twenty-five curb feelers, thirty radio antennas each bearing a flapping Mylar pennant, and mag wheels with chrome bullet spinners.

In the passenger compartment another set of decor conventions took hold teaming Ed "Big Daddy" Roth with Roger Corman to produce the set of a drive-in (as it were) B movie, *The Naugahyde that Ate Mexicali's Discotheque.*

The manufacturing of Jeepneys (and Jeepney accoutrements) was big business, as close as the Philippines came to heavy industry. About a dozen firms produced the buses. The largest was the Sarao Company.

Sarao was founded by Leonardo "Boy" Sarao Sr. in 1953. I talked to his son, Leonardo Jr., a sturdy, affable young man in his twenties and a serious Jeep aficionado. He showed me a dented but complete and all-original M38 that he was restoring at the plant.

Sarao was not the first company to make Jeepneys, Leonardo Jr. said, but it was the oldest remaining manufacturer. They'd long ago lost count of how many they'd produced.

The last of the real U.S. Jeep parts ran out in 1969 or '70. Since then the Sarao Jeepneys, like the owner Jeeps, had been based on Japanese mechanicals. Sarao used rebuilt C240 Isuzu diesel engines and axles, suspension, steering gear, and brakes from junked Isuzu light trucks. Everything else was made in the factory. "We make our own batteries," said Leonardo Jr., "same as Ford." Sarao employed 350 people and about four Jeepneys were completed every day, each having taken about a week to build.

Leonardo Jr. said his father was the first to decorate a Jeepney. In the beginning it was just some cheerful paint colors and the metal horses because Sarao Sr. had been a horse cab driver before the war. I said, "Decoration seems to have grown more elaborate."

"Oh, yes!" said a proud Leonardo Jr., and he told me "styling" was a collective family decision. His father and mother would sit down with him and his sister and four brothers. Leonardo Jr. didn't tell me what happened next at these brainstorming sessions. If the Saraos weren't obviously such decent, substantial members of the Philippine middle class, I'd guess they all smoked something.

The basic design of the Sarao Jeepney, though, hadn't changed in thirty years. "They've only become bigger," said Leonardo Jr. "The original one sat only nine."

The Sarao factory was four enormous, open, dirt-floored sheds. To shape body panels the workers use depressions hollowed out of the ground in roughly the desired shape. Then they threw a sheet of sixteen-gauge galvanized steel over the hole and began smashing it with hammers. Floor panels were sawed by hand from fourteen-gauge galvanized. Frame members and body parts were eyeballed together and spot welded where they stood. The engine shop was a cleared space in a heap of clapped-out diesel blocks. The mechanics squatted in the gloom and ground valves, fitted piston sleeves, milled heads, and packed bearings without a single power tool. All the paint spraying was done in the open and the upholstery was sewn on old Singers. The noise from panel beating, arc welding, compressor running, steel unloading, and employee shouting was enough to break a word processor's adjective key.

Although the factory was as primitive as a factory could get and not be called a farm, everyone swore by the Sarao product. A Sarao Jeepney would last, Jeepney drivers told me, five to seven years of being fueled with bunker oil and driven night and day over pavement like Warsaw Pact tank traps. And they were cheap. The most expensive Sarao Jeepney cost $7,000. When it was worn out it could be rebuilt for half that.

The adoration of the Jeep in the Philippines and the manner in which the Filipinos adorn their Jeeps doubtless have some academic meaning and may even really mean something. (Use the phrase "postcolonial cultural supersession" for extra credit.) Fortunately this is a car nut book and we don't have to figure out any meanings. If, however, there happens to be a reader who is both a car nut and a highbrow type looking for a PhD dissertation topic, let me recommend the study of Jeepney slogans.

These mottos are displayed prominently on every Jeepney. Tourists usually mistake them for the name of the vehicle. But a Jeepney's actual name is painted in modest letters between the fenders, and it's just a route description, e.g., "Pasay City—Rizal Park." The slogans are, as one driver explained, "a gimmick of the driver." Like the punt boat in the old *Pogo* comic strip, a Jeepney bears different slogans on front, back, and sides. The most common are "Socialite" and "Wonderful" but there are thousands of others, some of them spelled correctly.

I have not been back to the Philippines in a number of years, but I have been assured that Jeepneys are still a popular mode of transportation and that Jeepney slogans are still in use, though no doubt updated in topicality. The following were collected in Manila in the spring of 1986.

Student Lover
Sunday Lover
Lipstick Lover
I ♥ New York
A. Delrico's Fighter Wings
California Sheriff
Amityville Queen
Drunken Mastery
Earth Moons

Lucky Luck
Virgin Trooper
Virgin Class
Virgin Breaker
Aquino's Pride (Cory Aquino being the leader of the anti-Marcos faction and, subsequently, president of the Philippines)
Myla Melody Juju
First Time
Short Time
Sacrifice Valley
Rally Sport
Spoiled
Original Clean Liver
Hero Dynamic
General Dynamic
Sip Sip Tutu (a phrase meaning "Blow Job Puppy" in Tagalog, about the worst thing you can call somebody in the Philippines)
Black Out
Face Out
Beyond the Reach
Hello Kitty
Boys Don't Cry
God Knows
Successful Achiever
Immortal
College Girl
Beauty Maker
Emeritus Pride
Judge Advocate
Maricon (meaning "queer" in Spanish but who-knows-what in Tagalog)
Folk Rock
Simple Mind

Never Sleep
Ladies Conquer All
Uni-Charm
(and my personal favorite)
Three Jesuses

12

Taking My Baby for a Ride

I was on the bachelor track for nearly fifty years (with one brief and quickly corrected skid). The Offy roadster of my existence had gone two-thirds of the way around life's brickyard when I lost control, spun, hit Cupid's hay bale, flipped, and came to sprawled in the infield of happy matrimony, to coin a phrase.

Issue ensued, as issue will. And suddenly in 1997, in the ripeness of middle age, I found myself with six pounds, six ounces of adorable iggum-squiggums in my arms and no fit place to put her and her infant car seat.

My garage (and driveway and barnyard) contained a variety of motorized conveyances, all manufactured before the Clintons escaped from Arkansas. There was my 911. This was appropriate for most midlife crises but not this one. That is, the 911 was better suited to a second childhood than a first one. There was my roofless, doorless, windshieldless ex–press fleet Scrambler. There was Mrs. O's BMW convertible with seat belts in the back that looked like they'd come off the behind of a pair of 1960 Ivy League Bermuda shorts. And there was a Jeep Cherokee in about the same condition and of about the same vintage as the Cherokee that had been towed across the finish line by a taxicab at the end of the Jeep Canada-to-Mexico run.

Our Cherokee was, of course, what we used to haul Muffin home from the stork roost. It was a good, commodious, mechanically reliable vehicle. But the Cherokee, through no fault of its own, had faults. By 1997 Cherokees, as SUVs, seemed to have been designed about the time of the meteor impact that caused the extinction of the British sports car. This particular Cherokee had been used extensively for transporting filthy dogs, deceased fish and game, and outdoorsmen with aromas both dead and unhousebroken and for the smoking of cigars that smelled worse than all of these. The Cherokee had a permanent, embedded stink so bad that, in place of a pine tree–shaped air freshener, you could have hung a dirty diaper from the rearview mirror and it would have been an improvement.

Then there was the matter of a certain ex-wife who had totaled the Cherokee (and who wisely declined to accept it as part of her divorce settlement). Former husband having been off covering the 1991 Gulf War at the time, ex-wife took the advice of the local insurance agency (Dub's Auto Liability and Cold Beer) about where to get the car repaired (Dub's Fender, Body and Live Bait). As a result no Cherokee wheel pointed in the same direction as another. At fifty miles per hour this caused more of a shudder than the details of Monica Lewinsky's private life. Also something was awry in the headlights, the very same thing that had been awry in my Rent-A-Wreck Mustang years before. The Cherokee's left beam inspected the roadside for litter while its right beam was fixed on the constellation Cassiopeia.

Time to get a new grocery hauler, parent trap, Keds sled, family bus. Our new car had to be big because, although babies themselves are surprisingly small, their car seats, strollers, collapsible cribs, etc., are all built to accommodate late-career Marlon Brando. And there is no overestimating baby gear. To take Muffin on an afternoon outing required a supply of bottles, formula, Pampers, Handi Wipes, trash bags, spare Baby Gap wardrobes, blankets, Snuglis, rattles, teething rings, Velveteen Rabbits, and copies of *Goodnight Moon* equal in volume to the pack baggage carried by Roald Amundsen during his 1911 expedition to the South Pole.

On the other hand, our new car couldn't be *too* big because we were living half the year in Washington, D.C., where parking spaces were laid out in expectation that the Crosley Hotshot would become America's dominant form of transportation.

The second half of the year also had to be considered. Summer, fall, and ski season we were in New Hampshire, a state with roads so bad and weather so ugly that Roald Amundsen couldn't have made it to the liquor store. So we needed rough-terrain capability.

And yet we had to have good highway manners too. Driving between the slicks and the hicks, we covered five hundred miles of idiot-infested interstate. We wanted horsepower, handling, brakes, cup holders, and a ride that wouldn't make Muffin upchuck more than the International Tot and

Toddler Union's mandated minimum of once between each rest stop.

Keeping all this in mind (and, with a wee one in the house, keeping anything but prayers for nap time in mind was a task), I talked four gullible automobile companies into loaning me their products. Each vehicle was kept for about ten days, repeatedly upchucked in, and returned splashed with formula, smeared in fanny rash cream, full of trash bags, Handi Wipes, unmatched Baby Gap socks, Velveteen Rabbits with the stuffing coming out, torn-up copies of *Goodnight Moon,* and a dirty diaper hung from the rearview mirror.

We borrowed a Dodge Grand Caravan ES minivan with all-wheel drive, a just introduced M-class Mercedes-Benz, a Volvo V7OR AWD wagon, and a Toyota Land Cruiser. The test cars were given standard owned-by-busy-parents maintenance. (Tire pressure, oil, and coolant were never checked. Gas was bought from the nearest pump even if it sold kerosene, brevity of fill-up stop being the key because the only time Muffin slept was when the car was moving.)

All four vehicles failed in one important respect. The interiors could not be cleaned with a garden hose. When will the auto industry get over it with the deep plush carpets, velour upholstery, and delicate electronic do-jiggs in the dash? What Americans with children want is something that can be run through the car wash with the windows open (and maybe with the urchins left inside). While we're at it, please let's go back to simple, sturdy lap belts in the middle of rear bench seats. An engineering degree is required to rig an infant seat in a shoulder harness. If it isn't done right, and you leave a window open, you can find that the inertia locks have played out and that seat and scion are flapping outside in the breeze.

One more suggestion: a fender-mounted, flip-open exterior ashtray and cigarette lighter. These days, no decent, caring person fires a butt with a bambino in the car. But it wouldn't hurt to have a place where you could sneak a smoke while keeping an eye on the little devil.

I have discovered that what a family needs in a brat buggy is a thing that has voluminous interior space and modest exterior dimensions, that's car-like when a car's required and truckish when there's trucking to be done, that's good on slippery surfaces (including the garage floor with upchuck and fanny rash cream on it), and that doesn't cost as much as the majority interest in Procter & Gamble, manufacturer of Pampers, that I seem to have bought.

What I have also discovered is that this vehicle already exists. To my wife's and my dismay it's a minivan. The Dodge Grand Caravan was the best kiddie kart we tried. There was zip enough for any kind of driving you'd care to do with a tiny most-important-person-in-the-world aboard. The AWD worked well. (I tested it in the playground sandbox.) Seating was so ample that my wife and I started discussing those fertility drugs. Maybe, next trip to the obstetric ward, we'd come home with everything in it.

The cargo space seduced me into all kinds of fix-it projects. Not until I got the plywood, Sheetrock, and two-by-fours home did I recall that I don't know how to fix anything. And there were compartments, cubbyholes, pockets, and nooks sufficient for storing a dozen backup Velveteen Rabbits in case the current one went blooey.

And we wouldn't buy it.

I looked at my wife and said, "A minivan is what we need."

My wife looked at me and said, "A minivan is what we should have."

Then we looked at each other and said, "Nope."

We weren't the only ones who felt this way, obviously, or there would have been a lot fewer SUVs (like, none) on the road. And now, eleven years later—Mrs. O and I having abstained from minivan ownership through the whelping of three progeny—the minivan is a dying vehicle type, being replaced by something called a crossover, which combines all the humdrummery of a minivan with an SUV's preposterousness. What was it that was wrong with the poor, derided, soccer-mom, suburban-boob minivan?

Easier for me to say what wasn't. It wasn't the styling. To my eyes, the mid-'90s Chrysler family of minivans had better, cleaner, more fashion-forward lines than the Ferrari 456M. It wasn't snobbery. My favorite car that I've owned was a 1981 Subaru wagon. It wasn't machismo. I once traded in a Rabbit convertible for an Alfa Romeo Graduate. It wasn't fear of appearing to be a member of the AARP. I always rent Town Cars for that nostalgic "Avast, matey! Right full rudder!" road feel. And I'm not easily embarrassed by what I drive. My first set of wheels was my grandmother's 1956 four-door Ford Custom in salmon pink.

Mrs. O and I talked it over. The Dodge minivan just made too much sense. If you have children it makes sense to buy a minivan. But having children doesn't make sense. If you split your time between two houses five hundred miles apart, one in the arctic boonies and one in the political jungle, it makes sense to buy a minivan. But splitting your time between those two houses doesn't make sense. And besides, this is America, we're not *supposed* to make sense. We're supposed to make whoopee. The minivan made too much sense to lead to anything in the whoopee-making department. (A full-sized van might have been a different matter. "If the Van Is Rockin', Don't Come Knockin'" and so forth. But that's the subject for an essay about *practicing* to have children in a car rather than actually having them in there with you.)

There was probably something that Chrysler could have done about this sensibleness problem. How about supplying the minivans with waterfall front fenders and inboard headlights like the old Land Rovers, plus a spare on the hood and a safari roof rack? Or how about an NO_2 boost that I—on solitary midnight Pampers supply runs—could use to blow the doors off some Hair Club for Men member in a Viper?

Or, since Chrysler had at that time just been purchased by Daimler-Benz, how about putting a big, fat Mercedes star on the front? This worked for the next car I borrowed. I hate to break the news to the uber-boober denizens of suburbia, but the M-class Mercedes *is* a minivan. It's a refined, eminently off-roadable minivan upon which the Mercedes-Benz stylists have, perhaps, put in a little too much overtime. But there is no mistaking the fundamental slope-nosed, one-box, volume-maximizing shape.

There was zero danger of being called sensible in this—it was a Mercedes! But that had its good side as well. The M-class rode like your boss's executive office chair, steered like the prize dressage horse owned by your boss's wife, and stopped faster than your paycheck would if you got caught naked on any of these things.

The M-class was so well built and safety conscious—front airbags, side airbags, crash absorption frame that inflicts minimum damage on other vehicles—that it would have put Swedish au pairs out of business if it could have been trained to wear a bikini. It was reputedly very good in the bumps and stumps, though I didn't get to try this. (The miniature O'Rourke was doing most of the 4X4ing in the family at the moment.) And the 215 HP V-6 meant you could get to the next rest stop almost in time to avoid . . . Oh, hell.

The sole problem with the M-class was that Mercedes had worked so hard on making it compact that they had . . . well, they had succeeded. The M was, not counting height, as small as a Ford Mustang. The Volvo wagon was actually 5.3 inches longer than the Mercedes, and the Dodge minivan was 4.5 inches wider.

M/B put a lot of inside into this outside. On paper the M-class had 44.7 cubic feet of space behind its second seat—more than the Toyota Land Cruiser and within a large duffel and a case of booze of what the minivan had back there. This was a remarkable amount of cargo capacity. But the capacity turned out to be remarkably vertical. "No stacking when you're packing." That's the rule once you have a kid. Sudden stops could turn into a luggage London blitz on baby. Rear vision was obscured, allowing highway patrolmen to sneak up and ask why the heck you're doing a hundred with the family in the car. And when you opened the M's top-hinged tailgate, strollers, portable cribs, bottles, Pampers, Baby Gap inventory, and gummed bunnies got unloaded a little faster than you planned—right onto the pavement. My advice to Mercedes: give the design efficiency a rest. Kick back, loosen up, and add a foot to the back of this thing. (Which advice Mercedes would, eventually, take with its R-class, its GL-class, and its M-class redesign.)

The surprise rug rat ride was the Volvo V7OR AWD wagon. With a 236 HP turbocharged five-cylinder engine and 3,788 pounds of curb weight, it *could* blow the doors off at least the more cowardly Viper drivers. The Volvo made me wonder if there was anything else that the quiche-eating, Whole Foods–shopping, Clinton-voting Yuppies weren't telling us. If this Volvo was anything to go by, the Think Globally/Act Locally crowd may not be the dorks we thought they were. Maybe their bizarre behavior is the side effect of really good drugs.

Anyway, the Volvo wagon had a backseat that could accommodate two adults and a booster seat as wide as Hillary Clinton's . . . open mind. The wagon bed had only 37.1 cubic feet in it, but all of those cubes were safely useful. And the Volvo was even better than the Mercedes for braking, handling, and steering with one hand while reaching around the headrest to extract your cell phone from Muffin's mouth. The Volvo's turbo five made a nice noise, too, just audible over the cute googoos, cooings, *pffffffffts*, and burps emanating from the backseat. The engine sound was reassuring to a guy who wanted to fulfill his parental responsibilities while still feeling that he was a member of the car nut fraternity.

Alas, the Volvo was too small for our travel habits and our one-client day care center. But I would have recommended it, if you had a less materialistic child and you didn't spend as much time as a migrating gray whale moving bulk over distance, the way we did.

The Toyota Land Cruiser was what we chose for O'Rourkes-on-the-road. And we may even buy one as soon as Muffin's college fund has enough in it to be filched. (Do I hear a faint whine from decades hence? "I had to go to a school advertised on the back of a matchbook because my father couldn't bring himself to get a minivan.")

The Land Cruiser was pure joy, as well padded as Dad, as smart as Mom, and almost as beautiful as Muffin. We took it on an 1,100-mile round-trip from Washington to a region of North Carolina so remote that the locals considered the characters in Charles Frazier's novel *Cold Mountain* to be sissified city folk. The Toyota's 230 HP V-8 charged the hills like a motorized Teddy Roosevelt at San Juan. The handling was as confident as Teddy and his cousin Franklin put together. And the Land Cruiser could get in and out of muck better than the then-current president. We could fit all our stuff onboard and it stayed onboard when we opened the doors. And though the seating position was as high as a guitar player in an alternative rock band, we swept along slither coils of road without any sport-ute effects that demanded Dramamine.

Nothing could be said against the Land Cruiser, except by the therapist Mrs. O and I were seeing because we wouldn't buy the Dodge minivan. The Toyota was a better-appointed, more feature-laden vehicle and with swankier trim and upholstery than the Dodge, but for half again as much money it should have been.

The Land Cruiser could, no doubt, traverse the canyons of Mars. But, being honest with myself, how often did I take my car to the red planet? In every day-to-day practical way the minivan was a better deal. It was only 7.1 inches longer and two-fifths of an inch wider than the Toyota, but (with third seat out) its stuff and junk room was 58 percent greater. It wouldn't haul a 6,500-pound trailer like the Land Cruiser, but it would tow a ton and three-quarters, which was almost enough Pampers to get us from D.C. to the cutoff for the Garden State Parkway. The minivan had more rear leg room and better fuel economy than the Land Cruiser, and its power to weight ratio was almost as good. (If you don't count torque and, since I've never really understood torque, I didn't.) They both rode and drove like cars, albeit the Toyota rode and drove like a better one. And the Land Cruiser, with its frame and body construction and greater heft, was presumably somewhat safer. But, since progeny arrived, I'd become the world's safest driver anyway—something I accomplished by turning the wheel over to my wife.

The one strong argument I could make in favor of the Toyota was clearance—a New Hampshire road-rut-friendly 9.8 inches versus the minivan's San Bernardino lowrider-style 5.4. But this meant taller sills, and Muffin was putting on the pounds. I tried to convince Mrs. O that hoisting our daughter, daughter's accoutrements, and the shopping in and out of the Land Cruiser would be a swell postnatal workout program. She responded (out of daughter's earshot, naturally) with an Anglo-Saxon verb. Me as the predicate.

Unless Pampers came through with a major modeling contract for Muffin (and we're *still* waiting; some would say eleven is too old for a child to be in diapers, but we think Muffin will thank us later, after her career as a model is launched), the Land Cruiser was out of the question. Concerning the minivan, Mrs. O and I battled our inner demons. They won. So the Dodge was out of the question. We stuck with the Cherokee. We were all pretty grumpy about it. But in those early days of parenting, before we'd learned the ropes (you use the ropes to tie up the kid in front of the television), we were all pretty grumpy anyway. So the world was probably a better place for us having kept our old car, because in our old car the world could smell us coming.

13

ReinCARnation

We got a new family car, a Land Rover Discovery II. This was the result of a mystical experience I had in India. Speaking as a past owner of a British car (1960 MGA), a mystical experience is the least of what it takes to get you to buy another British car. Fellow past owners of British cars (everyone in Britain, for example) will back me up on this.

Extraordinary things can happen while you're traveling across the Indian subcontinent. You bring a lot back from the journey—amazement at the antiquity of civilization, diarrhea, outrage over poverty and caste discrimination, fever and vomiting, colorful snapshots, fresh insights concerning the lunacy of Gandhi, a suitcase full of tacky dhurries and cheap brassware, the desire to own a Land Rover Discovery II, and spiritual enlightenment. (I need to check and see if Rent-A-Wreck's Guatama of the Garage, Dave Schwartz, owns any British cars. But even Dave may not be that enlightened.)

Personally, what I attained was something more like reverse enlightenment. Now I don't understand the entire nature of existence. My conscious mind was overwhelmed by a sudden blinding flash of . . . oncoming truck radiator.

Nirvana, from the Sanskrit word meaning *blowout,* is the extinction of desires, passion, illusion, and the empirical self. It happens a lot in India, especially on the highways. Sometimes it's the result of a blowout, literally. More often it's a head-on crash.

I traveled from Islamabad to Calcutta, some 1,700 miles, mostly over the Grand Trunk Road. The Grand Trunk begins at the Khyber Pass and ends at the Bay of Bengal. The road was celebrated in Rudyard Kipling's *Kim* and dates back at least to the fourth century B.C. (especially in the matter of stoplights and lane markers). Of all the wonders on this ancient route nothing made me wonder more than the traffic accidents.

But first came a phone call from Bill Baker, he of the Rolling Organ Donors Motorcycle Club. Bill had now risen in life to the position of director of communications programs at Land Rover, responsible for garnering worldwide publicity. When Land Rover introduced the Discovery II in 1998, Bill decided to take the worldwide part of his mandate literally and drive a pair of Discoverys around the world.

"This," Bill said to me on the phone, "will prove they're tough, durable, and can operate under thousands of feet of seawater. Scratch that last part. We'll use a boat. As I was saying, this will prove they're tough, durable, and that automotive journalists can be talked into anything including driving across the most crowed part of the earth during the hottest time of the year at the pace set by Craig Breedlove on the Bonneville Salt Flats."

I told Bill to count me in. I flew to Pakistan and met the Land Rover expedition when it arrived, by way of Baluchistan, fresh from confounding the fundamentalist Shiite clerics of Iran. We stayed in a nice hotel, a place that later became the target of an Islamic extremist terror attack. (But what place in Pakistan hasn't?) There were eight of us: expedition director Iain Chapman, who is an ex-officer in the British army and the former head of the Camel Trophy off-road program; Land Rover engineer Mark Dugmore; expedition photographer Nick Dimbly; car journalists Jeremy Hart, Todd Hallenbeck, and Franco Gionco from Britain, Australia, and Italy, respectively; and Bill and me.

The drive southeast toward the Indian border began pleasantly enough. Traffic was light. It's remarkable how short toll booth lines are in a country with no money. Groups of squatting men flicking whisk brooms kept the turnpike well maintained. And the pavement surface was excellent—if you don't mind a berm six inches lower than the asphalt so that if you swerve to miss one of the whisk broomers and put a wheel off the road, all the other wheels go into the air.

This did not happen. Although we almost wished it had when we found ourselves trapped in the downtown Lahore train station parking lot. Somehow we'd gotten into the special queue for crippled beggars, bullock wagons, goatherds, and local buses.

"Can you tell us where the border is?" we yelled at a policeman busy directing traffic by hitting it with a long stick. The policeman replied, in perfect English, "No."

"Fortunately," said Bill Baker, "we have the Garmin GPS II Personal Navigator that can show us a route to anywhere on earth and show us our exact position within three meters."

"Well, if it can show us all that," Todd Hallenbeck said, "why didn't it show us we were headed up the arse of that ox on the hood?"

"We were too busy," said Baker, "using the BT Mobile Vehicle satellite phone that delivers full global coverage and allows us to call anywhere in the world."

"Call room service," said Jeremy Hart, "and order ice." It was forty-seven degrees Celsius in Lahore.

"How hot is that in regular temperature?" I asked. No one knew. I picked up the BT Mobile Vehicle satellite phone and called my German mother-in-law in Connecticut. She's used to the metric system. "Hi," I said, "I'm in Lahore. Tell your daughter I'm fine. How hot is forty-seven degrees?"

"*Pffffft*," said my mother-in-law, "it doesn't get that hot."

Mark Dugmore did the math. It was 116½ degrees in Lahore with 100 percent humidity, which meant that breathing was like drinking coffee through your nose. Our Discovery II had climate control, of course. But once we'd lowered the window to yell at the policeman we couldn't raise it again because there was part of a goatherd and most of a crippled beggar caught in the opening.

Anyway, the Garmin GPS did, indeed, show us our position to within three meters. The problem was that the streets of Lahore weren't three meters wide. In fact one was so narrow that I think we got off the street entirely and into someone's house. But the GPS directed us to the border. Turn right at the armoire. Left at the kitchen sink.

Approaching the Indian frontier from Pakistan, it was clear that the land of the unfathomable was nigh. We went down the single, solitary connecting road between the two countries and there was nothing on it. Not even military fortifications were visible, just one company of crack Pakistani rangers in their jammies because it was nap time.

The only other wayfarers at the Pakistani customs post were two dirty backpackers from Switzerland who were acting like the things that pop out of Swiss clocks every hour. No one was going to or fro. They can't. *Pakistani and Indian nationals are only allowed to cross the border by train,* said my tourist guidebook. This utter lack of customs traffic had not prevented the establishment of fully staffed customs posts on both sides of the boundary.

Getting out of Pakistan was a normal third world procedure. The officials were asleep, lying on the unused concrete baggage-inspection counters like corpses in a morgue—a morgue posted with a surprising number of regulations for its customers. The number-one man roused the number-two man, who explained the entire system of Pakistani tariff regulation and passport control by rubbing his thumb against his forefinger. He then gave a performance in mime of documents being pounded with a rubber stamp.

"Fifty dollars," said the number-one man. I opened my wallet, foolishly revealing two fifty-dollar bills. "One hundred dollars," he said.

Things were very different on the Indian side of the border. Here they had not just an unused baggage-inspection counter but an unused metal detector, an unused X-ray machine, and an unused pit with an unused ramp over it to inspect the chassis and frames of the vehicles that don't use this border crossing.

Our party consisted of people representing four nationalities, in two Land Rovers, with the satellite phone, GPS, several computers, and a trailer filled with food, camping gear, and spare parts. The rules concerning entry of such persons and things into India occupy a book large enough to contain the collected works of Stephen King.

The Indian customs agents were delighted. They'd never had an opportunity to consult their book about so many items. Bandying legal niceties, they fell into happy debate among themselves. Every now and then they'd pause in their arguments with one another to argue with us. An agent would turn a page, point to a paragraph, and say, "You are doing what with these vehicles?"

"We're testing them," we'd reply.

"Oh no, you are not. That would require special licensing."

"We're transporting them," we'd say.

"Definitely no, that is a different permit."

The Land Rovers had already passed the customs inspection of twelve nations, including Bulgaria, without hindrance, delay, or more than moderate palm greasing. The Indian officials heard this explained and clucked and wagged their heads in sympathy for the hundreds of brother customs agents from London to the deserts of Iran who had lost an opportunity to look up thousands of items in a great big book. Everything had to come out of the cars and trailers. Everything had to go through the metal detector, even though the detector didn't seem to be plugged in. And everything had to come back through the X-ray machine, which the customs agents weren't watching because they were too busy looking up items in a great big book.

All this took four hours, during which the seven or eight agents on duty met each hint at bribery with the stare you'd get from an octogenarian Powerball winner if you suggested the twenty-year payout option. The fellow who was recording, in longhand, everything inside our passports did take two cigarettes, but he wouldn't accept a pack.

None of the cases, trunks, bags—unloaded and reloaded in 105-degree heat—was actually opened, except for a wrench set. Perhaps there is one size of wrench that requires a special permit in India. The satellite telephone *did* require a special permit, which we didn't have. The briefcase-sized sat-phone went unnoticed. (Engine compartments and under-carriages were inspected, but no one looked under the seat.) Our tire pressures must be checked in case the all-terrain radials were packed with drugs. The Indian government tire gauge wasn't working. We offered our own. We were halfway through checking the tires when we realized nobody was accompanying us. I walked around behind the customs building to take a leak and found drugs to spare. I was pissing on thousands of dollars' worth of wild marijuana plants.

The customs inspection could have gone on forever except that, in India, everything—including the endless cycle of death and rebirth—stops for tea. The customs agents shut their book.

The staggering traffic and whopping crowds of India materialized. We still had 250 miles to go that day to stay on schedule. A brisk pace was required. Think of it as doing sixty through the supermarket parking lot, the school playground, and the Bronx Zoo.

For the greater part of its length the Grand Trunk runs through the broad, flood-flat Ganges plain. The way is straight and level and would be almost two lanes wide if there were such things as lanes in India. The asphalt paving—where it isn't absent—isn't bad. As roads go in the developing world this is a good one. But Indians have their own ideas about what the main thoroughfare spanning the most populous part of a nation is for. It's a place where friends and family can meet, where they can put charpoy string beds and have a nap and let the kids run around unsupervised. It's a roadside café with no side to it—or tables or chairs—where the street food is smack dab on the street. It's a rent-free function room for every local fete. And it's a piece of agricultural machinery. Even along the Grand Trunk's few stretches of toll-booth-cordoned "expressway," farmers are drying grain on the macadam.

Kipling called the Grand Trunk "the backbone of all Hind," claimed that "such a river of life . . . exists nowhere in the world," and said, "It's the Indy 500 with all the infield spectators on the track during the race. And, instead of drivers putting Budweiser on their sponsorship decals, they're drinking it." Or, if Kipling didn't say that, it was only because he'd never been to the Indianapolis 500 so the metaphor eluded him.

Nor was Kipling much on Beatles references. Given visits to the Maharishi Mahesh Yogi, it's easy to see how the Fab Four came up with "Why don't we do it in . . ."

The road is a store, a warehouse, a workshop. We saw a blacksmith who had pitched his tent on a bridge. Under the tent flaps were several small children, the missus working the bellows, and the craftsman himself smoking a hookah and contemplating his anvil, which was placed fully in the right-of-way. The road is also convenient for bullock carts, donkey gigs, horse wagons, pack camels, and the occasional laden elephant—not convenient for taking them anywhere, just convenient. There they stand along with sheep, goats, water buffalo, and the innumerable cows (all sacred, I presume) sent to graze on the Grand Trunk. I watched several cows gobbling cardboard boxes and chewing plastic bags. No wonder the Indians won't eat them.

Dashing through this omnium-gatherum is every kind of motor vehicle you can think of. Or, rather, you can't think of them. Who *would* think of a big automobile factory—India's largest—manufacturing a brand-new 1954 Morris Oxford (the Hindustani Ambassador)? Who'd conceive of a rejected American Bantam design for a World War II scout car rolling off production lines fifty-five years later (the Mahindra Jeep)? Who could envision a Royal Enfield motorcycle with a diesel engine? Let alone the ubiquitous Tata truck, which seems to be a replica of what drove the Burma Road in the war against the Japanese except with a too-tall wood-frame cargo bed and a hideous demon painted on the differential? Tata tailgates bear the message (wholly gratuitous): "Please Blow Horn."

One type of Indian vehicularity was a total mystery. It had three wheels, bodywork shaped like a tongue depressor, a grille from a Chrysler Airflow, and a single-cylinder engine with a bore four times its stroke. This power plant was attached to one side of the front wheel steering fork, giving the conveyance the stability of a motorized unicycle. No nameplate was visible. (Who can blame the manufacturer?) We called it an "Ugly." The Uglies were used as taxis, transporting as many as fifteen or eighteen people—for about a hundred yards before the Ugly expired, tipped over, or got squashed by a Tata.

All daytime driving in India is done at full throttle. And Indian drivers respond to nightfall by picking up the pace. Indian pedestrians make a special effort to be present and milling in the right-of-way after dark, bringing their household goods and chattle with them. The dimmer switch has not been discovered in India. Night driving proceeds exclusively by highbeam, usually only one of them—if there are any lights on the vehicle at all. Chances are there aren't.

Among the many things that suddenly appeared out of the gloom and right in our face was an unilluminated, reflectorless tractor-trailer with a smiley-face death's head and a sign reading "High Explosives. Expert Advice Given. No Smoking."

The first time you look out the windshield at this melee you think, India really *is* magical. How, except by magic, can they drive like this without killing people?

They can't. Jeeps bust scooters, scooters plow into bicycles, bicycles cover the hoods of Jeeps. Cars run into trees. Buses run into ditches, rolling over on their 1940s-style breadloaf tops until they're mashed into unleavened chapatis of carnage. And everyone runs into pedestrians. A speed bump is called a *sleeping policeman* in Jamaica. I don't know what it's called in India. *Dead people lying in the road* is a guess. There's some of both kinds of obstructions in every village, but they don't slow traffic much. The animals get clobbered too, including sacred cows, in accidents notable for the unswerving behavior of all participants. The car in front of us hit a cow—no change in speed or direction from the car, no change in posture or expression from the cow.

It's the lurching, hurtling Tata trucks that put the pepper in the masala and make the curry of Indian driving scare you coming and going the way dinner does. The Tatas are almost as wide as they are long and somewhat higher than either. They blunder down the middle of the road, brakeless, lampless, on treadless tires, moving dog fashion with the rear wheels headed in a direction the front wheels aren't. Tatas fall off bridges, fall into culverts, fall over embankments, and sometimes Tatas just fall—flopping on their sides without warning. But usually Tatas collide, and usually with each other. They crash not just in twos but threes and fours, leaving great smoking piles of vaguely truck-shaped wreckage. What little space is left on the road is occupied by one or two surviving drivers camping out until the next collision comes. Inspecting one of these catastrophes, I found the splintered bodywork decorated with a little metal plaque: LUCKY ENGINEERING.

In one day of travel I tallied twenty-five horrendous Tata wrecks. And I was scrupulous in my scoring. Fender benders didn't count. Neither did old abandoned wrecks or broken-down Tatas. Probable loss of life was needed to make the list. If you saw just one of these pileups on I-95 you'd pull into the next rest stop with clutch foot shivering and hand palsied upon the shift knob, saying, "Next time we fly." But in India you shout triumphantly to Mark Dugmore, Todd Hallenbeck, and Franco Gionco, "That's twenty-five fatals! I had the over! I win today's truck wreck pool!"

Taking the wheel in India was, however, less fun. I had a tendency to beat my forehead against the horn button and weep, "I have a family. I'm fifty. That goat didn't have its turn signal on. My glasses are smudged. I hate the food. We're all going to die."

Fortunately, expedition leader Iain Chapman and Land Rover engineer Mark Dugmore knew what they were doing. Luke 18:25 should be revised to read, "For it is easier for a camel to go through a needle's eye than for a rich man to enter into the kingdom of God, unless the rich man has the good sense to hire Iain Chapman and Mark Dugmore." Plus we had, apropos of Chapman's experience with the Camel Trophy, a camel right there in the road. The younger journalists—Dimbly, Hart, Hallenbeck, and Gionco—were steely nerved as well. And Bill Baker, who is in fact older than I am, was an amazing driver.

Bill, that was particulary amazing when you pulled out from behind two side-by-side Tatas and discovered that the oncoming lane was occupied by two other Tatas with a Premier Padmini microvan wedged between them—closing speed about 120 mph and road shoulder blocked by a dense contingent of women and children.

I have no memory of how Bill got us out of that. But I do remember thinking it was odd what was said in the car at the time. There were no swear words or calls to God or Mommy, just a joint statement on the vagaries of Indian traffic: four people, in unison, going "Whoa."

I also don't remember being crushed to death by a coal truck. We were trapped behind a stupendously overloaded, hilariously top-heavy Tata. Its leaf springs were in the autumn of their suspension life. Every time the truck hit a bump it would tip on two wheels. Bill waited until a bump tipped it away from us, then tried to pass. The truck hit a contrapuntal bump. The last thing I recall was an acre of bituminous-laden Tata bed descending upon us.

Maybe I died and was reincarnated as a life-form that wanted to buy a Land Rover Discovery II. Maybe my mind was fogged by gratitude to the Discovery for letting me experience nirvana without getting my third eye poked out. Whatever, when I came out of my "Whoa" trance I decided to purchase a Discovery. Storage space was ample, as India's customs agents will confirm. The A/C was equal to the subcontinent's worst climatic efforts, as the crippled beggar in Lahore can testify. The Discovery had a body-on-frame construction built like the proverbial brick thing of which there were hardly any in India. (And when you do find one, it has a bowl of water instead of a roll of toilet paper. Bring Handi Wipes.)

The Discovery II was doubtless crashworthy, something we—amazingly—did not test. Although we did experience a side mirror fold-in from an express bus, got a Lambretta into the tail gate of the trailer, and had several sacred cow brushbacks (touched by the Pot Roast of God).

We tested the Discovery's off-road qualifications, though not on purpose. We'd go off road abruptly and at high speed because of horrendous events in front of us or because of sudden pavement disappearance. This is not the preferred "tread lightly" method of exploring the wilderness in a sport utility vehicle. Nonetheless the Discovery has excellent rough-terrain capabilities including the all-important capability to not flip over.

The trailer was also great off-road, where it spent a lot of time going straight up in the air due to the remarkable things it ran over on Indian roads. Despite being loaded with spare wheels, tool chests, and jerry cans of diesel fuel, gasoline, and purified H_2O (Indian weight-loss miracle: one tablespoon of tap water with every meal and eat what you want), the trailer planted its landings with gymnastic grace and precision.

One of our Discoverys had a five-cylinder direct injection diesel engine with manual shift. The other had a four-liter gas V-8 with an automatic. The V-8 delivered immediate speed and the diesel gave almost as good even though it was dragging the trailer. Diesel revs had to be kept above three thousand to get adequate power, but both cars had enough acceleration to flee traffic embroilments. And—when escape to safety was impossible—they had their computer-assisted brakes. We could move ahead quick as stink (not a meaningless cliché in India) and could stop faster than the pair of Tatas we saw going in opposite directions who snagged each other's rear wheels and tore each other's axles off. Plus we could maneuver with the agility of a President Clinton policy position. As proof of these assertions, I give you the fact that I lived to write this. So I bought a Discovery II and I'll hear nothing against the make or model. Bill Baker took it around the world without a major problem. (And what happened back in the United States when I took it around the block is none of your business.)

We had to be in Calcutta by the afternoon of June 25, to get the Discoverys into a cargo container for the next leg of the global tour. We left Islamabad on June 20. Our route was 1,710 miles. In five and a half days, we clocked seventy-eight hours of driving time. Thus we crossed the subcontinent at twenty-two miles per hour—on average. This average was achieved by going a million miles an hour for a total of about one of those hours and sitting as still as road kill the other seventy-seven.

Coming east from the border we traveled to the dirty and disorganized town of Chandigarh—pronounced "*Chunder*-gar," Todd Hallenbeck noted, as in the Australian slang for blowing lunch. Brief rest was had at the Budgerigar Hotel (it's motto, no kidding: "Welcome to your nest"). A parakeet in every room? There was something that size in mine but it was a member of the order Insectivora.

Then we made a dash up to Shimla and back through the Himalaya foothills, the Himachals. These foothills are about the size of the Rockies. Highway engineers customarily use switchbacks to decrease grade inclines across mountain slopes. In the Himachals the switchbacks are arranged to maximize vertical ascents and abysmal plunges. Heaps of smoldering Tata wreckage decorated the bottoms of ravines.

The Discovery II had a rather eerie suspension system called Active Cornering Enhancement. ACE kept the car almost perfectly level no matter the swerving, hairpinning, or off-camber S-bending. As a result, the insane miscellany on Indian roads came at the Discovery's windshield with steady, relentless horizontality, like the world's worst arcade game. Which Jeremy Hart, Todd Hallenbeck, and I have patented: Drive-Inda-Ya™. You get 1 point for hitting an Ugly, 2 points for creaming an Ambassador, and, if a Tata clobbers you, it's not "Game Over," you're reborn. As a sacred cow. Bonus.

Shimla, the famous hill station and summer capital of the British raj, built at a higher elevation than Kathmandu, was a standard Indian mess of sheet-tin roofing, catawampus concrete block walls, and imperial leftovers. Along the mall there's a row of dusty British-era shops that the British—seeing mountains all around them and not knowing what else to do—built in alpine style. But the town had a view to die for (or die of, if you leaned against the parade ground's flimsy railings).

Atal Bihari Vajpayee, then prime minister of India, was headed to Shimla. Preparation consisted of someone loudly testing the PA system.

HELLO HELLO HELLO ONE TWO THREE FOUR FIVE
SIX SEVEN EIGHT NINE TEN MICROPHONE TESTING
HELLO HELLO HELLO HELLO HELLO HELLO HELLO

For an hour. This was the crowd warm-up. The speech must have been a dilly. Meanwhile, behind handsome batik curtains, tribal women in full native dress, with nose jewelry the size of baby shoes, were repairing the pavement.

We almost, but not quite, plunged downhill to Dehradun, home of the Indian Military Academy and also the "Windi Ass Shopping Centre." The Hotel Madhuban ("Please do not open window to keep mosquitoes out") was all right, but it didn't have hot water. And all you have to do to make hot water in India this time of year is leave it outside for ten minutes.

Next, we went south to Agra for a peek at the Taj Mahal. It's one of those satisfying tourist destinations that looks just like it's always looked like it would look. An impressive pile built with public funds while a famine scourged the countryside, the Taj was commissioned by Shah Jahan to memorialize his favorite wife, who died in 1629 giving birth to their fourteenth child. If Jahan had really wanted to show his love, he could have cut back on the ginseng and powdered rhino horn.

We had our first glimpse of the famous mausoleum at sunset, from a heap of trash and offal on the bank of the Yamuna River. Mixed into the garbage around our feet were hundreds of miniature clay images of Krishna. These are tossed into the water by devotees upsteam in Mathura, the god's supposed birthplace. The holiness of India is impressive. The ground is littered with divinities.

The bridge across the Yamuna into Agra was also interesting —two-way traffic on a one-lane bridge going both ways at once. Three-way traffic was threatened. Splash.

Then it was back on the Grand Trunk to Varanasi, the most holy place in India, where millions of pilgrims come to wash themselves in the purifying Ganges and also to cremate corpses in it. Everybody got up at five in the morning to see this done except me. I figured that, when it came to scary things in the water, the hotel coffee would do.

Varanasi was squalid even by Indian standards. Expedition members had their own reactions. Todd Hallenbeck, an adopted Australian who was born in California, retained an American can-do sensibility. "Gosh," he said, "you see so many things you'd like to fix."

Franco Gionco, with Latin sophistication, was inclined to excuse the accumulated dreck. "But it is an ancient civilization, very old."

"Certainly smells past its sell-by date," said Jeremy Hart.

Iain Chapman gazed upon all the oddity and impoverishment and made his pronouncement upon India in general: "Surreal pity."

East of Varanasi the driving got harder yet, unhelped by the fact that we were in left-hand-drive cars in a country that drives on the left. A spotter had to be on duty in the death seat saying, at each attempt to pass, "Yes," or "No," or, "Oh, God, no!"

Opportunities to overtake were so few that spotters started modifying their pessimistic assessments. Sometimes the spotter would use the laws of physics and comparisons of relative mass: "Go ahead, nothing but Vespas coming." Sometimes the spotter would try to gauge the legal and social ramifications of possible collision: "Are pigs sacred?" And sometimes the spotter would get distracted by the random nattering in the car.

"Should Prince Andrew marry Sporty Spice?" someone in the back seat would inquire.

"Yes, definitely," the spotter would say, causing the driver to . . .

"Whoa."

This is the India ordinary travelers never see—because they're in their right minds. And we didn't see much of it ourselves. The scenery was too close to view, a blur of cement-block shops and hovels in unbroken ranks inches from the fenders. Yet my map showed open country with only occasional villages meriting the smallest cartographic type size. There are a lot of people in India: 966.8 million as of 1998. I don't know what they want with the atomic bomb. They already have the population bomb, and it's working like a treat.

Nevertheless India, with a population density of 843 people per square mile, is not as crowded as the Netherlands, which packs 1,195 people into the same space. Nobody comes back from Holland aghast at the teeming mass of Dutch or having nightmares about windmills and tulips pressing in on every side.

Poor people who depend on agriculture for a living, as 67 percent of Indians do, take up room. If 67 percent of New Yorkers depended on agriculture for a living, someone would be trying to farm the dirt under the floor mats of your Yellow Cab.

Everything is squeezed together in India to keep it out of the picnic-blanket-sized rice field that's the sole support for a family of ten.

Every nook of land is put to use. At the bottom of a forty-foot-deep abandoned well, which would be good for nothing but teenage suicides in America, somebody was raising frogs. City public restrooms employ the space-saving device of dispensing with walls and roofs and placing the urinal stalls on the sidewalk. No resource goes to waste, which sounds like a fine thing to advocate next Earth Day—except, in the real world of poverty, it means that the principal household fuel of India is the cow flop. This is formed into a circular patty and stuck on the side of the house, where it provides a solution to three problems: storage room, home decor, and cooking dinner.

Therefore, what makes a drive across India insane (and smelly) isn't overpopulation, it's poverty. Except this isn't really true either. The reason for those ranks of shops and houses along the Grand Trunk, and for the cars, trucks, and buses bashing into each other between them, is that people have money to buy and build these things. And the reason for the great smoldering dung funk hanging over India is that there's something to cook on those fires.

When the British left in 1947, India got itself an economy in the socialist closet, an economy in the political bag. The Indians called it the "license-permit-quota raj." The *Economist* magazine once stated, "This has no equal in the world. In many ways it puts Soviet central planning to shame." Indian industries were trapped and isolated by the government. Like an aunt locked in the attic, they got strange. The results can still be seen in the Tata trucks, Ambassador sedans, and motorcycles that Evel Knievel would be afraid to ride. But in 1992 India began to surrender to free-market reforms. Imports were allowed, foreign investment was encouraged, and customs regulations were (amazing as this seems to those who have been through Indian customs) simplified.

By 1998 the Indian economy had been growing for half a decade at about 7 percent a year. As many as two hundred million people had been added to the Indian middle class—a number almost equal to the total middle class of the United States.

India is still very poor. Small boys with hammers make gravel by the side of the road, an activity that must seem worse than school even to small boys and isn't much of a skill-building vocational opportunity either. The people on the Grand Trunk looked in need but not in wretched misery (until they stepped in front of a speeding Tata). There are plenty of flat bellies in India but few of the distended kind that announce malnutrition. And the beggars, whom Western visitors have been taught to expect in legions, arrive only in squads and platoons. A kid selling trinkets in Agra was irked to be mistaken for such. "I'm not a beggar," he said. "You want to buy, you get." Then he named a thievish price.

What is happening in India is what happens every place where an agrarian economy changes into a modern one. The first stage of prosperity is ugly. (Remember the 1950 which-way-did-they-go Studebakers?) This is the ugliness that caused William Blake, at the beginning of the industrial revolution, to speak of "dark Satanic mills"—dark satanic mills that were giving people cash, social mobility, and an opportunity to escape a hundred generations of chopping weeds with hoes. Hoeing is not as dark, maybe, as working in a mill, but it's plenty satanic, as anyone with the smallest garden knows.

The quaint and orderly India of old is still there, just beyond the clutter of the Grand Trunk Road. In West Bengal we visited a beautiful farm village full of amusing thatch architecture and cute peasant handcrafts. Here the handsome patina of tradition glowed upon lives that were quiet, calm, and as predictable as famine and the dowry needed to marry off the ten-year-old daughter.

The villagers were friendly enough. But what if a carload of grubby car journalists came into my driveway and Nick Dimbly began taking happy snaps while I was scrubbing down the barbecue grill? I preferred the chaos of the Grand Trunk.

The road is a trash basket, as all roads in India are. I saw a dressy middle-aged woman eat a chocolate bar on Nehru Road (the so-called Fifth Avenue of Calcutta). She threw the candy wrapper at her feet with a graceful and decisive motion. And the road is the john. You never have to wonder where the toilet is in India, you're standing on it. The back of a long-distance bus had a sign in Hindi and an elaborate pictogram, the import of which was *Don't crap on the pavement, and wash your hands after you do.*

By day four we were accustomed to the voluminous detritus, but somewhere around the town of Dhanbad (pronounced as it ought to be) we encountered mile upon mile of garbage stretching to both horizons. We were riding through this in awed silence when Jeremy Hart said, "I . . . I don't know what came over me . . . I just put my empty cigarette pack into our litter bag."

Iain Chapman, who was driving, laughed so hard he had to pull over. We pitched all the detritus in the car out the window, litter bag included.

Then the monsoon arrived, eliminating all daylight and firing boiled egg–sized raindrops into the slime on the Grand Trunk Road. "You know you've got pollution when the rain foams," said Bill Baker. The temperature dropped nineteen degrees in five minutes. Which was nice. But if we'd opened the windows to enjoy the frigid eighty-four-degree weather we would have drowned.

Our last night on the road we stayed in an insalubrious government guesthouse. My bathroom was already being used by some of the other guests, each with six legs and a body the length of a hot dog roll. "That's a *good* thing," said Iain. "It means no cobras in your toilet. They would have eaten the bugs."

Just when I thought I wasn't getting it about India, I started to get it less. The next day, we encountered a communist rally.

Hundreds of agitated-looking agitators waved red flags and brandished staves. We were a ripe target for the anger of the masses—eight capitalist prats in Land Rovers with a trailer full of goodies protected only by a tarp. We were ignored. It seems the ideological fury of the Communist Party of India (Marxist-Leninist) is directed primarily at the Communist Party of India (Marxist).

The latter runs Calcutta. According to my guidebook, "They have somehow succeeded in balancing rhetoric and old-fashioned socialism with a prudent practicality. . . . Capitalism is allowed to survive, but made to support the political infrastructure."

Not that you'd know this by driving into Calcutta, where the infrastructure doesn't look like it could support another flea. Certainly the Howrah Bridge over the Hooghly River can't. It carries sixty thousand motor vehicles a day, and they were all there when we tried to get across at five P.M.

Packed along the filthy opposite bank of the Hooghly were temples to scary gods, a ratty colonial fort, a coal power plant barfing cones of smudge, and the dreariest kind of glass-box office buildings. The city appeared to be an educational diorama: the History of Mess.

I retain nothing but a few disordered and bedlamic images of our entrance into the city: An intersection with a crushed traffic warden's shelter in the middle. A main street with more human beings than I'd ever seen. (One out of five people in the world is an Indian. And, believe me, that person was standing in Nehru Road on June 25, 1998.) A shop that sold what looked like department store mannequins, but they had four arms. A herd of sheep being driven through the traffic. And a very dirty banner advertising "World Environment Day." (Canceled due to overbooking is my guess.)

We were all wrecks, but the Land Rovers were not. From Islamabad to Calcutta they hadn't even had a flat. (Although a swell tire-repair trick had been learned from the Tata drivers. Put a couple of washers on each side of a puncture, run a bolt through, and tighten the nut.)

Jeremy Hart, Todd Hallenbeck, and Franco Gionco flew home. Bill Baker and Nick Dimbly went on to Perth to arrange the next leg of the expedition. I stayed with Iain Chapman and Mark Dugmore to help them load the Discoverys into a cargo container. This took twenty minutes or—adjusting the clock to Indian daylight wasting time—four days.

First the port was closed. Well, it wasn't really closed. I mean, it was sort of closed because the port of Calcutta has silted in and is nearly useless. Only about three ships were there. This didn't keep hundreds of stevedores, shipping clerks, and port officials from coming to work. But there were city council elections that day with attendant rioting. So the police had to suppress voters and weren't available for harassment at the port.

Then the port was closed because it was Sunday.

Then our shipping agents fell into an argument about when to pick us up at the hotel the next day. Not that they disagreed with one another.

"We will go to get them at nine-thirty in the morning," one said.

"Oh, no, no, no, no," said another. "It must be nine-thirty in the morning."

"How can you talk like this?" asked a third, stamping his foot. "The time for us to be there is nine-thirty in the morning!"

We had about ten shipping agents. There's no such thing as hiring an individual in India. In a Bihar village it took the services of two shops, four shopkeepers, and a boy running for change to sell me a pack of cigarettes.

While waiting for the port to open, I wandered the streets of Calcutta. The late-nineteenth-century Writers Building is crumbling and dirty although a row of large, carefully tended potted plants decorates the sidewalk below its windows. Trees, products of less intentional horticulture, grow out of the cracked Edwardian edifice of the nearby Standard Assurance and Life headquarters. Even Calcutta's New Market, built in 1985, seems about to fall down and probably doesn't only because—being nothing but a pile of moldering concrete in the first place—it can't.

Calcutta is a byword for squalor. Most Americans suppose that to tour its precincts is to flush oneself down the toilet of humanity and amble through a human septic system. This isn't true. There aren't that many flush toilets in Calcutta. Anyway, parts of Washington, D.C., are dirtier (Congress; the White House) and Calcutta smells no worse than a college dorm.

The poverty is sad and extensive but at least the families living on the Calcutta streets are intact families—talking to one another instead of themselves. I did see some people who seemed really desperate, addled, and unclean. But these were American hippies at Calcutta's Dum Dum airport. I was standing in the ticket line behind an Indian businessman who stared at the hippies and then gave me a stern look, as if to say, These are *your* people. Isn't there something you can *do*?

Calcutta's pollution is more visible than it's fashionable for American pollution to be—smoke and trash instead of microwaves and PCBs. The food sold on Calcutta's streets may be unidentifiable, but it's less likely than New York City hot dogs to contain a cow rectum. The crowding is extreme but you get used to it. You get used to a lot of things: naked ascetics, elephants in downtown traffic, a single file of costumed girls linked by electric wires, with one carrying a car battery and the rest having blue fluorescent tubes sticking out of their headdresses.

I was waiting to cross the busiest street in Calcutta when a four-story temple complex on wheels went by, complete with high priest, idols, acolytes, clouds of incense, blazing torches, and banging gongs. And what I noticed was that I wasn't noticing it. Imagine the pope (and quite a bit of Saint Peter's) coming down Broadway at rush hour and you thinking, *Should I jaywalk or wait for the light?*

There's a certain pest factor in Calcutta, mostly from the touting of roving market bearers. But it's not without its entertainment value. Bearer No. A-49 from the New Market told me not to listen to any of the other bearers because they would get me into their shops and cut my throat. So be sure you get Bearer No. A-49. Accept no other. Lesser merchants, squatting on the street, sell everything from new Lee jeans to brightly colored pebbles and pieces of broken mirrors. The poster wallah's selection included views of the Taj Mahal, photographs of kittens tangled in balls of yarn, and the gore-faced goddess Kali holding a severed human head by the hair.

In the midst of this is the Oberoi Grand Hotel, with guards stationed at the gate holding sticks to use on touts and beggars. At the Oberoi everything is efficient, crisp, clean, and pukka (except when the electricity goes out). The Indians inside seemed as perplexed by the chaos of India outside as I was. I told Alex, the restaurant manager, about the muddle at the port. "Oh, this country," he said, "there are no two ways around it."

We had parked the Land Rovers and trailer in the hotel courtyard. The shipping agents came by to inform us that everything in the vehicles had to be clean and packed exactly as described on the customs documents. Iain, Mark, and I set about amending seventeen hundred miles of dirt and equipment disorder. It was a hundred degrees in the courtyard. A dozen members of the hotel staff gathered to watch us. I don't think they'd seen Westerners do actual work. (And—as far as my own experiences go in the offices and stores of America and Europe—neither have I.) Removing the trailer tarp we discovered an ax had come loose from its lashing and punctured a container of beef stew and a can of motor oil. The trailer bed was awash in petroleum and what Hindus euphemistically call brown meat.

On Monday we went back to the port, where the customs inspectors ignored everything about our cleanliness and packing except the ax. "What is this?" said the chief inspector.

"An ax," said Iain Chapman.

The officials conferred at length and decided it was so. Then there was a seven-hour delay because of an engine serial-number discrepancy. The customs inspectors were worried that we'd stolen one of the Discovery IIs from Rover. "*We're* from Rover," said Iain. "These are the only Discovery IIs in Asia, and they can't be stolen because they're both right here." The inspectors returned to their office to ponder this. We sat on the dock.

I asked one of our shipping agents why so many of the Tata truck drivers had decorated their front bumpers with one dangling shoe.

"Oh, for the heck of it," he said.

Finally the Land Rovers were rolled into the cargo container. Things do eventually get done in India. My theory about why they do is that, although making business matters complicated is a great source of fun there, you know how it is with fun. Sooner or later it's time for different fun, such as making family matters complicated. "I am a twenty-one-year-old man involved in a physical relationship with my thirty-six-year-old unmarried cousin for the past six years," read a query to an advice column in a Calcutta newspaper. "It all began when I raped her."

I was sad to see the Discovery IIs go. They weren't broken, an anomaly in this land. And they never burned or exploded, which is more than I can say for Iain when, leaving the docks, the police tried to arrest us because we had padlocks in our possession.

"What the hell kind of thief comes back with the locks instead of the swag?" Iain asked them. Maybe an Indian one, if it would complicate matters.

I remained in Calcutta for a few days after Iain and Mark left, in sort of a paralysis of awe at a dundering muddle of a place that seems in total disorganization but where I couldn't even get lost because everyone with a clean shirt speaks English. And they speak it in a style that is a reminder of India's claim upon the language. There were Indians speaking English when most of America was gibbering in Gaelic, German, or Italian on the wrong side of the Ellis Island fence. Placards ask that Calcutta's subway be treated WITH RESPECT AND AFFECTION. Street signs read, I USE FOOTPATHS, DO YOU?

Indian journalist Gita Mehta says India turns out five million university graduates a year. That's four times the number of bachelor degrees awarded annually in the United States. Yet the ancient guild of scribes still does brisk business outside Calcutta's general post office. Scores of men hunker on the sidewalk writing and reading other people's letters. Forty-eight percent of Indians are illiterate, including almost two-thirds of Indian women.

You walk by a newsstand—a news squat, to be precise—and see the Calcutta *Telegraph*, the Calcutta *Statesman*, the *Asian Age*, the *Times of India*, and stacks of newspapers printed in Hindi and other languages. The *Telegraph* ran a know-how feature on particle physics. A *Statesman* op-ed page had an article on energy efficiency: "The heat rate of the power plant, in layman's terms, refers to how much kilo calorie of heat is required to produce 1 kwp of power." You think you're in a nation of Einsteins until you read the advice columnist's answer to the rapist: "At this stage of life you ought to detach yourself from this cousin to secure a healthy life. Initially your cousin provoked you in the act, and hence it cannot be called rape."

In the midst of Calcutta's street stampede (not a figure of speech, considering cows), there are young hawkers with what look like shoe-shine boxes. What's offered for sale isn't a wingtip buff. The youths crouch in the hubbub, juggle the tiny wheels and springs of wristwatches, and set the timepieces running again. There is a whole street in Calcutta lined with stalls too small and ill-equipped for lemonade sales. Here, artisans with flame-heated soldering irons rearrange the logic on the latest computer circuit boards. Then you look up and see a man walking around wearing a bucket upside down over his head.

14

The Geezers' Grand Prix

Coming down the Mendocino coastal range on a one-and-a-half-lane semipaved road dropping 2,700 feet from Buck Peak to Point Arena, the brakes gave out. They'd been soft for a couple of days, but now the pedal went to the floor at seventy miles an hour. On one side, ready to swallow an oversteer spinout, was a hungry ravine. On the other side, set for smacking an understeer slide, was an angry wall of rock. In the middle was oncoming truck traffic. My codriver, unflappable Detroit investment banker Fred Schroeder, closed the little plastic lip on his Starbucks cup—never a good sign. And I was driving a priceless item of automotive history.

The modified 1939 Chevrolet coupe had belonged to Juan Manuel Fangio. This was the last extant specimen of the

Chevys in which Fangio got his start during the 1940s. They were built by his genius mechanic brother, Toto. Juan Manuel ran them in the Carreteras, the incomparably punishing South American long-distance road races. One course went from Buenos Aires across the Bolivian Andes to Lima, Perú, and back—ten thousand kilometers mostly on dirt and gravel. Surely I could make it ten miles to Point Arena. Best not to think about the two solid axles, the leaf spring suspension, the yard-long clutch throw, school bus steering wheel, no power anything, and mechanicals old enough to get IRA disbursements without tax penalties.

But the spirit of Fangio was with me, he who won five world driver's championships after the age of forty. Or, more likely, the spirit of Fangio was with his car. The Chevy went down the mountain with adult authority—no toddler body roll, no childish darting into the middle of the road, no infant squeal of tires. It just *went,* down switchbacks as tangled as life, down grades as precipitous as the known alternative. Meanwhile the unskilled driver was yanking the tiller 360 degrees hand over hand, pounding the chassis to find brake pressure with one foot and pumping up revs with the other, crashing into second and then first, looking for a little anchorage from an engine with its tachometer punching redline and blasts and backfires exploding from its exhaust pipes.

The Chevy itself was blissfully calm. And it elevated me into a state of sweaty tranquillity. The machine, the pavement (though I wished there were more of it), and I became one, serene and focused. I was keenly aware of, yet indifferent to, the woes of the material world, some of which were coming straight at me overloaded with hay bales.

I got us to Point Arena in perfect unity of being and nothingness, also in one piece. The Fangio Chevy emptied my mind like no Zen you ever heard of. Of course it would have emptied my wallet too, if I'd put it in a ditch.

I have discovered the middle-aged, overfed, comfortably off car nut's road to inner peace. (And it has nothing to do with India.) The secret is driving vintage automobiles too fast. The path—the Tao, if you will—is the California Mille, a four-day, thousand-mile, all-out classic car run across the valleys, over the mountains, and along the coastlines on the most spectacular back roads in northern California. No dumpy ashrams are visited. No tedious meditation is practiced. No pointless kabbalah babble is heard. (Although there's plenty of praying: "Lord, don't let me go over the cliff!")

The California Mille was established in 1990 by San Francisco auto enthusiast Martin Swig. It commemorates the Mille Miglia, raced from 1927 to 1957 through the middle of Italy at astonishing speeds in equally astonishing Italian traffic: Brescia-Rome-Brescia. To qualify for the California version, a car must have been eligible to compete in the original. Swig and his friends decided to found their Mille, as Martin put it, "Before some jerks got the idea first." In other words, Martin wanted an event in which ex-president Clinton could not enter his Mustang.

The California Mille starting line is Nob Hill, with the drivers flagged away from the forecourt of the splendid Fairmont Hotel. Did I mention that I also discovered truth, wisdom, and beauty for the middle-aged car nut at the California Mille? Especially beauty. We fellows in our most expansive years of life ("Honey, the cleaner shrank these khakis.") don't get much credit for artistic sensitivity. We fall asleep during the ballet. At gallery openings we head for the bar to make friends with José and see if he's got anything better than lukewarm white wine. But gaze upon the starters' grid at the Mille and see the finely honed aesthetics of curmudgeonly men.

Looks like a million dollars, and we're talking certified checks. There were the ten Ferraris, a prancing horse Augean stable of them (but sparkling clean)—lustrous Barchetta, radiant Berlinetta, resplendent 375MM Spyder driven to victory at the Nürburgring by Alberto Ascari. Of Jaguars, a whole cathouse was on hand—SS100, XK120s, a C-Type, and the XKSS progenitor of the E that sits in the permanent collection of New York's Museum of Modern Art. AC Ace Bristols appeared, the most graceful sports car of the 1950s with bodywork later to be borrowed by the Shelby Cobra. Mercedes 300SLs worked their sturdy Teutonic charms, especially that Lorelei of price, the Gullwing Coupe, which has lured many a man into Chapter 11. Porsche 356s and Speedsters hunkered, pretty as poison gumdrops. And Porsche Spyders too. If looks could kill . . . And with James Dean they did. There was an Aston Martin DBR2 showing compound curves beyond the dreams of Frank Gehry and a gill-slitted Maserati 200SI that could star in *Jaws IV* if anyone were idiot enough to put it in the water. Plus dozens of other ravishing cars, seventy-two all told, an orgy of vehicular pulchritude including a *La Dolce Vita* of Alfa Romeos with their labially suggestive grilles culminating in a Zagato 1900 double-bubble-silhouette coupe. God bless you, Anita Ekberg.

Why the appeal of *old* cars? Aren't there beautiful new cars to be driven? Perhaps. But modern automobiles are filled with electronic weasel works and the mice mazes of computerhood. We old guys can't understand them. And when it comes to contemporary beauties that we can't understand, we have our second wives.

Fabulous wives, I may say, many of them along as codrivers and one, Esta Swig, in her own Alfa Tipo IV.

Then came truth. Moment of same, to be precise: when I had to drive one of these things. My worst experience with the Fangio Chevy was in downtown San Francisco, getting it up the barely cable-car-climbable California Street from the Fairmont's garage to the starting line. The friction point on the clutch pedal is so far out from the floorboards that my left knee was waving in the air like a Balinese dancer's. There's no hand brake. The engine runs grumpy when cold and gas has to be kept on, but to heel-toe between the brake pedal and the accelerator would require the shoe size of a Yeti. I stalled in traffic. The Chevy has a floor-mounted starter button. I now needed not one but two more feet than I was born with. And when I did get restarted, frying clutch smoke billowed behind me.

The green flag dropped. I was off into the whimsical motoring of San Francisco's eccentric population. The Chevy is right-hand drive, per the rules of the road in prewar Argentina. It came equipped with two playing card–sized mirrors clipped on the windshield pillars, but I had broken one off already by opening the driver-side door wide enough to get my duck-shaped self into the little canvas rally seat. (Oh gosh, was that the very mirror that Fangio looked into and saw . . . Yow! Taillights! I'm in the wrong lane!) The shift lever, on my extra-clumsy left side, is goal post–length with first down distances between gears. A change into second put my fist into the passenger's lap for an untoward intimacy with Fred Schroeder. Going to third I bashed the instruments, which, except for the tach, were wonky anyhow because of a last-minute conversion from a six-volt to a twelve-volt battery. Fourth and I whacked myself in the . . . *blippity-blip* went the turn signal. It's not self-canceling and thus had been indicating, for blocks, that, besides being in the wrong lane, I intended to plow into a row of parked cars.

And so forth in a swivet across the Golden Gate, through Marin County, and into the Sonoma Valley where, finally, there were gridlock-free curves and bends. I began to feel a little confidence in my hulking ride. It overtowered the lithe elegance of fellow competitors, outsized even a 1928 4.5-liter LeMans Bentley and a massive 1955 Chrysler C 300. But the Chevy had qualities to equal its heft. It tracked like a train through the esses and with nothing Amtraky about the ride.

We went over to the Napa Valley and up, being passed by Ferraris and their ilk to be sure, but I was getting faster. In the tight turns near Clear Lake I found I could keep pace with Miles Collier who was driving a Cunningham C-1, the prototype of Briggs Cunningham's brilliant sports/racers of the 1950s, the only C-1 in existence. Then I noticed that Mr. Collier and his wife were wearing Panama hats that stuck, without fluttering, above the brim of their windshield. They were not, maybe, really pushing the C-1. "I think we're going about thirty-five," said Fred Schroeder.

I made my first pass not quite on a blind curve but on a very nearsighted one. There was power enough to spare from the Chevy's Blue Flame Six, but the effortless business of driving that we daydream our way through in a new car was effort-intensive in 1939. Even the gas pedal required an emphatic shove. It made me appreciate the esteem in which a good wheelman was held by 1930s gangsters—not to be compared to the Crip or Blood finger-steering a Lexus in a drive-by shooting today.

On the arcs and crescents east into the Sacramento Valley I hooked in behind Max Hobson in his 1931 Chrysler

LeMans roadster. This, on its vermicelli-narrow tires, is even more of a handful than a '39 Chevrolet. I couldn't keep up. But it wasn't really my fault. My aged cohort isn't slowing its pace going down the road, or going to the bathroom either. There's a distinctive rhythm to midlife male high-speed driving—fifty-five minutes of to-hell-with-the-brake-lights and five minutes in the weeds beside the highway. At the drivers' meeting before the Mille, Martin Swig suggested a signal for us to give to other participants if we stopped because we needed a urologist rather than a mechanic.

The route looped west into the mountains on roads as grueling as going to work for a living. Being temporary chief executive of the Fangio Chevy, I had panicky decisions to make at each crossroad, disastrous wrong turns lurking on every side, crookedness coming at me seemingly from all directions, peaks and dips of NASDAQ dimensions to survive, deadlines to meet. (What's the line through that curve? Don't get dead.) I was actually living in the metaphors used for business life. And I was feeling the fear businessmen my age actually feel about the absurd trust that the world puts in us. We trade the stocks and bonds on Wall Street, run the Federal Reserve, control the IMF.*

And my situation was even worse. My pal David E. Davis Jr., dean of American automotive journalism, had loaned me this car. He was friends with Juan Fangio. Fangio, when he was dying, in 1995, asked the trustees of the Centro Cultural y Tecnológico Museo del Automovilismo "Juan Manuel Fangio" to give the Chevy to Davis. When David E. went to Argentina to accept the gift, Toto himself drove the

*I wrote this in 2001 when, due to the dot.com crash, the financial situation was bad enough. But what would things be like when we old guys began to really lose it and get Alzheimer's in, oh, say, around 2008?

car right into the museum's lobby. David E. has spent a bazillion restoring it. And now David, who was somewhere behind me in a magnificent Mark IX Jaguar, would see his dream dashed to pieces—no figure of speech—at the bottom of a canyon. But we graying fifty-somethings get up and go into the office anyway and manage the bazillion-dollar portfolios whether we're frightened or not. Or, in this case, we clamber back behind the wheel after a quick break. (Thumbs up for a call of nature!) And we hardly ever let on that risking other people's money is nine-tenths of the fun.

Fred took over when we returned to I-5 in the valley. And we had a problem. We could not go seventy-five. At seventy-four and a half miles per hour a violent shudder set in. Something to do with worn rear shocks and spring harmonics, we said to each other with the usual car nut capacity, when talking car talk, to blow more smoke than's been inhaled. Anyway, steering wasn't affected and the Chevy stayed straight. But we were dice in a backgammon cup. There was only one thing to do—go a hundred. The shudder vanished. Truckers, low-riders, and dads ferrying Cub Scout–pack minivans gave us the full bladder signal as we passed everything in sight.

At Red Bluff we turned east into the Cascade Range on logging roads picketed by stands of enormous pines. Navigation, hitherto handled with aplomb by Fred, fell to pieces under me among the big trees. "Turn right at the big tree!" I shouted. "The other big tree! Not that big tree! This big tree! Look out! You're headed right for . . . a big tree!"

"Maybe you'd better drive," said Fred. He relinquished the controls just in time for the long northwest run up the Hat Creek Valley where there were enough twists in the road to keep me from going a hundred, and pride (and vibration) wouldn't let me dip below eighty. We arrived at the Best

Western in the town of Mount Shasta . . . "Shaken, not stirred," Fred told the bartender. We had driven 446 miles on the first day. Most of the aging machinery had survived and all of the aging drivers. A banquet was spread. The wisdom of hoary gearheads was exchanged. And don't think that we lack it. Juan Fangio made a toast in 1986 to a sport "based on permanent values of manliness, bravery, mobility, and honesty." Who but a veteran car nut would think to include the cardinal virtue *mobility* in his list of ideals? Although most of the wisdom I heard that night in Mount Shasta was along other lines. "Always," said the sage next to me, "walk a mile in another man's shoes. You're a mile away, and you've got his shoes."

Deeply dined, with healths thoroughly pledged, we took our cognacs and cigars into the parking lot to survey our aristocracy of transport. Is a little snobbery incompatible with inner peace plus beauty, truth, and wisdom? I was walking with Camilo Steuer, who had flown from Bogotá to drive his 1955 Alfa Spider Veloce in the Mille. "These are cars," said Camilo, "of the soul, not of gold chains."

No offense to the memory of Dale Earnhardt but motorsports could use some class. It is the traditional responsibility of the gentry to do the dangerous, foolish things in life. Wars became vulgar when just any old person was drafted to fight them. Not that the California Mille is really dangerous or that I'm a member of the upper class. But there's such a thing as a natural gentleman. Fangio was a humble mechanic from the potato-growing town of Balcarce. And if danger and folly are the provenance of oligarchy, then my incompetence with the Fangio Chevy made me at least a duke.

A duke with, the next morning, an ignominious speeding ticket, a mere sixty in a forty-five zone. This in a town with the humiliating name of Weed, where I was written up by a young twerp of a highway patrolman who was oblivious to the car's regal bearing, uninterested in its noble pedigree, and not impressed by the lordly note of the Chevy's engine. "You're pretty loud too," said the twerp.

This was the only unexalted moment of the remaining three days. But now that I've found truth, wisdom, and all that stuff I realize how egocentric and unevolved it is to dwell on my own bliss. So I'll stop right here with the recitation of the delights I experienced in the California Mille. I'll say nothing about the ecstatic thrills of the two-thousand-foot climb to Gazelle Summit on the wiggles, steeps, and skinnys of escarpment roads where the Weed speed limit seemed like space launch velocity—and a launch into space was available at every hairpin. I won't report that there's Elysian scenery in the remote Scott Valley running north through Xanadu gorges to the wondrous Klamath River, which I won't even mention despite the fact that it's a fly fisherman's paradise though somewhat cluttered with whitewater rafting bozos, but they might be amusing to catch and release too.

I kept making Fred drive and Fred kept making me drive because neither of us could chase nimble Porsches while steering a ton and a half of Chevy and, at the same time, drink in the glories of nature (and the Seiad Valley Volunteer Fire Department's excellent cup of coffee). And neither of us could decide whether driving or gawking was the most fun. But I won't speak of that. In fact, just to name the geological features of Route 299 to Humboldt Bay would be to flaunt the good time I was having (and on expense account, at that)—Nixon Ridge, Lord Ellis Summit, Tip Top Ridge.

I want the reader to be as happy as I am. And it would

only make you feel bad that you weren't there if I said we stayed at the luxurious Eureka Inn or that the Fendale loop out to California's Lost Coast is so sublime it must be kept a state secret from everyone who owns an RV or that, at the Little River Inn south of Mendocino, proprietor Mel McKinney has the best cigars this side of the Hotel Nacional in Havana. Likewise I'll avoid any reference to Humboldt Redwood State Park and its stately Avenue of the Giants. (Nice but, personally, I think, too many trees.) I won't tell you that we traveled an additional three hundred–odd euphoric miles beyond Humboldt in a heaven-to-heaven zigzag between mountains and sea until we arrived in jubilation at the groaning boards in the pleasure gardens of Napa Valley's Far Niente restaurant. And I'm certainly not going to brag about how I got better at driving the Fangio Chevy.

I got much better. I almost got good. I apprehended that the Chevy, despite an undercarriage as clunky as a trolley's and a suspension design dating to the days when a table model radio was bigger than a NASA mainframe computer, was perfect in its handling. The back end didn't push. The front end didn't pull. The faster I'd go the better I went. Bad brakes? So what. If I couldn't stop when I ran out of road, well, who wanted to stop?

My joy increased with every hour until I attained satori on the Point Arena road. Never mind that the car is stronger than I am and has more guts. So much so that I would have been hard put to screw things up. The point is, I'm enlightened. I finally understand the message that all the great teachers, saints, and visionaries have been trying to convey to man, particularly to middle-aged car nut man: "Buy an Alfa Romeo 8C 2900A [first, second, and third place in the 1936 Mille Miglia] and let the wife and kids go on welfare."

15

Call for a New National Park

I recently returned from vehicular purgatory, or, as it's called locally, Hong Kong. Here sad transgressors very like ourselves, who've committed the sin of lust for fast cars, suffer the penance of having nowhere to go fast.

Hong Kong is a great place to make money. And the first thing a person of our kind does with money is buy something such as a Maserati Quattroporte. My Hong Kong pal Dave is our kind of person, and he's been making money. He picked me up at Chek Lap Kok airport in a Maserati Quattroporte. The travails of purgatory—says Dante's long, boring poem of the same name—produce a patient, humble soul resigned to divine will. I guess Dave hasn't been in Hong Kong with fast cars long enough, although it's been more than twenty years, and he once owned the only 1965 Mustang in the colony and it had the 289 four-barrel and the four-speed stick. Alas, Dave didn't seem any closer to the pearly gates now than he had in the pony car. He shouted, "Capitalized-top-line-of-the-keyboard it! We're on an eight-lane expressway! And look at the speed limit! Ninety kpm!"

Since we were, at that moment, going zero kpm, I didn't quite see his point. Hong Kong has the universally familiar squeezed-tight expressway congestion, negotiated at the speed of a toothpaste tube's last dollop emerging.

In fairness to Dave, though, once you're off the expressways Hong Kong's congestion is familiar with an exponent of seven million. That's the number of people in Hong Kong, all crossing the street in front of us.

The New Territories are crowded. Kowloon is crowded to the point of making Times Square on New Year's Eve a haven for agoraphobics, and Central on Hong Kong Island is worse. Hong Kong Island is also so hilly that it renders San Francisco a comparative Kansas. The hills produced an extra Tantalus torture in the dragon-squiggle curves and surf-spritzed hairpin turns around Repulse Bay. Every centimeter of this splendid driving turf was clogged with motor vehicles, among them not a few AMG Mercs, Turbo Porsches, Aston Martins, and Ferraris. All were moving at the same clip as Iraqi government reform, and they were packed so close together that they almost touched. *Crunch*. And sometimes did.

"There's one stretch of road," said Dave, "about three kilometers long, way up by the Chinese border, where there aren't any traffic cameras."

The situation gave Dave heartburn. It gave me an idea. We're facing an only slightly less severe version of Hong Kong car constipation here in the United States. We need relief. And since we, unlike Hong Kong, are a democracy, we can demand government action. Plus we've got a new president who's promising everybody everything. Come on, Obama, give us car nuts *our* bailout.

What I propose is a linear national park. We need a road, or network of roads, where we can drive the way we'll be allowed to drive in heaven after we succumb to apoplexy caused by being stuck for six hours on I-95 when a Prius full of vegans swerves in front of a livestock truck and an oil tanker, causing America's least wanted barbecue to be hosted at the off-ramp to the Washington beltway.

The government should set aside and preserve a number of our nation's "blue highways" such as those that Fred Schroeder and I traveled on the California Mille. The chosen roads would be the less used and most skill demanding—not to say death defying. Upon these designated rights-of-way all the usual traffic laws would apply except there would be *no* speed limits. The grizzly gawkers, hiking trail sloggers, trout pesterers, and such all have their federally mandated paradises. Now we'd have ours. We'd be late-apexing, heel-toeing, and power-sliding at the right hand of God. (Actually, at His left hand, unless we're driving a Brit classic.)

Mr. President, a highway preserve would benefit our nation in so many ways. It would be a public works program, giving America's economy much-needed stimulus and keeping your poll numbers sky high. Don't forget, you've got those dreaded midterm congressional elections coming up next year. We lead-feet vote. Or we would if we could get through traffic and find a parking spot.

Mr. President, conserving traffic wildlife would be not only a source of jobs and a source of spiritual uplift, it would also be a dynamic new health care program—*mental* health care. Because if I don't get to drive like crazy soon I'll go insane, increasing the nation's Medicare costs.

Mr. President, before you protest that in these safety-smitten days such a speed-happy legislative package is as likely as a Jeb Bush victory in the 2012 presidential election, hear me out. I want the nation's first R-rated road to go through the South Side of your hometown. The Cannonball Baker Motorsport National Park (or—naming rights will be available—call it Tony Rezko Trail if you want) is intended to be a major antipoverty initiative. It should start somewhere midst the unemployable swamp Yankees of inland Maine or upstate New York; dash to the sooty and caved-in-upon denizens of central Pennsylvania's coal towns; sweep west into the benighted rust belt with a pit stop in the pit that is Detroit; roar to Chicago to do a half dozen laps on a new state-financed speedway around the Reverend Wright's old church; come back via the bare ruined choirs where late Ohio's factories were; head down through Appalachia, home to seventy-five years of poverty programs, which have begotten, you guessed it, poverty; make a long loop traversing the ghettos of Washington, Baltimore, Philadelphia, Newark, and New York while moving (it is to be hoped) faster than a speeding bullet (or bullet train); return south to pause for fuel, tires, and sundry repairs in the vicinity of Senator John Edwards's privations and disadvantaged home life; push west again, bringing to the hookworm and pellagra belt the deliverance—as it were—of tourist dollars; experience some off-roading more extreme than the Baja's off the debris-clogged roads of New Orleans and into its hair-raising abandoned neighborhoods; then make the toothless mouths of the Ozark natives gape; blast onward to carry some population into the rapidly depopulating Great Plains states; and hasten at last to Nevada, Arizona, and California for time trials on the S-bends of subdivision streets where park fees will save the faux-Tara porch columns, lawyer foyers, three-barge garages, media rooms, and granite-topped kitchen counters with their granite-headed mortgage holders from the subprime meltdown crisis.

This national park will be a paying concern. We car buffs are willing to spend goodly sums to purchase our liberty. And America's troubled carmakers and all the businesses dependent upon them will vie for sponsorships. The insurance companies may balk at first, until they realize that a thousand enthusiasts going 180 mph is safer than one working mom going thirty miles per hour while text messaging.

We'll make the park roads into limited-access routes wherever possible. Where access can't be limited we'll treat park roads the way grade-level railroad crossings have been treated for a hundred years. We'll install warning lights and bells and crossing gates. Accidents will—as they still do at railroad crossings—happen. Think of the job creation for your trial lawyer buddies from Harvard. We park users accept the risk. As for the "innocent victims," consider the usual stories of people being hit by trains. These incidents tend to be Darwinian—or, to put it in liberal political terms, "pro-choice."

When our national park is established, no doubt the usual busybodies will get busy. We'll have to wear helmets and Nomex, and five-point harnesses, and I suppose child and infant seats are out of the question, at least if they're occupied. Probably we'll be required to take some Skip Barber–type course and pass a test and get a medical exam and go for a check ride—the rigmarole with which pilots are familiar.

Still all that is no buzz kill compared to our current situation. When are carmakers going to quit with the cup holders and start installing urinals? Otherwise we men over fifty are never going to be able to drive anywhere in our cities or suburbs.

Even in rural New Hampshire, where I live, the problem is dire. We don't have too many cars on the road but we have too many with lights on their roofs. I blame it on 9/11. After the World Trade Center attack Patriot Act largesse was showered on small town police departments. New Hampshire's small towns used the money for extra traffic patrols in case Osama bin Laden has one taillight out. Last December some shavetail local copper, about the age of my average tape cassette, gave my wife a speeding ticket *on Christmas morning*. This on a clear, dry, deserted country road absurdly posted at a Hong Kongish forty miles per hour. And my wife was driving us to Mass, for Christ's sake (in this case literally).

President Obama, tear down this shameful legacy of the Bush regime. And, fellow car nuts, call or e-mail the White House and demand that America's new inclusive politics include us. Otherwise we'll have to move to Hong Kong. Financial meltdown or no financial meltdown, Hong Kong is still a great place to make money. If we're going to be stalled in traffic in our Maserati Quattroportes, let's at least *have* Maserati Quattroportes.

16

A Ride to the Funny Farm in a Special Needs Station Wagon Complete with Booby Hatch

Or, for an old-fashioned family vacation, let me recommend piling three kids into a Ford Flex station wagon in LA and, forgetting about Disneyland, go instead across the Mojave. Eschew Circus Circus in Las Vegas in favor of the wildlife refuge of the Sheep Range mountains. View spectacular scenery in Utah's Zion and Arches National Parks while avoiding every "Genuine Wild West Ghost Town," Native American tchotchke shop, water park, and other locale of childish interest. Traverse the Rockies continually explaining to the kids—from Grand Junction to Denver—the marvels of North America's geology. Then stay in a hotel without a pool.

It's just what you're looking for, if what you're looking for is a Prozac ℞. But that's as it should be. The ultimate test of a car model is psychiatric. We all know this—we who had as our first love a salmon pink four-door sedan, an MGA, or an old Alfa that would rust if its beauty provoked a moist glance.

I wanted the Flex to produce sessions on the Freudian adjustable seatback of psy*car*logical analysis for potential car buyers such as my wife and myself. Gosh, what subconscious horrors were summoned during this therapy. Mrs. O and I worked through our anger at parents who wouldn't stop at a "Genuine Wild West Ghost Town," our guilt about making Dad halt every twenty minutes because "I have to go," our mixed feelings about our siblings (a mixture between loathing and detestation). "She's touching me!" Some memories weren't even repressed. We'd gotten no farther than Rancho Cucamonga before I was shouting—in a perfect echo from the front seat of fifty years ago—"Don't make me pull over and come back there!"

The Ford Flex itself may need mental health attention. It isn't making much sense. It's babbling as a product. For one thing Ford already has plenty of Sport Futility Vehicles, cross-dressing SUVs, and minivans in false mustaches, many of them needing immediate sedation. Then there's the Flex's modernist functionalism, lacking in only one aspect of the utilitarian: utility. Seems like you could go off road with it. And you can, on your lawn. It has 5.9 inches of ground clearance (versus a Jeep Wrangler's maximum of 10.2). Or, with the Flex's slabby sides, maybe it could double as a handyman's special. Except the biggest sheet of plywood that will lie flat inside is three feet, four inches by a little short of seven feet. What is that? The European Union's new mandatory plywood dimension? The maximum cubic feet of cargo space in the Flex, with all seats that will fold folded, is only

60 percent of a Chevy Suburban's. This is a lot of stowage subtraction for a vehicle that's just 10 percent shorter than the Bowtie behemoth. And if what you really wanted was a minivan but you lacked the humility to buy one, get a Toyota Sienna and a Glock, and see if any NASCAR dads talk smack to you. But it takes more than the foregoing to create a truly conflicted automobile. You have to add in my family's immediate and unconditional love for the Flex. Whatever crazy thing Ford is doing, we are enablers.

My wife is an aficionado of classic modern design. She dislikes the rubbery anonymity that coefficients of drag impose on contemporary bodywork and dislikes more the blob-job add-ons of bulgy bumpers and wheel-well flares. And she really hates the "commuting is a battlefield" buncombe of Hummers, Dodge Nitros, and Jeep Commanders. She adores the Flex. "Clean lines," said Mrs. O, "great proportions, and the contrasting roof color keeps the whole thing from taking itself too seriously."

"This car's great!" said ten-year-old Muffin. "It's making everybody look at us—like we're celebrities!" (Muffin, I'm afraid, is fated for a career in the performing arts.)

"Real big truck!" said Buster, our four-year-old. Buster's a sucker for anything on wheels, but he's a quantitative fanboy. More is better. He's asked me several times if we could get a semi-tractor-trailer for our family car. "Real big truck" is his highest accolade.

And Poppet, our eight-year-old, broke into tears. She does that a lot. In this case she grew emotional over the Flex's seating bounty. Seeing the space assigned to her in one half of the split-seat third row, she wailed, "I could have brought Joker!" (Poppet has an inappropriate object of affection in the form of a plush toy cheetah that is full scale and horribly accurately detailed. More than once Dad has had a couple of drinks and Joker has slipped his mind and he's tiptoed in to give Poppet a beddy-bye peck when the night-light was illuminating Joker just so and a nasty shock ensued.)

I agreed with everyone about the Flex, except Poppet since we would have had to buy another plane seat to get Joker to the West Coast. The Flex's styling is excellent. Like a lot of modern design—e.g., the lava lamp—it's better when you're there and in the spirit of the thing than it is in photos. I'm particularly fond of the strakes—or perhaps, more properly, the corrugations—along the sides of the car. I imagine these stiffen the flat body panels. But "form follows function" is good styling advice even for functions that are imaginary.

And Muffin was right. It's pleasant to have folks admire your ride. The more so in the case of the Flex, which attracted sensible-type admirers who didn't have too many tattoos and were probably employed.

But I agreed most of all with what Buster said, or was trying to say. The Flex harks back to motor vehicles of a simple and straightforward nature. And it does so, per Buster, not just for us over-fifties.

Without using any homesick retro-styling cues, the Flex puts us in mind of Chevy's original Suburban, the post–World War II Jeep Station Sedan, a woody from back when there were weight and structure reasons for the wood, and, more than anything else, the International Harvester Travelall. The Travelall was a mode of transport so simple and straightforward that it shocked the tail-finned natives. "Yow, a car you buy at the tractor dealership!"

In other words, the Flex is a station wagon, but a station wagon that lacks the lame-o factor that infected station wagons in the 1950s and reduced them to objects of pity by the time of the Chevy Chase *Vacation* movies. After that the public humiliation spread to minivans. Instead, the Flex has that *useful* look. (As with the swell old machines that the Flex evokes, "Useful for what?" remains a valid question.)

There's a large touch-screen computer consol in the middle of the Flex's dash. This will do anything from providing map directions to filing your federal income taxes. Or so we think. Our Flex came with lots of extras but no manual. The manual hadn't been published yet. As a writer I can understand how it takes time to craft that special style of car-manual prose and then send it to Mumbai and have it translated into Hindi by one class of sixth graders and translated back into English by another. But this meant that the extras on our Flex were mostly extra confusing. Figuring out trip mileage required more time at the computer than an average college freshman puts in on her Facebook page during an entire school year.

When you shift into reverse the computer turns into a TV with a minicam in the tailgate at the perfect level to play chicken with your spouse's knees while he's marshaling the luggage. (Note to wife: Am I overinsured?) The camera is also useful for parallel parking, to the extent that anyone attempts to parallel park things the size of a Flex. I know I can't do it. I always wind up with the left front fender blocking a lane of traffic and the right rear bumper in a sidewalk café's chair ordering a mocha latte.

Anyway, a careful driver never backs into what's behind him. He sideswipes what's next to him, such as the fire hydrant he forgot about because he was busy carefully backing up.

The Flex will be criticized by Al Gore and that ilk as being too big. But that ilk's kids are grown, allowing the ilk to squeeze into weenie hybrids. (Will Al Gore fit?) We, on the other hand, have to take our three offspring with us plus, more often than not, our three dogs. In point of fact the Flex is too small. Thanks to the third-row split we could fit in a week's worth of shorts, T-shirts, and flip-flops. But it was a game of inches. The nicely wide and unobstructed floor pan behind the Flex's last row of seats needs to be deeper, to let two average-sized roller bags lie down. That way we could have eaten in restaurants other than the kind with signs saying, "No Shirt, No Shoes, No Sweat—Drinks ½ Price for Shirtless Ladies."

The Flex was handy in traffic, nimble on the highway, and immune to crosswind effects despite having the shape of the box it came in. The braking was adequate for the kind of driving that's done with your complete chromosomal heritage to civilization in the back. However, the above assessments should be understood as relative. We are a truck/tractor/wheels-with-locking-hubs family, inured to the shortcomings of lumpy machinery. We have not one but two Chevrolet Suburbans (and a close personal relationship with the Saudi royal family). My daily driver is a beat-down 1999 model with an odometer that looks like an Obama campaign online fund-raising figure. If I wanted to make any sudden stops in this I'd have to get a boat anchor, weld its chain to the frame, and throw the anchor out the window every time I hit the brakes.

My wife adored the desert. "Clean lines," she said, "great proportions, and the contrasting sky color keeps the whole thing from taking itself too seriously." The kids felt otherwise. Children hate scenery. It just sits there. Scenery doesn't make goofy faces or funny noises or have any candy or pay attention to children at all. Scenery doesn't even cry when you hog the backseat. Say to your kids, "Oh, look, there's ______! Gosh, that's so______!" And they'll fill in the blanks:

dumb old stones	stupid
loser cows	bogus
a boring sunset	whatever

Probably their little minds would have popped from tedium except their little minds had been popped already by Muffin's iPod, Poppet's DVD player, and Buster's Leapster. They sat out a good deal of the week's car riding in a (relatively) quiet daze of personal electronics. This left Mrs. O to appreciate the landscape, me to enjoy the Flex, and both of us to ponder the question, "Why bother to take kids anyplace?"

The reason for taking kids places is to give them new things to whine about when they get there. Such as who gets to sleep on the cool fold-out couch in the motel room, and why do we actually have to go see Zion National Park instead of staying in its gift shop and ice cream parlor?

Zion Canyon is, by the way, a brilliant destination for the child-encumbered. It's off I-15, half an "I need a bathroom" from the Arizona border in lower left Utah. The Park Service has devised a system that both forces kids out of the car and yet keeps parents from having to hike with the crabby little devils. Closely spaced shuttle buses run up and back the canyon road making frequent stops. You can get out and take a leisurely look around or trek deep into the wilderness and die of thirst and hunger. Then you can catch the next shuttle bus ten minutes later.

The scenery (think Ansel Adams + Georgia O'Keeffe + Grateful Dead concert drugs) was so good that even Muffin and Poppet had to admit it was almost as interesting to look at as *High School Musical*. Buster enjoyed arguing about the park ranger. "Wear your hat," I said to Buster, who turns into a boiled shrimp at the touch of a sunbeam. "See," I said, pointing to a park ranger's Smokey the Bear headgear, "rangers where *their* hats."

"No they don't!" said Buster. "They wear masks in different colors and go 'EEE-AHHHHH!'"

The Park Service officer sighed and said, "That's the second time today I've been confused with a Power Ranger."

We took the leisurely look around rather than the thirst-and-hunger option. We watched two rock climbers scaling thousands of feet of cliff face and were told that it would take them two days to reach the top. They'd have to tie their sleeping bags to pitons and sleep like dead flies hanging in a cobweb. The children agreed that there are, after all, worse ways to travel than by car with your family.

We saw many kinds of birds, which Dad pretended to be able to name. "That's a Fannie Mae, kids, watch it plummet to earth. Its mate is called a Freddie Mac." At the end of the canyon road I insisted that we take at least a little bit of a real hike. We headed up a flat, easy trail along the Virgin River for almost forty feet before our three New England–bred children simultaneously discovered cactus. Go west, young man. And bring tweezers.

After Zion we continued up I-15 then east on I-70 to Arches Park near the Colorado border. The Flex's fuel economy wasn't bad—22.3 mpg by my calculation. But keeping a gas log while making sure three children don't get run over in the service station and/or shoplift ten pounds of Skittles from the minimart is more art than science so someone should check my math.

Roads were dry, traffic was light, I cranked it up. Over seventy-five mph I felt the Flex was hunting a bit, quartering back and forth in its lane, though only slightly. I blamed the tires, then front-wheel offset, cast, and camber, but really the problem is a small zone of lazy slob steering when you're pointed straight forward and want the car to track with a minimum of senior management input.

The only other gripe of note is that the Flex's driver-seat headrest is as comfortable as a pillowcase stuffed with cans of tuna fish. I gather this is the result of a DOT friends-of-the-lawyers whiplash hysteria and is probably required by the federal Equal Rights to Uncomfortability bill. It didn't bother me much, with my Neanderthal posture, but Mrs. O sits up straight like she's driving with a copy of Emily Post's *Etiquette* on her head. By the time we reached Denver she would have attacked the headrest with the Flex's tire iron—if we'd had a car manual and were able to find that item of equipment.

There's also the matter of the Flex's dopey name. I think back to the station wagons of my boyhood. They were called things like Explorer, Nomad, Country Squire, Voyager, and Sierra. Flex is a name for a brand of pedal-operated kitchen garbage can or a mutt from the pound who's adept at opening it. The Studebaker Conestoga had a better moniker.

Arches National Park is even more kid-compliant than Zion. You can drive right through the amazing display of nature with you and your youngsters never leaving the car. I just turned around and yelled at them every so often, "Darn it, would you at least say 'wow' or something?"

We did stop and climb up to sit in the opening under one of the natural stone spans that give the park its name.

This was okay with the kids because it looked like they were in a scene from *The Lion King*. Nearby was Balanced Rock, which is exactly as it is said to be and big as a hedge fund manager's foreclosed house. Balanced Rock was a reminder that real life is no Chevy Chase movie, never mind how well station-wagoned you are. Chevy would have triggered an Unbalanced Rock and crushed half a dozen RVs. Much to my children's' disappointment, I lack Chevy's talent.

We finally gave in to popular demand and stopped at a roadside "gem store" outside Moab. The children were wildly excited to buy pieces of authentic fossilized dinosaur bone. I'll give another $60 to anyone who can tell these from road gravel.

We ascended into the Rockies, where a fundamental difference between boys and girls was exhibited. Only Buster was interested in my information that if you stand right on the continental divide and take a leak, half winds up in the Pacific Ocean and the other half in the Atlantic.

The Flex comes with a transmission feature called "Overdrive Cancel with Grade Assist," which provides engine braking going downhill and keeps you in a lower gear going up. This is a great advantage when driving through the mountains. Or I suppose it is. Lacking the manual we couldn't locate the button for it.

For the same reason we couldn't get the touch-screen computer climate control figured out. The best we were able to do was make each section of the car the temperature that its occupant didn't want. The consequent grousing caused Mrs. O and I to almost wish for the sweltering pre-A/C days with all of a station wagon's windows open and wind noise drowning out the family complaints.

Not really. The Flex is a huge improvement on station wagons of yore. There's no rear-facing "barf bench." And there's no roll-down glass in the tailgate. In those days of aerodynamic innocence we didn't realize that the rear window was an exhaust gas intake port with potential for making third-row passengers deceased as well as nauseated. Speaking of nausea, our kids didn't speak of it. Or not often, anyway, despite hours of heads-down engagement with digital doodads. In thirteen hundred miles we had no chucks that fully upped. I credit this to the Flex's good ventilation, its low belt line that keeps the horizon in view, and a suspension soft enough to prevent tummies from being shaken like warm Coke bottles but too firm to give children the old crossing-the-English-Channel coil spring experience.

And yet, good as the Flex is, the argument in favor of a minivan arose again, as it had ten years before when Muffin's birth sent us looking for our first family car. Mrs. O and I rediscussed our mutual aversion to the worthy, practical, good-looking minivan. Back in the '90s we'd thought that a minivan was too sensible for us. Now we realized that a minivan was too virtuous for us. Minivans have the virtue of space efficiency. This means you can pack in a lot of kids, so you're asked to pack in a lot of kids. You're at the mercy of every soccer team, school field trip, and church picnic. I was once a young man living in New York and I was the only person my friends knew who had a pickup truck. Every weekend was devoted to moving someone into a new apartment. Owning a minivan is like that. And what makes having all those kids packed in so nerve shattering is that the minivan's generous passenger compartment allows the kids to socialize. They run around loudly enjoying themselves, causing the distracted minivan driver to back into the soccer field goal posts whether the minivan has a rear view camera or not.

The Flex may be able to carry as many kids as most minivans but it doesn't advertise the fact. And once the kids are in the Flex their range of interaction is limited. Minivans are Montessori schools. Station wagons are Holy Cross K-through-8. Stay in your seats. Keep your hands to yourself. I've got a nun.

Poppet cried again when we left the Flex at the Denver airport. Reluctantly climbing out of her third-row nest she sniffled, "I love this car so much—as much as my whole family."

Ford is welcome to use this quote for promotional purposes. But keep in mind that Poppet had just spent a week traveling through the middle of nowhere with her brother, sister, mom, and dad. By this point she probably would have said that she loved broccoli "as much as my whole family."

17

Big Love

The last time gas prices were going through the roof, or maybe it was the time before last . . . it's hard to keep the cycles of petroleum-cost rafter-bashing and basement-busting straight. At the moment they're giving away a free fill-up with the purchase of any bank or financial institution. But tomorrow the bill for a gallon of regular may require a restructuring of the international debt market. Don't you dare, however, tell your congressman that you want stable gas prices. If a politician gets to decide what gasoline costs, you know where he's going to stick that price, anatomically speaking.

As I was saying, the last time gas prices were going through the roof, the London *Sunday Times* called me and said they were devoting their automotive section to . . . you got it in one, denouncing cars. Specifically the *Times* was vilifying large SUVs. Would I care to be the piñata at the party and write something in favor of nonsustainable, resource-sucking, planet-boiling, road-hogging murder wagons?

The whole world is angry at America for driving SUVs. Why do we Americans love these monstrous and threatening devices? Barging through traffic in a sport utility vehicle is hardly sporting. The utility of the things is open to question. And they are vehicles mainly in the sense that the Alaska pipeline is a vehicle for oil—most of this pipeline's capacity being needed to keep one Cadillac Escalade topped up.

It has to do with sex. We Americans are not as sexually sophisticated as you foreigners. Therefore a lot of the sex we have results in procreation. We need a place to put the kids. Our families are big. The Bush family, for example, is so big that one presidency wasn't enough for them, let alone one SUV. Dozens of huge, black Chevrolet Suburbans full of Secret Service agents were—until recently—required to escort the Bush family around. During the Bush administration, an American who had a huge, black Chevrolet Suburban of his own could pretend to be a Secret Service agent. He could let those scampish Bush twins, Jen and Barb, know that it was all right with him if they got up to all sorts of high jinks on his watch. Wink, wink. Nudge, nudge. Maybe the Obama administration will offer similar opportunities with Michelle. She's the bomb.

We have big families, and we're big people. How big I needn't tell you who are annually trampled in Trafalgar Square and butted across Hyde Park by herds of Guernseysized American tourists. Michelle Obama, in fact, is considered the Twiggy of America. Even our wispy left-wing intellectual types are . . . you've seen Michael Moore.

We're big people from a big country. We like our elbow room so well that we carry it around with us. We can't stand to be squished together as if we were sitting in the backseat of a Nissan Micra or living in England. And in our big country we're in a big hurry. When we drive an immense Lincoln Navigator we get to where we're going sooner, or at least the front part of our car does, though it may be a long walk to the bumper. Plus, you know what kind of a mess the kids make on long trips. With rear footwells the size of Loch Lomond, we never clean up the soda cans and candy wrappers. We trade in for a new Navigator at ten thousand miles.

An SUV is very safe in a collision—safe for me, because I drive one. You, who don't, are crushed like a garden slug. Although, in fairness, SUVs are equipped with features designed to improve survivability for occupants of the other vehicles involved in SUV crashes. High ground clearance gives you—if you jump out of your Opel Astra and throw yourself flat on the pavement—a better than even chance to survive being run over.

There *is* something of a safety problem with SUVs flipping and landing in ditches on their roofs as a result of encounters with curbs, potholes, or too thickly painted highway center lines. But we Americans don't mind this, given our national propensity to turn the world upside down. Also, we regard these incidents as an answer to the oft-voiced criticism that SUVs aren't really used off-road. This is a baseless attack anyway. America is a country with widespread muck and mire, as you may have noticed in our recent presidential election campaign.

Perhaps we SUV owners don't go into the wilderness very often. But such is the weather in America that the wilderness frequently comes to us. Bushes, trees, surf, sand, and whole chunks of scenery are delivered to our places of residence by hurricane and tornado winds. Our mobile home may blow away but, by gosh, our Dodge Durango is right there in the driveway where we parked it.

America is a practical nation. SUVs provide practical solutions to the problems Americans face. Americans have a lot of baggage—backpacks, fanny packs, laptops, beer coolers, blame for everything that's wrong in the world. Try armor-plating your Mercedes Smart Car.

Americans have cumbersome hobbies. Tie an ultralight aircraft on your Ford Ka's luggage rack, put a Jet Ski and a dirt bike in the back, and tow a dune buggy. Now you're ready for a typical American afternoon in the park. We don't go in for train spotting or darts.

Animals on the road are another consideration. You have cats, dogs, bunny rabbits. We have moose. (And Sarah Palin.) Hit a moose in your VW Polo and the People for Ethical Treatment of Animals will be picketing to save *you.* (Survive hitting a moose and you run the further risk of Sarah Palin showing up at your house and offering to cook.)

Americans demand convenient parking. Conveniently, SUVs can be parked—*squash, crush*—anywhere.

SUVs provide America with economic stimulus. Replacing parking meters, fire hydrants, street signs, gates, fences, decorative plantings, HANDICAPPED ONLY markers, bumpers, fenders, hoods, and trunk lids that have been backed into by SUVs is a multibillion-dollar business in the United States, and provides tens of thousands of jobs.

Americans are very competitive. America's state and local transport authorities make roads longer and wider. America's automobile companies make cars longer and wider.

And Americans love media attention. Being on television so defines American life that there is now more "reality TV" in America than there is discernible reality. SUVs are easier for television station helicopters to spot during the live televised car chases that all Americans dream of being featured in.

America is also an idealistic nation. Americans drive SUVs for the good of mankind. Think of the vicious wars fought over petroleum resources. SUVs turn oil into dirty air. Nobody fights wars over dirty air. When all the oil is gone the people of the Middle East will be able to go back to being "Sand French." And the sooner America's SUVs use up that oil, the sooner global warming can be halted. Meanwhile, melting of the polar ice caps threatens to put Washington, D.C., under ten feet of water. Is that a bad thing? And whether it is or isn't, you Brit sightseers will be needing an SUV to make your way through the swamped Mall to the submerged Air and Space Museum.

There is, of course, the Freudian aspect of SUVs. Driving an SUV is an affirmation of manhood, an expression of machismo, an undeniably phallic experience. That said, my wife has a much larger SUV than I do. Her GMC Yukon XL was made in America. My Land Rover Discovery was made in Britain. Out of consideration for the amour propre of male writer and male readers alike, perhaps we should drop this subject. (Personally, I think American women like vast SUVs because, standing beside one, they look svelte by comparison. Ouch! No, honey, the Kia doesn't make your butt look big. Honest.)

Speaking of hurt feelings, you'd be better off in England if you had leviathan SUVs like we do. You could have avoided the entire fox hunting ban kerfuffle. Get a Ford Expedition EL. There's room in the back for the horses, the riders, the dogs, *and* the fox. You can slip the whole lot right past the furious people in anoraks.

It's this kind of preservation of freedom that's behind America's passion for SUVs. The real truth is that we need sport utility vehicles to carry our concealed weapons. Sticking them down the waistband of our pants doesn't work with AK-47s, .50-caliber machine guns, bazookas, and so forth. Why do Americans love *these* monstrous and threatening devices? Because the whole world is angry at America for driving SUVs—and for a few other things we've done lately. We may have to shoot everybody. If anti-Americanism gets any worse, Oprah will be giving away Hummers.

18

The Other End of the American Car

Good-bye to all that, fellow car nuts. Barak Obama has been elected, Congress is overrun with Democrats like cooties on a spelling bee winner, and the Supreme Court will be next to go. Poor Chief Justice John Roberts did the best he could to save us by muffing the oath of office. But they forced him into a do over. And it's only a matter of time before Roberts is exposed as having once written a legal brief where "she" wasn't used as a collective pronoun—thereby proving Roberts's deep-seated phallocentric bias, anti-inclusive prejudice, and insensitivity to hurtful language. When Roberts is impeached Al Gore will be named to replace him and the Fun Suckers will be fully in charge.

We have the ugly mug of liberalism right in our face or, rather, the armpit of liberalism's left wing. The progressives are back, the community activists, the collectivists, the socialists, the Bolshie scum—call them what you will. Reagan throws pinko politicians out the door of human liberty and they come back down the chimney of climate change. Globalization tosses pinko environmentalists out the window of free-market opportunity and they crawl back through the rat hole of fiscal crisis. Pinko economic reformers will be given the bum's rush in their turn. But they'll be back in yet another guise. It's a battle that won't be won in my lifetime.

I'm not saying there's no hope. Young lads of good courage and lasses brave at heart, spit upon the hand that offers you the keys to the Prius. Freedom will dawn again.

The beauty of communism is that like all great projects of social engineering it contains within itself the mechanism of its own destruction. I know because I drove one.

A few years ago I was on a horseback trek across the Chatkal Mountains (another story entirely) in the former Soviet republic of Kyrgyzstan. Kyrgyz-where? Well you might ask. Kyrgyzstan is the southeasternmost of what used to be the U.S.S.R.'s central Asian provinces. It lies between Kazakhstan and China (more alpine than the latter and less the subject of a comic movie than the former). If you were to go due south about five hundred miles from where I was you'd be in India. Kyrgyzstan is the place that Sean Connery and Michael Caine ended up ruling in the movie of Kipling's *The Man Who Would Be King*. I didn't actually see any polo played with a human head but I'm not saying it doesn't happen.

Anyway, I was on a horse. I like horses well enough—although better when they win, place, or show—but what I loved was our support vehicles, which traveled down the logging skids and sheep trails of Kyrgyzstan's wilderness. These were a pair of magnificent seven-ton, six-wheel-drive 1984 Zil trucks, Soviet army surplus left over from the Afghan war. One truck carried all our tents and gear and the other contained a complete camp kitchen.

We would ride our horses along the mountain ridges all day while the trucks made their way through the mountain valleys. They'd meet us each night. We'd come down from the heights with the setting sun and find the tents pitched, a trestle table with vodka bottles set in a row, and a lamb turning on a spit. I was off the horse and into the trucks as quickly as I could. They were wonderfully engineered machines. By that I don't mean that their engineering was wonderful. It was wonderfully big and wonderfully simple, so simple that it was comprehensible to me. And wonderfully repairable in the middle of nowhere.

We'd passed beyond the end of the road into a place with no power lines, no phone towers, not even any vapor trails of airplanes in the sky. We met only a few people, nomads grazing their flocks in summer pastures, living in felt yurts. We found one small village with one old blacksmith who had one small boy operating the bellows of his forge. He could make engine parts for the Zils—such were the tolerances and metallurgy involved.

The Zils were classic vehicles, almost unchanged in appearance from the World War II Red Army trucks. They were built on ladder frames with roly-poly 1930s-style cabs in front of plywood sheds with ordinary house windows, barn doors at the back, and a stove pipe out the roof of the camp kitchen. "It comes with just cargo container," said driver Valerii Katalukin. "It must be modified."

Valerii and his codriver Andre Akimenko put me in the driver's seat and let me run through some of the plentiful shift positions—five unsynchronized gears and two much less synchronized axle speeds. We drove around in a riverside meadow undeterred by boggy footing at speeds ranging from the preferred pace of my trek horse (less than zero) to the fastest rate at which I'm comfortable on a horse (grudging trot). Wheel, pedal, and gear lever efforts were as large as the Zil but not without a coarse-grained precision.

The Zil's engine was a six-liter V-8 with a 1950s Ford look. There was a Ford engine about this size, a 352 cid, introduced in 1957 as an option in the Ranchero pickup. The Ranchero, however, had two four-barrel carburetors and three hundred horsepower while the Zil had one two-barrel and 150 hp.

The detuned V-8 had a good deal to do besides moving fourteen thousand pounds of truck plus whatever was loaded onto it. Each Zil had a hydraulic system so that it could be fitted with a tractor bucket, plow blade, or backhoe. Three different wrist-thick V-belts spun from pulleys at the front of the engine, one to run the hydraulic pump, one to turn an air compressor, and one to operate the radiator fan and the ninety-amp alternator. A second drive shaft powered a twenty-ton winch with seventy meters of steel cable wrapped around an oil drum–sized reel on the front bumper.

We obtained firewood for our camp by finding a dead pine in the forest, wrapping the winch cable around it, and yanking the whole tree out of the woods.

Why not diesel if all this power was needed? Valerii and Andre laughed. Russian winter temperatures turn diesel fuel into a mold of Jell-O shimmying on a plate.

I looked under the truck. The three live axles were

mounted on leaf springs with torsion bar assists. If the engine was nabbed from a '57 Ford, then the suspension was nicked from a Plymouth of the same era.

The Zils were primitive. But when America's Fun Suckers nationalize the car companies they will be surprised by the primitivism that will ensue, as no doubt the Soviet Union's nationalizers were. GM, Chrysler, and Ford will be run by Nancy Pelosi. The Fun Suckers and the climate-cleansing creeps think government-spec cars will run on wind power from the breeze that cars encounter when they drive down the road. They think cars will run on tofu farts. They think cars will run on solar energy. And maybe they will, if you roll up the windows and take away the bottled water and lock your family in the car on a hot, sunny day and figure out how to harness the energy of furious death throes. They think cars will run on six AA batteries. And that might work too. Put half a dozen batteries in a sock, hit a gas station cashier over the head, and steal thirty gallons.

What will actually happen when the government owns the car companies is that organized labor will wield renewed and enormous power. The very air in the factories will have to come from the atmosphere on a fully unionized planet. Executive pay will be curtailed until the car companies are driven insane looking for managerial talent. That kid with the head set at Burger King. He seems focused and decisive. "Three Whopper Meals to go!" Engineers and designers will be hired because they're related to the governor of Illinois. Styling will be done by the same commission and committee process that produces public monuments such as the Vietnam Memorial. Your new Impala will be a simple slab with the names of everyone ever killed in a traffic accident engraved on it.

The Fun Suckers believe that a motor vehicle created by politics will be a cross between a biofuel golf cart and the thing the Baby Einstein kids fly. A motor vehicle created by politics will be a Zil. And FYI, Al Gore, fuel economy in a Zil is five miles per gallon on the highway and 3¾ mpg off road.

To us beleaguered car nuts, though, Zils rolling off the assembly lines in Detroit is not bad news. This is a device we can deal with. It will be easy to trim its weight and not hard to bring that engine's horsepower back to three hundred. We can even improve gas mileage if we want. Meanwhile we've got twin forty-six-gallon fuel tanks. And the Zil is not without sophistications of a kind. It has coolers for both engine oil and hydraulic fluid. And it has fully waterproof two-piece spark plugs. The plug design is ancient. I found a drawing for a similar type in a book called *Self-Propelled Vehicles* published in 1907. But the design works. Andre told me that, supplied with a snorkel, the Zil can operate completely underwater. There's a centrifugal oil-bath air cleaner to filter out the worst dust in the world (which Afghanistan has). The Zil's air compressor feeds a self-inflation system for the truck's six tires. Tire pressure can be changed on the run by half an atmosphere—about 7½ psi. Tires can be deflated to negotiate sand or pumped up to roll over obstructions. And air can be kept in tires punctured by bullets.

The tires themselves are mounted on twenty-four-inch wheels. A wheel mount weighs 330 pounds and stands forty-seven inches high. The Russian tires looked okay with an aggressive tread pattern and the kind of soft composition that works well on ice. But Valerii told me they only last a year. A little American know-how and a visit to the tractor-trailer junkyard should get us better unsprung weight and tread life. The Zil's sixteen-inch ground clearance is disappointing, no better than a Hummer's. But the Zil can climb a forty-five-degree incline and can tilt, Andre assured me, an astonishing sixty degrees before it flops over.

"He is best driver," Andre said of Valerii. A Kyrgyz native, Valerii had been driving Zils in central Asia for twenty-three years. He was an enlisted man in the Soviet army from 1979 to 1981, serving in a Vladivostok transport division that used Zils to move bombs.

"To learn to drive Zils I was in school six months before I was really good," Valerii said. "I was lucky because I could feel it very quickly, center of gravity. I learned to drive local trucks at fourteen." When we encountered a mile-wide landslide it was Valerii who drove each truck across the crumbling ground above an abyss while Andre walked along beside him shouting how much earth was giving way from beneath the downhill wheels.

And landslides may be an issue for us car nuts. With the Fun Suckers ruining everything, we'll have to head for the hills. Yes, I know, we've spent years trying to head for the hills, in New Hampshire, Colorado, and Northern California. The Fun Suckers keep coming after us on their cross-country skis that suck the fun out of skiing. Keeping fit so she can torment us until she's a hundred, Granny D telemarks into our rifle sights while we're trying to shoot a moose. Other Fun Suckers litter our bird covers with granola crumbs as they "Hike for Peace" and block our four-wheeler routes by holding 5K fun runs to raise public awareness about the dangers posed by lack of broadband Internet service to rural minorities and the poor. They get "centered" and "positive" and "spiritually attuned" by taking raft trips though the middle of our best trout pools. They build spas for holistic healing next door to where we were trying to get off the grid and then they complain about the noise our electric generators and snowmobiles make. Now that Volvo has built a credible all-terrain machine in the form of the XC90 (with scads of air bags to protect the passengers in case they drive into my goose-hunting pit blind and squash me), there seems to be no way to escape the Fun Suckers.

Yet nature geeks, outdoorsy bores, and advocates of protecting the endangered rabid raccoons in our garbage cans will never be able to go where our Zils can take us. The Zils took the Russians to Kandahar (and, better yet, got them out again). Maybe Afghanistan wouldn't be our first choice as hills to head for. But there is no DOT there, no NHTSA, no CAFE, no emission controls, no annual vehicle inspections, no seat belt laws, speed limits, crash standards, or random roadblock checks for DWI (although there's not much Afghan I to DW with). The Zils can take us plenty of other places as well. And here's one more piece of good news from Obama's Russian commie role models: Zils are still being made at a factory outside Moscow. They cost only about $30,000 new. You can get a good used one for six or seven thousand. And you can see the dealership from Sarah Palin's house.

Interview: P. J. O'Rourke

Courtesy of Gregg LaGambina, The A. V. Club

These days, loving your car might as well fall under the military's "Don't ask, Don't tell" policy. Everyone's proud of their strangely shaped lightbulbs, compost piles, and hybrids humming like hairdryers—it's good to go green, but the self-congratulatory backslapping can be unbearable.

Energy efficiency be damned; famous contrarian P. J. O'Rourke still has his foot firmly pressed on the gas pedal. The political satirist's latest collection comprises decades of his auto-fixated contributions to *Car & Driver*, *Automobile*, *Esquire*, *Forbes*, and others. Its title is fairly self-explanatory: *Driving Like Crazy: Thirty Years of Vehicular Hell-bending Celebrating America the Way It's Supposed to Be—With an Oil Well in Every Backyard, A Cadillac Escalade in Every Carport, and the*

Chairman of the Federal Reserve Mowing Our Lawn. Recently, the former Foreign Affairs Desk Chief for *Rolling Stone* visited with *The A.V. Club* to discuss Ann Coulter, Clint Eastwood, the idiocy of Prius owners, and why we'll soon be begging the Bolivians for lithium.

The A.V. Club: How do you feel about Barack Obama becoming the de facto president of General Motors?

P. J. O'Rourke: I think it's a really, really bad idea. It's one of these situations where Dad burns dinner, so you say, "Oh, I know. Let's have the dog cook!" The only people that could possibly be worse at running a car company than the current crop of car executives—who have proven themselves to be plenty bad—would be a politician. There are lots of levels of fear and complaint about the government getting involved in business. First and foremost, of course, is incompetence. We actually have experiential evidence about this. In England, all the English car companies were beginning to circle the drain in a series of well-deserved failures and bankruptcies, earned by making lousy products with very poor production at high prices. So, the government, back in the '70s, nationalized all the British car companies. The result was British Leyland, a name that perhaps doesn't resonate much with you. Many of your friends probably drive Humber Super Snipers, or perhaps not. [Laughs.] That's certainly one thing that we're headed for. The other thing is that there's a very good reason that governments aren't supposed to compete with private-enterprise companies. Governments have monopolies on certain things, like eminent domain and deadly force. What's another example of an organization that gets into the same business that you're in, except that their guys have got guns? That would be the Mob. Ford is like the last honest trash collector in the New York metropolitan area, the last one that's not mobbed-up. How long is that gonna go on for?

AVC: In your book, you refer to the 2010 Obama-mobile. What will that car be like?

PJO: It's gonna run on alternative energy, it's gonna have a small carbon footprint, and it's gonna be sustainable. When I was a kid, we called it a Schwinn.

AVC: And it will run over blind people, because they can't hear it coming around the bend.

PJO: And then there's that! [Laughs.] Electric cars are a little creepy in that respect. They make no noise.

AVC: How many cars do you own?

PJO: If I mowed the lawn, the total might differ. [Laughs.] But I think at the moment, we've got five cars and a tractor.

AVC: What's your favorite?

PJO: My old 911. I've got a 1990 Porsche 911. It's just a Carrera, a very simple, straightforward little thing that goes like stink. I love it. It's been incredibly reliable for all these years.

AVC: Would you agree that the planet basically has lung cancer and needs to quit smoking? Is that a fair analogy?

PJO: No, I don't think so. There are plenty of problems in the world, and doubtless climate change—or whatever the currently voguish phrase for it all is—certainly is one of them. But it's low on my list. I spent almost twenty-five years as a foreign correspondent, and the world's primary problem is poverty. And I don't mean, like, "our kids are gonna have to go to public school and I'm gonna have to give up my spa membership" poverty. I'm talking about "not enough to eat" poverty. In the first place, it's a moral imperative that we fix that. In the second place, we're gonna be in a world of hurt if we don't get it fixed, because there's going to be billions of people out there—they're hungry, they're mad. One thing that they can get their hands on is guns. We've seen a little bit of it so far; we could see a lot more of it. First and foremost: feed people. If it warms the planet slightly . . . I live in New Hampshire. We're in favor of global warming. Eleven hundred more feet of sea-level rises? I've got beachfront property. You tell us up there, "By the end of the century, New York City could be underwater," and we say, "Your point is?"

AVC: Do you worry that some people might dismiss your more serious points because they'll just assume you're joking?

PJO: No, I don't worry about it. It's much better to have your arguments dismissed because you might be joking than to have your arguments dismissed because you're not telling the truth. I'll pick "I'm kidding" anytime over "I'm lying."

AVC: There's a line in the first essay in this collection where you refer to "a general feeling of not giving two fucks about man and his universe." That might be construed as the thesis for this book.

PJO: [Laughs.] Well, one has one's moments, although I like to only have them after 7 or 8 in the evening. It's not good to think like that before cocktail hour. Someone was asking me, "What do you think about Ann Coulter? How are her opinions different from yours?" I said, "You know, they're not. There's nothing that Ann Coulter has said that I haven't said, it's just that I say it at 3 in the morning dead drunk, and she says it at 3 in the afternoon, stone-cold sober." It's kind of a nuance thing. [Laughs.]

AVC: You love cars, but in the book, you chastise Los Angeles for having too much car love. It's almost as if you're writing about sex, and L.A. represents the porn industry.

PJO: Yeah, that's a very good parallel. I wish I'd drawn it myself. I am a great admirer of women, but that doesn't mean I like *Hustler*. Los Angeles is sort of the *Hustler* magazine [of car love]. And I'm as fond as the next person of a lively set of photographs.

AVC: Shouldn't you be celebrating Los Angeles, considering that you can't do anything in that city without a car?

PJO: Los Angeles is many places in one place. If you get outside the world of show business and its satellites, there's a whole world of car nuts in the Los Angeles area. Southern California is a nice place, if you could cut out the show-business cancer. It just keeps spreading.

AVC: In your defense of SUVs, you introduce the theory that they'll use up the oil faster and actually curb global warming.

PJO: Listen, everyone in the Middle East would be back to being sand French, you know? They'd be off the map. We can't use this stuff up too fast. There's no doubt about it. Then, of course, if you use it up, you've got to come up with something else to replace it. I'm not guaranteeing what we come up with will be better for the planet. There is ethanol, for instance, which actually nets out with more pollution at greater expense, and more harm to the environment than petroleum, but we'll come up with something.

AVC: Are you fearful of a future of quiet, electric cars?

PJO: I'm certainly not fearful. I'm sixty-one years old. I'm not that fearful of the future, *period*. I'm not going to see that much of it. [Laughs.] But, no, that [Chevy] Volta sports car is supposedly hot property. There's nothing inherently lame about electricity. I've got a basement full of power tools that all operate with electricity, and they're manly items. And when you see a great big locomotive hauling a mile of freight cars, that's a hybrid. A lot of people don't understand that. Those big GM locomotives—that is a diesel engine running a generator that sends electric power to the actual motors that are in the wheel carriages.

AVC: So what's taking GM so long to make cars like that?

PJO: It's a clumsy, heavy, expensive technology. It works better in a locomotive. A lot of things work better in a locomotive. Cars would be safer on rails! The problem with making a hybrid that works is, it's going to be a heavy vehicle, and it's going to be expensive to build, and is it gonna net out to be more efficient? It kinda depends upon how you do the math on making the batteries, and how much battery power it carries, how you dispose of the batteries when they're done. It's tricky. Somebody pointed out to me the other day—and I haven't checked this fact—but apparently Bolivia is the key source of lithium in the world. So we're gonna trade the Saudis for the Bolivians.

AVC: They've been feeding us with a different kind of energy for years.

PJO: They have, and that hasn't been good for the internal peace of Latin America, so you can only imagine what a lithium-and-cocaine dependant economy will be like. [Laughs.] That is a *great* idea.

AVC: Some people argue that Prius owners are dangerous because they don't care about cars, and therefore are terrible drivers.

PJO: They're bad drivers because they're idiots. And we know they're idiots because they bought a Prius.

AVC: What's wrong with a Prius?

PJO: Slow, expensive, it's got no room. I have three children and three dogs. *You* put them in a Prius, you know? People who have a Prius obviously have no life! No wife, no kids, no pets—there's no room in there for anything! A recent issue of *Car & Driver* has a test of a Honda Insight, a Toyota Prius, and then they pulled out of mothballs an old GM Metro from the '90s, this pathetic three-cylindered automobile that sold for about 1,800 bucks. It got better gas mileage than the Prius or the Insight.

AVC: But you have to agree, for a variety of reasons, that we should find a way to curb our dependence on oil.

PJO: No! I don't at all. I mean, yes, pollution is a problem, and there's the whole problem of the spoiling of the commons, but we've addressed the pollution problem on a variety of different levels in a variety of ways, and it's worked pretty well. I'm old enough to remember when the air over American cities was a lot dirtier than it is now. You've probably never woken up early on a winter morning to the acid stink of coal smoke in the air, which was everywhere when I was a little kid. My grade school was heated with coal. Not only was coal used to generate electricity, it was without any scrubbers in the stacks. We can address this problem. Most of the people who have grabbed hold of climate change and greenhouse gases, pollution, oil dependency—they have another motive, and their motive is to attain the appearance of virtue without having actually done anything virtuous. Or if they're in politics, the whole point of politics is to achieve prestige and power without merit. These are just nice opinions to have. They're utterly meaningless. It's just a way for people to be pious jerks. This going on and on about how terrible a carbon-based economy is, these people are full of crap. They don't know what they're talking about. Their motives are not necessarily good just because they say they are being good. It's peace, love, and understanding. To which

I can just say, "Shut up." Human liberty, rule of law, and free markets fix this stuff. It isn't necessary to go around being the Mia Farrow of the ecosphere. [Laughs.] I'm really tired of virtue.

AVC: With the future of cars and journalism both in doubt, where does that leave you?

PJO: Clint Eastwood has done it all with that film *Gran Torino*. I've been channeling that character ever since I saw the movie. I've decided that my motto in life is "Get off my lawn." It's the right answer to everything.